Open to Disruption

Open to Disruption

Time and Craft in the Practice of Slow Sociology

Edited by

Anita Ilta Garey
Rosanna Hertz
Margaret K. Nelson

Vanderbilt University Press
Nashville

© 2014 by Vanderbilt University Press
Nashville, Tennessee 37235
All rights reserved
First printing 2014

This book is printed on acid-free paper.
Manufactured in the United States of America

Library of Congress Cataloging-in-Publication Data on file
LC control number 2013039763
LC classification number HM571.064 2014
Dewey class number 301.072—dc23

ISBN 978-0-8265-1984-9 (cloth)
ISBN 978-0-8265-1985-6 (paperback)
ISBN 978-0-8265-1986-3 (ebook)

Contents

Part III: Reflections on Disruptions: Time and Craft

Introduction

On Being Open to Disruption

Margaret K. Nelson and
Rosanna Hertz

> Experience is not so much what happens to you as what you make of
> what happens to you.
>
> *Aldous Huxley (paraphrased)*

For all the discussion about the research process in social science, few accounts open up that process to inspection.[1] Rather, most published descriptions of the research process take a standard narrative form: an idea for study, followed by data collection, analysis, and writing. This narrative assumes a smooth, continuous arc that invariably ends with publication (otherwise we wouldn't be reading it). Someone has finished a project, sent it off into the world, and is now ready to move on to the next item on the academic agenda. The trajectory of the arc appears set from the beginning. The dynamic way in which our craft actually evolves is rarely chronicled and the backstage stories remain hallway talk at professional meetings or uncomfortable silences we keep to ourselves. And, not surprisingly, given the current pressures on academics to publish—pressures experienced especially by those without tenure but increasingly by those with tenure as well—the arcs revealed in published accounts encompass ever shorter periods of time. We could take some of our own scholarship as examples; we could find many more among our colleagues.

The essays in this collection describe work that took longer than whatever might be considered usual, even if that "usual" is only in the mind of the author. These are essays about taking time. But they are *not* essays about planned longitudinal research. Although some of the studies described ended up taking a very long time (even decades in some cases) and thus came to constitute longitudinal research, in no case was this the original intention.

These essays are about something unanticipated, something disruptive. They discuss the complexities of inventing concepts that, as yet, have no name and no scholarly history. They evoke the excitement of breaking disciplinary boundaries. They explore the consequences of becoming aware of and open to new possibilities for collecting data and to new ways of thinking about, analyzing, and writing up our findings. They acknowledge circling back to work we had considered "done" and allowing ourselves the possibility of thinking about it in a different way. They are about unfinished business that gnawed at us until curiosity or "chutzpah" led to a return to the field. In short, these essays are about what have been called "crucible moments," those moments when individuals sense that they will continue to grow and their art, "whatever form it takes, will continue to evolve" (Thomas 2008, 17–18). What holds the essays together is that in each case, although sometimes grudgingly in the beginning, ultimately the author not only allowed disruption to occur, but even met it with openness.

Even so, almost to a person, the authors of these essays expressed uneasiness about some aspect of this disrupted process. Susan Bell, for example, speaks of blushing when her work was praised because it had taken so long for her to complete it: "For many years I would not name the starting date, hoping to avoid the stigma of being so slow and preferring to pass as a 'normal' scholar, one who managed to publish at least one article or book chapter per year." Annette Lareau is equally explicit about how embarrassed she was about questions about her book, *Unequal Childhoods*, during the many years she was working on it. And Naomi Gerstel is surprised by, and still worries about how others read, "gaps" in her impressive résumé.

Writing about this disrupted process was difficult too. And it was not "just" the discomfort of taking longer than "normal," or of noticing one's own years of skimpy output, that made acknowledging disruptions publicly so emotionally complex. In some cases the emotional content came from writing about personal disruptions that were private—sometimes deeply painful; sometimes deeply pleasurable; sometimes both. In some cases, the emotional content came from writing about open disruptions to (or near misses of disruption to) significant relationships with people who began as the "objects" of study and ended up being friends. In some cases, the emotional content came from writing about the difficult lives of the people being studied. And, in still others, the prevailing standards of the academy, combined with one's own sense of professionalism, made the acknowledgment of oversights and inadequate technique feel like public humiliation. But in almost every case, whether in oral or written form, the authors expressed satisfaction with having had the opportunity to have a say. One author, as she struggled to get her words down on (virtual) paper, said in an e-mail, "This is a new adventurous type of writing for me." Another commented on a range of issues, including emotional intensity and reflexivity and her fear that the writing might be insufficiently scholarly: "I want to tell you that this piece has been a bit emotionally difficult for me (I imagine this is fairly typical of such long-term involvements), and I found myself really needing to write this piece. But it is highly reflective, and not terribly academic."

As is the case for the scholar just quoted, these essays are all "highly reflective."[2] With almost surprising resonance, one to another, they consider how a disruption (e.g., taking more time than usual at one stage or another, circling back to issues they thought had been resolved, learning new methods, or deliberating about word choices) altered the process so that the narrative arc not only *felt* different but *was* different from what other scholars described (even if it merely looked longer). And they reflect on how that new arc, at the very least, helped them reach a different level of understanding of their project and, in its most provocative incarnations, helped them write something more serious, more profound, and more honest to themselves and those they studied. A few weeks before she submitted a first draft of the paper she was writing with Carol Stack, Linda Burton commented on her awareness of these issues: "The paper looks different than I thought it would look, but I love it. In it you see the real Carol and Linda and how we struggle with making sense of our ethnographies and doing justice to the lives of girls, women, boys, and men in our studies in the context of the politics of science."

There are some common themes. From one perspective, what several write is really quite simple: they say that once the research process was disrupted, one thing led to another. That is, no matter what the initial reason for the disruption—and these reasons varied—the earth didn't stand still either during the time it took a scholar to find her or his intellectual footing or during the hiatus before a scholar returned to an unfinished project.

Disruptions created an ever-moving research target. Albert Hunter wrote about the same place for many years, but that place underwent such major transformations that in a very real sense it no longer was the same place. The

Hare Krishna movement Burke Rochford joined in prayer in 1975 had transmuted into a major world religion with generations of congregants by the time he wrote about child abuse there. The women Bell interviewed as adolescent "DES daughters" faced their own problems of giving birth to healthy children as they matured. The maid's daughter, a twenty-three-year-old college graduate when Mary Romero first met her, was a middle-aged adult with children of her own when Romero ended the project twenty years later.

The world around these "subjects" changed as well. Joanna Dreby comments movingly on the changing significance of being documented, as the immigrants she studies worry more now than they did half a dozen years before about being deported. Timothy Black captures how individual lives intersected with broader social systems and the changes that occur over time (such as changes in the labor force, the growing role of the criminal justice system for marginalized people, and the increasing social insecurity that characterizes the recent past). Marjorie DeVault wanted to "study—and bring into view—some of what women knew but didn't have words for." Pamela Stone starts out with a subject no one wants to fund, and ends up writing about a phenomenon that had central billing in the *New York Times Magazine* as well as on multiple blogs. Meanwhile, new technologies became both the means for keeping up to date with these changes *and* the subject of these changes themselves.

Especially intriguing are the discussions about the changing nature of relationships with those individuals who constitute the topic or subject, if you will, of the research. Lareau worried that "Mr. Williams," grouchy and exhausted after a long day of work, would one day "come home, get mad at his wife, and end the study." Karen Hansen's experience of a long period of research was different: she found that her repeated visits to the North Dakota reservation where she was collecting data meant that, after some time, she was no longer a "stranger" to those she interviewed. Hunter writes, "Many of the people who would enter into my research as subjects were the same individuals I had known in my youth, yet they were now different people."

As relationships stretched out in time, they also deepened, to varying effects. Some scholars, like Burton and Stack, felt they could get to the heart of certain issues only *because* of their long-term relationships with the people about whom they were writing. Some felt their responsibility more deeply and that sense of responsibility slowed them down or gave them pause. Some could find no easy way to finish a story; some found that their research relationships morphed into a quite different set of ongoing friend-ships and responsibilities in everyday lives that had no endpoint. Of course, these changing relationships with respondents cannot be separated from the changes experienced by one's self. Dreby, for example, writes, "Every return to this place is an exercise in self-reflection, of how I have changed as a mother and a woman, of how my relationships have changed, and of how my children have grown across these movements through time and place. Returns are highly personal. They involve influential characters in my for-mative years, tugging at my insides for reasons I cannot explain." And while Dreby talks about her "returns" as being "scholarly returns," it is clear that there is something more to it than that: each time she returns to the site in which she conducted her research, she finds herself reflecting upon the length of time she has known each family, recalling the life events she has shared that mark her relationship to the people, and considering both how she has aged and her children grown. These changes in subject matter, the world, and ongoing research relationships are the focus of Part I.

The intellectual world in which scholars wrote altered as well. Analytic frames changed under scholarly feet. Gerstel notes that what was once "sex roles" became reconceptualized as "gender"; understanding the family increasingly involved looking beyond relations between spouse and part-ners or parents and children to examine kin connections. Bell describes how daughters exposed to DES in utero created new knowledges, institutions, and practices "rooted in their embodied experiences of having cancer, wor-rying about having cancer, becoming and not becoming mothers, and the lifelong effects of endocrine-disrupted, synthetic chemical–infused bodies." Hunter's understanding of the significance of Evanston's becoming "wet" (after decades of being a "dry" town) relies on a student's insight and the cul-tural symbolic turn in contemporary sociology. Burton and Stack indicate that the discourse on men in families, throughout the 1960s and beyond, never quite provided them with an audience that would listen, without a political ear, to what they were observing in African American families. More specifically, their chapter reveals that the scholarly literature on African American men locked those men into "public personas" that were difficult to challenge with ethnographic data. Just as Burton and Stack had to wait for a shift in politics before they could present their analyses of African American male youth, Hansen had to wait for the theoretical concept of settler colo-nialism before she could use it to frame her study of Scandinavians and Native Americans at Spirit Lake.

Changes in prevailing methodologies were equally, if not even more, common. A project begun with the notion that one could apply an almost positivist vision of methodology ended with an awareness of, and reliance on, a more self-reflexive stance, encouraging participants to become partners of sorts in the research process. For some, this meant throwing out the guidelines that had characterized their graduate training. When Romero's interviewee, Olivia, took over the interview and steered it the way she wanted and for as long as she wanted, Romero sat back, initially stunned, and only later realized she had stumbled onto another approach to interviewing, one that in this case opened up rich narrative material. Will C. van den Hoonaard found that his old understanding of cartography was no longer sufficient and that he had to dive into the churning waters of interdisciplinary—and international—study. Stone, familiar as she was with a quantitative approach, had to retool to understand why women had "opted out" of their careers. DeVault discovered conversation analysis and learned to evaluate "talk" in a new way. And Bell moved from the standard use of the interview—decontextualizing the excerpted quote—to a narrative analysis of those interviews along with visual materials and performative evidence. These changes in analytic frames and methods constitute Part II of the collection.

In some cases, what we call "disruptions" were, in and of themselves, the direct cause of changes in perception and understanding. Emily Abel, for example, came to understand religion in a new way as she dealt with the aftermath of breast cancer; that new understanding seeped into her analysis of the nineteenth-century caregivers she was writing about. Hunter experienced his community in new ways as he raised a second family. And a number of others, including Gerstel, Hertz, and Bell, comment, albeit in different ways, about how becoming mothers altered their understanding of women's lives and issues of care.

In still other cases, what we call "disruptions" had fewer direct but no fewer consequential effects. Delays helped produce confidence in an individual voice; as they matured, scholars became more certain that they wanted to tell the story that made sense to them rather than the one their respondents might want them to tell. Hansen bristled when a respondent answered her question "Is there anything [else] I should know?" with the sharp retort, "Ask me. You're the one who wants to know. Ask me. If I know it I'll tell you." Over time, she came to an alternative understanding and embraced ownership: "Ultimately, the interviews were mine. I directed the conversation; I asked the questions; I was motivated to publish. My challenge was to ask the right questions." At the same time, some scholars also became more humble about their own abilities and aware that the story that makes its way into print is always going to be partial—the best anybody could do at a given time. And some became more frustrated with separating their activism from their academic activities; some allowed their political beliefs to inform their scholarship more openly as they became more fully engaged in what our students call the "real world."

Some disruptions were less the result of external events than created by scholars themselves. Scholars invented terms to describe what existed but as yet had no name, as did Gerstel when she wrote about "commuter marriages." Scholars also expanded or stretched the meaning of current terms, as did DeVault as she gave substance and meaning to the everyday language of "feeding the family" and advanced feminist understandings of "invisible work." And scholars breached disciplinary boundaries, as did Hansen when she navigated a route through the fields of sociology, history, and the study of Native peoples. As people moved beyond their comfort zones, these kinds of disruptions created deep internal turmoil, even as they reverberated out to alter the intellectual landscape. The reconsiderations occasioned by or introduced through disruptions are the central theme in Part III.

To be absolutely clear, little of this happened by design. For the most part, disruptions were "purely" serendipitous. Margaret Nelson is surprised to find that the same person has been caught three separate times in her research net; Rosanna Hertz is taken aback when the child of the family she lived with twenty years before in another country almost literally shows up on her doorstep. Dreby is astonished to realize that the child she has come to interview was not yet born when she attended that child's mother's baby shower, a moment memorialized in a photograph of Dreby "measuring Leticia's round belly with sheets of toilet paper." Stone drops a child off at a playdate and muses about why the mother is no longer employed. DeVault pats herself on her back when she is applauded by an audience of Taiwanese faculty and graduate students, only to discover a few days later that they had not understood a key phrase in her talk. Each of these serendipitous moments made authors reflect back on what they had done before, as well as propelling them forward into what they had to do next.

These reflections offer ironies to be savored—and ironies to be regretted. Gerstel explores inequality wherever it appears in the lives of the workers she interviewed and acknowledges that she can be attentive to this issue because of the "cumulative advantage" of a paid semester off to fashion a major grant proposal and a sabbatical year at a posh research center with the luxury of uninterrupted time to focus on writing up her analysis. And she writes about disruptions in both her life and in the lives of the men and women she studied. The events of 9/11 would have disrupted the ability of Ari (the son of the family Hertz had lived with two decades before in Israel) to work in the U.S. underground economy; they also made Hertz pause before agreeing to sign legal documents saying that Ari was working for her family. The same events made Stone wait a year before conducting more interviews because she did not want an artificial emphasis on family. A decade later, as Stone arranged space in her busy life to write about the disruptions that afflicted her study of disrupted lives, Hurricane Sandy threw her careful arrangement to the (literal) winds.

These various themes combine to produce a deeper story about the comfort and protection of the "usual" narrative arc (whether or not it is ever fully enacted) and, by way of contrast, the risks and uncertainty of the disrupted one. In its own irony, the pressure to get work out—imposed by a dissertation committee, a promotion review, an editor's deadline, an internal time clock—creates safe space: we each do the best we can before a project is due; the ticking clock creates a familiar structure. So, too, do the constraints of disciplinary boundaries and well-worn concepts. Disruptions do not just lengthen the research trajectory. They also bump us out of that safe space into a place without clear-cut norms. Does anyone know what rules apply when we stop asking, "How can I get this done?" and start asking an entirely new set of questions: How do I know when this is good enough? How do I decide when this story is finished? Now that my usual methods have been debunked, what approach do I take? Have I used the right words to describe the phenomena I observed? If mistakes were made, and could be made again, how could I possibly be secure in my judgment that this time I have it right?

Gerstel writes, "So many of the synonyms the thesaurus gives for 'slow' indicate problems." They also stigmatize. The meanings of "judgment" do not carry the same connotations, but they are almost contradictory as they range from sparkling capacity ("genius," "grasp," "incisiveness," "ingenuity") through reasonable skills ("rationality," "sanity," "soundness") to a cautious approach to the unknown ("prudence," "apprehension"). Because you cannot teach judgment, these essays are not advice manuals; they don't tell us *how* to become better at what we do. But they do tell us about occasions of learning to become better by deviating from whatever rules guided us in the past. They tell of risks taken—of working past a cautious approach to the unknown, through reasonableness, to achieve something newly incisive, newly ingenious. There is no moral. But there is open acknowledgment of the chaos of normlessness and of the emotional intensity experienced in the midst of that chaos. And taken as a whole, and even if the authors do not acknowledge it themselves, these essays are testimony of the solid, good judgment that ultimately emerged as these wise scholars drew on their own maturity and their own life experiences to find their way out of that chaos.

In the physical sciences and math, it is said, the best work is often done when one is in one's physical prime. Lareau fears something similar could be true in the social sciences, not because of the benefits of youth per se, but because it is only early in one's career (maybe even while collecting data for a dissertation) that one can find the uninterrupted time to engage in extensive fieldwork. Taken as a whole, both Lareau's own scholarship—and the essays included here—suggest a more complex understanding of age, time, career, and achievement. And, we would add, we think that this understanding does not just rest on the fact that so much of the research described here relies on qualitative data. As Gerstel notes, "doing *both* qualitative and quantitative analyses in a focused way demands constant revision and rethinking" (emphasis added), a sentiment Stone seconds. Nor does it rely on the fact that these issues are raised by sociologists: scholars in other fields (some of which are represented here) might also experience disruptions in their lives, their understanding, and their methods; scholars in other fields might find that the ground they thought was novel or new had already been cultivated by someone else or that the burning question of one day appeared far less significant at another moment.

Time alone does not produce better scholarship. Scholars could take (and have taken) years without producing anything better than what they started out with. And not all disruptions have happy or positive outcomes.[3] But what the authors of these chapters intuitively knew when they were invited to write (or were cajoled into writing) for this collection is that while the disruptions to their scholarship led to their taking an unusual amount of time to finish a given piece of work, it was their openness to those particular disruptions and their subsequent willingness to accept normlessness that opened up opportunities for them to develop their craft. In the end, then, the projects in this collection are testaments to authorial mindfulness, self-reflection, humility, risk-taking, and honesty. They are the products of time *and* craft, disruption *and* openness.

In higher education today, much of this—the time, the craft, and the openness—is threatened by the emphasis on productivity and the reliance on external grants obtained by individual faculty members. We have seen the speedup ourselves, even in our own liberal arts colleges where what was once sufficient for achieving tenure (excellent teaching and an article or two) is now laughable. Of course, excellent teaching remains a criterion, but on top of that is the expectation of at least one book and a new research project well underway with published articles in peer-reviewed journals. Increasingly, both colleges and universities now toss aside the first book (mere dissertation output) and require a second. And in both types of institutions, the counting continues unabated for each year of one's career: Is there enough here for a raise? Has this person met the standards for promotion to full professor? Is there sufficient new scholarship to help the department maintain its status in the world? This type of thinking has the potential to extinguish the kind of valuable scholarship described in these essays. Moreover, even as money is drying up in the social sciences, and the awarding of grants in those disciplines has become more competitive than ever before, faculty members are judged by (and rewarded according to) whether or not they have supported their institutions in just this way. But most grant applications assume more knowledge, and the ability to craft more specific hypotheses, than is possible in the initial phases of the kind of exploratory research showcased in these essays. Of course, even under the conditions of speedups and expectations about external funding, research trajectories will still be disrupted, but in the absence of the safety net the academy has provided in the past, these disruptions will be occasions of endurance alone, rather than fertile ground for innovative ideas.

Reading the chapters of this book, we have come to believe that the academy could even go beyond providing a "mere" safety net. We suggest changes that could be made by institutions—and by the individuals who work in those institutions—that might encourage the production of the kind of innovative scholarship described here. We acknowledge the utopian quality of some of these ideas; we believe that utopian thought can provide a framework for productive discussion and effective action.

As part of the speedup, most academic institutions (our own included) now require regular reviews of each faculty member's scholarly accomplishments. We see major problems here: in the frequency of these reviews, in the criteria for what "counts" within them, and, conversely, in what gets overlooked by current counting practices.

The first of these could be easily addressed. Reviews might be less frequent; they might also be initiated by an individual faculty member rather than occurring according to some preordained time frame. One factor that might be taken into account as institutions and individuals decide when the next evaluation will occur is whether or not a faculty member has experienced a type of disruption (e.g., divorce, the birth of a child, illness) discussed in some of these essays. Clearly, it is inappropriate to apply the same time frame in all cases.

The other questions raised by institutional reviews are even more complex and troubling. Institutions vary in their practices. But in some institutions (including both of ours), faculty members are asked to report only on those pieces of scholarship "published and appearing" at the moment of the review. This emphasis on publication means that a project in the works is ignored even though it represents considerable effort. Similarly, a project in the pipeline (e.g., accepted for publication in a journal that has a large backlog) cannot be mentioned even though it might represent the culmination of many years of work. Alternatively, assessment materials might ask for information about projects begun, progress made, and projects finished during a particular period. In that way, institutions would be acknowledging that no one collects data and writes a book or article of any merit in a short period of time. Such practices would allow scholars to find the *best* form for their material (i.e., whether it should be presented in a book or an article) and not just the one that could be produced (and then published) most quickly.

This current emphasis on outcome over process is especially problematic because, as so many of the authors represented here suggest, speed is particularly difficult for scholars who collect their own data. They write about how long it takes to discern the rudiments of different cultures, to form relationships with informants, to develop trust, and to "hang out" with respondents. They indicate also how long it takes to craft adequate research memos, to transcribe interviews, and to visit archives. These practices have no parallels in the scholarship of those relying on the secondary analysis of data. And for those who have not been able to garner the external funding to underwrite research assistants and otherwise facilitate data collection and analysis, the time necessary to accomplish those tasks can stretch on indefinitely. Of course, whether one is molding qualitative or quantitative data, craft takes its own sweet time. None of this time is acknowledged when completed publications are all that count.

Academic institutions are also increasingly using criteria we find problematic. One of these is the special attention paid to the ordering of names, and the accounting of the unique contributions of each person, on a coauthored piece. The scholars writing here have suggested that coauthorship can be a source of intellectual enrichment; others note that coauthorship can help them overcome the loneliness of being the sole representative of a field at a given institution. (The three editors of this collection are all well aware of these benefits.) When we list others on our publication, we frankly acknowledge that no scholar works alone; when we put down our names alone, we neatly conceal that fact. Current institutional practices not only promote the latter practice of concealment, but also have the potential to turn collaboration into competition and to encourage individuals to make claims of ownership over ideas that have collective origins.

Most recently, at one of our institutions, as is already the case at so many, the "impact factor" of a journal is being used to assess the quality of our research. Our concern here stems directly from issues raised in the chapters in this volume. Particular topics included here (such as Stone's analysis of the labor-force behavior of professional women, and Burton and Stack's studies of the caretaking actions of young, African American men) did not initially receive the credit they deserved because they did not fit with prevailing political agendas. Similarly, what was once regarded by many as being marginal (such as DeVault's investigation into what a family ate) or invisible (such as Romero's forays into the experiences of the maid's daughter) have now become central topics of inquiry, but they too were initially mocked. For some of the authors, this mockery led to destructive self-doubt. But in so many cases the initial judgments were particularly misleading.[4] While we understand that those working in the "hard" sciences might also have their work poorly evaluated when they buck prevailing frameworks, we believe that biased assessments are probably issued more frequently in social science. Hence it is especially likely there that individual articles might in the long run turn out to be far superior—or far inferior, for that matter—to a journal's current or future reputation. Not surprisingly, at all but the top-ranked institutions, administrators are eager to proclaim that the yearly rankings by the *U.S. News and World Report* should not be viewed as definitive; we suggest that these administrators might be equally willing to regard "impact factor" assessments of journals with skepticism.

As we discuss the issues of what counts, and how it is counted, we need also to consider the issue of what gets obscured in assessment practices. Here we draw attention first to two areas of concern drawn from our own experiences over the past few years (choice and collaboration) and then to two distinctive areas of concern (skill acquisition and activism) raised by other authors in this volume.

Our own experience first. Over the past several years, as we worked on this manuscript, as well as on other projects while fulfilling our teaching obligations, we have had to make careful choices about resources of both time and money. Both have limits: we did not submit papers to conferences that conflicted with important moments in our teaching schedules, we withdrew conference submissions because we had already run out of money, and we failed to take advantage of opportunities to conduct interviews with respondents because we had neither the time nor the money to travel easily to their homes. When we are not asked about opportunities foregone, but only about those "accepted," we look less productive (and less successful) than we know ourselves to be. Even more important for our intellectual development is our participation in collective endeavors that play no role in reviews. We have already discussed coauthorship and its benefits. Other such occasions (e.g., study groups) allow individual scholars to keep abreast of changes in the discipline and, in a democratic fashion, bring together junior and senior faculty on a topic of common concern. In fact, some of those represented in this collection initially met through such opportunities and one of us recently spent considerable effort in re-creating this opportunity for a new group of scholars. But whereas postdocs are (now) available at the early stages of one's career, the efforts to create and participate in less formal networks have no place on one's CV.

The authors in this volume highlight two other issues. First, adequate assessment of scholarship might also ask whether a particular project required—or led to—the acquisition of skills such as learning a new methodology or language, embracing a new analytic framework, or crossing into new disciplinary territory. Ultimately, of course, an institution profits enormously when a faculty member engages in this kind of professional development: new skills can enhance a faculty member's teaching; the institution can bask in the reflected glory of a scholar's pathbreaking work. At present, however, the initial costs of these self-improvements are borne by the individual faculty member alone and they are totally ignored when the counting begins. The same is true of shifts in direction of interest: a scholar hired to teach a particular area might develop into one who can teach and publish in a far broader range of intellectual activity. Yet, because current practices of assessment discourage these shifts, faculty tend to become more and more narrowly focused. Curiously, for those of us at liberal arts colleges, incentives *are* available for the development of new courses. However, what we—and those elsewhere—need are equal incentives for the development of new areas of intellectual inquiry.

A couple of the authors in this volume make an additional, important point about activism. Bell's chapters for *Our Bodies, Ourselves* and Hunter's civic engagement in his local community have helped educate the broader public; while other contributors to this book do not explicitly mention this kind of activism in their essays, we know of them providing expert testimony and writing op-eds. But these activities are considered free-time hobbies or the pursuit of personal aggrandizement rather than essential uses of professional knowledge.

In short, we are suggesting that institutions do more to encourage and support risk-taking and innovation. As we have indicated, we believe that many current policies do just the reverse, even though some institutional policies encourage *students* to take risks as they make the transition from high school. At one of our institutions, for example, during the first semester of college, students are given shadow grades in a "pass-fail" system so that they can exercise new intellectual muscles in a stress-free environment. A parallel kind of support might be available to the faculty who are finding their way in new fields or embarking on particularly complex projects.

To be sure, the proposals outlined here cannot ensure positive results for every new endeavor: not all new projects will be fruitful; some projects will never see the light of day. Moreover, although we have emphasized the gains to be realized through supporting creative intellectual activity and responding well to the kinds of disruptions scholars experience in their real lives, we recognize that some "disruptions" are just that: caretaking, illness, depression, and bereavement do not necessarily bear intellectual fruit. Institutional openness to disruption must embrace these realities as well.

Finally, we believe that a more "open" institutional stance will need to be balanced by a more "open" individual stance. We acknowledge that the kind of scholarship described in these essays is unlikely to be a possibility *before* tenure. Quite simply, the risks are too high. But difficult as openness might be even after tenure, we do encourage it. The scholars represented here came from many different types of institutions; they also had varying levels of prominence before (and after) the disruptions they describe. As these essays show, they all paid a price for bucking the system: for some, the price was the invisible one of shame and embarrassment when their individual timetables did not conform to institutional expectations; for some, it was the equally invisible one of experiencing a normless chaos. We have all internalized the academy's demands, and this internalization keeps us in line and unwilling to take some potentially worthwhile leaps into the unknown. "Take your time" and "trust yourself" are the easy mantras of advice manuals. Needless to say, they are far more difficult to enact. They are also impossible to dictate.

In the last essay in this volume, Lareau suggests that this collection of essays itself might become the "cheering team" for scholars stumbling along their way through complex research projects. It is in this spirit that we initially embarked on this project. We will be gratified if, in its final form, scholars rely on it for their own encouragement. We will be gratified as well if scholars use it as evidence that institutional change is necessary. We cannot forget that because institutions merely "rent" our reputations, but do not own them, our individual enhancement serves their purposes as much as (if not more than) our own.[5]

When we embarked on this project, we called it simply "slow sociology" and we made reference to Stacey (2007) and to the slow movements in other areas of life (e.g., slow cooking, slow journalism). We thought of the positive impacts on our lives when we slowed down—when we allowed ourselves to take the time to "get it right"; we also believed that others could profit from our experiences. We discussed these ideas at panel presentations at two recent Eastern Sociological Society meetings and the word spread. Other sociologists also wanted to write about their own experiences with "slowness," as did a historian (Emily Abel) and an anthropologist (Carol Stack).

We initially organized the chapters of this volume into three sections, each referring to a way that the normal arc of the research process could be disrupted: at the initial stage of data collection (resulting in a long time in the field); during the period of writing and reflection (resulting in a long gestation); and at the point of reflection on, or reassessment of, initial ideas (resulting in reconsiderations). We solicited essays from scholars to "fit" into one of these designations. As the essays came in (and maybe even before then), we came to realize that these were not clear delineations: as our discussion above suggests, one thing led to another, and a disruption for any reason might lead to another form of disruption.

We didn't entirely throw out that initial framework, but have reconceptualized its elements to work in conjunction with the themes we found in these essays, even as we acknowledge that no individual essay fits squarely in one—or rather *only* in one—section of the collection. Even more significantly, as we read the authors' chapters for this volume, we recognized that slow sociology was not a broad enough focus. Various essays (as well as our discussions of those essays) continue to use the concept and language of our initial formulations. However, taken as a whole, these essays go well beyond slowing down.

Notes

The authors thank Emily K. Abel, Anita Ilta Garey, Naomi Gerstel, and Karen V. Hansen for their thoughtful readings of and helpful suggestions regarding this introduction. We also thank Michael Ames for his excellent stewardship throughout the entire process of creating this collection.

Epigraph: The exact quote reads, "Experience is not what happens to a man. It is what a man does with what happens to him" (Huxley 1990). We chose gender-neutral language.

1. Other collections that open up the research process in different ways include Hammond 1964; Glassner and Hertz 2003; Deflam 2007; and Goetting and Fenstermaker 1995. See also the "Backstage" column that Rosanna Hertz and Naomi Gerstel edited for *Contexts* (2004–2007).

2. See, for example, Callaway (1992, 33), who described the process as "a continuing mode of self-analysis and political awareness." For a more theoretical piece on feminist reflexivity, see Hemmings 2012, which addresses the "affective turn" that feminist theorizing has taken over past years.

3. We are grateful to an external reviewer for reminding us of this point.

4. In both of our institutions, assessments are made by college-wide committees that include representatives from a broad range of disciplines. This seemingly democratic practice can also cause particular problems for social scientists. The fact that everyone thinks they can assess that scholarship—because "good" social science should be readable—makes us particularly vulnerable to the evaluation of being trivial (mere common sense) and epistemologically problematic.

5. See Stinchcombe (1990, 338).

References

Callaway, H. 1992. "Ethnography and Experience: Gender Implications in Fieldwork and Texts." In *Anthropology and Autobiography*, edited by J. Okely and H. Callaway, 29–49. New York: Routledge, Chapman and Hall.

Deflam, M., ed. 2007. *Sociologists in a Global Age: Biographical Perspectives.* Hampshire, UK: Ashgate.

Glassner, B., and R. Hertz, eds. 2003. *Our Studies, Ourselves: Sociologists' Lives and Work.* New York: Oxford University Press.

Goetting, A., and Fenstermaker, S., eds. 1995. *Individual Voices, Collective Visions: Fifty Years of Women in Sociology.* Philadelphia: Temple University Press.

Hammond, P. E., ed. 1964. *Sociologists at Work.* New York: Basic Books.

Hemmings, C. 2012. "Affective Solidarity: Feminist Reflexivity and Political Transformation. *Feminist Theory* 13: 147–61.

Huxley, A. 1990. *The Perennial Philosophy.* New York: HarperCollins.

Stacey, J. 2007. "If I Were the Goddess of Sociological Things." In *Public Sociology: Fifteen Eminent Sociologists Debate the Profession in the Twenty-First Century*, edited by D. Clawson, R. Zussman, J. Misra, N. Gerstel, R. Stokes, D. L. Anderton, and M. Burawoy. Berkeley: University of California Press.

Stinchcombe, A. L. 1990. *Information and Organizations.* Berkeley: University of California Press.

Thomas, R. J. 2008. *Crucibles of Leadership.* Cambridge, MA: Harvard Business Press.

PART I

Changing Subjects, Changing Relationships, Changing Worlds

T he essays in the first section talk about what happened when scholars spent a long time engaged in collecting data about—and thereby interacting with—the people who, and the places that, constituted the focus of their research.

Timothy Black begins his chapter by expressing his own surprise that the research he began in 1990 was still his major focus—that he was still, in some sense, "in the field"—twenty-four years later. As he continues, he explains how during those two decades he (i.e., Black) changed, his relationships with the three brothers changed, and the world in which they all were attempting to make lives for themselves changed as well. Black thus describes a long time in an ever-changing field with ever-changing participants. His essay introduces three key thematic issues. One is that in long-term ethnography there are pivotal moments, or "junctures in the course of research that lead to new directions of inquiry." A second theme is that intense, ongoing relationships create multiple opportunities for rich, thick description. Finally, Black demonstrates the intersections of macrosocial forces, institutional dynamics, and individual lives as he considers how much has changed as his study transmuted into a "journey."

Burke Rochford's essay also describes a long time in the field: for three and a half decades, the Hare Krishna movement, known formally as the International Society for Krishna Consciousness (ISKON), has been at the center of his scholarship. During those thirty-five years, he was not "simply" in the field, collecting information for one major manuscript: he wrote two books and numerous articles. In his essay, in partial contrast to Black, Rochford focuses less on how the world and the participants of his study changed and more on his status as both an insider and a researcher whose writings were perceived as being critical of ISKON, which thus threatened to disrupt the relationships with many people he had come to consider friends. He muses, in his conclusion, about the nature of the relationships formed through long-term ethnography, dwelling especially on the issues of perceived trust and perceived betrayal.

Joanna Dreby's chapter describes how she gained trust with a new generation of immigrants when she returned to a former research site after a hiatus of over a decade. Her chapter also echoes back to the last theme raised by Black as she describes the changing context of immigration, reporting that in her current work she recognizes greater fear and anxiety over the possibility of deportation. In an interesting comparison to both Black and Rochford, Dreby writes about comings and goings—what she calls "returns"—rather than ongoing relationships, and how these returns allow her new insights into herself, her relationships, and her scholarly understanding. We could think about these issues in terms of photography: Leaving the field freezes one's respondents in time. Upon returning, one has to catch up and acknowledge that the snapshot no longer holds. Returns thus "disrupt" earlier visions of the lives of respondents.

In his review of his many studies of Evanston, his hometown, **Albert Hunter** demonstrates concretely a changing world and changing analytic frameworks with which to assess that world. A key focus of his essay is his varied types of ties within the community—ties that both allow him access to behind-the-scenes events and, from time to time, undermine his legitimacy as an "objective" scholar. Another key focus is how changes in his personal life left him in different locations within the community and provided access to different types of knowledge. In the end, he reflects on how "local engagement" has been both "giving back" and a way to advance his career, even if these two goals are sometimes in dynamic tension.

Although she is more focused on a single study (rather than on a new one, like Dreby, or repeated ones, like Hunter), as she too comes and goes from her research site in an initially foreign culture, **Karen Hansen** finds that repeated visits to the Spirit Lake Reservation, extending over a decade, transform her from a stranger to someone familiar. She thereby gains the trust that so many other essays in this section raise as an issue of concern. And, like Rochford, she comes to realize that good scholarship means gaining trust in one's own voice as well as gaining the trust of those one studies. Finally, Hansen introduces a theme that becomes more prominent in the next section, as she writes about searching for and articulating a new research frame.

1

From a Study to a Journey

Holding an Ethnographic Gaze on Urban Poverty for Two Decades

Timothy Black

I n 1990, when my research began in Springfield, Massachusetts, I had no reason to expect that twenty-four years later I would still be recording fieldnotes and tracking the lives of the boys I met then—in particular, three Puerto Rican brothers: Julio, Fausto, and Sammy, one year apart in age.[1] The trajectories of their lives extended my work into different social spaces (schools, streets, job training, workplaces, courtrooms, prisons, drug treatment facilities, and churches) and across a range of social contacts (family members, friends, neighbors, girlfriends, street associates, teachers, counselors, attorneys, and some city leaders). These spaces and faces transformed a study into a journey.

Much of what I have learned is due to the breadth of my study—time situates analysis. First, it allows for new directions to emerge in the course of the research. Emergent themes and the flexibility of field research are commonly valued qualities of ethnographic research, but when practiced over a lengthy period of time, multiple themes emerge that can provide fresh insights and broader analytical connections, and push beyond balkanized divisions within the discipline. Second, thick sociological description is written from within and through webs of relationships. When thick description is sustained over a long period of time, the positioning within relationships changes, the duality of researcher-respondent is transmuted, and knowledge claims become relationally, or interpersonally, grounded. Third, long-term ethnography helps us document the intersections of macrosociological, institutional, and individual dynamics, illustrating the interconnections between social and individual changes, which are rarely apparent immediately but take shape over longer periods of time.

Pivotal Moments

Ethnographic study is shaped by relationships in the field, inspired and uninspired observation and documentation, imaginative sociological construction, and serendipity. It becomes a journey, however, through a series of pivotal moments over long periods of time. Urban ethnographies typically focus on *place*—a social space in which external forces shape local conditions, while internal cultural strategies and routines negotiate these forces. Across time, these ethnographic studies see a community in motion, shaped for instance by housing and educational initiatives, economic and employment trends, policing tactics, and health strategies, and lived through the hierarchies of race, ethnicity, social class, gender, and/ or sexuality. Time in the field allows for emergent directions of study that can augment our understandings of place and its related complexities, but longer time in the field provides the opportunity to move our gaze beyond the confines of place, as relationships take us beyond a singular social space and require that we make sense of the intersections between these varying social spaces.

Pivotal moments are junctures in the course of research that lead to new directions of inquiry. I distinguish these junctures from what we may refer to as *emergent themes*. Emergent themes suggest a bounded study in which the unexpected occurs and theses are modified, or else an unstructured study in which our observations and predispositions "find" a topic or issue to study. Pivotal moments convey movement, or eruptions, that foster new directions of inquiry, new social spaces to comprehend, and definitive departures from the familiar. There have been many pivotal moments in the course of my journey—too many to document here—but I will describe a few to illustrate.

My study began in a high school where I developed relationships with a few boys who were considered likely to drop out of school. I documented their school and job experiences, their family and neighborhood dynamics, their relationships with institutional authorities, and their social networks, which became the basis of my doctoral dissertation. Shortly after I defended my dissertation, Fausto, the middle Rivera brother, went on a ten-week robbing spree that ended in a failed bank heist. Little did I know at the time that his incarceration would become the first pivotal moment in a twenty-four-year research journey.

I began making visits regularly to the prisons where Fausto was incarcerated, as my research remained in motion. These Sunday trips to the prisons were all-day affairs. I picked up Fausto's older brother, Julio, early in the morning, drove to the eastern part of Massachusetts, and spent long days in waiting rooms and visiting areas before returning to Springfield. During this time, my relationship with Julio developed. Julio was a high school graduate who had lost his job in 1993. Unable to find another one, he turned to Jorge, a childhood friend and a drug dealer, to fill the gap. In 1996, Julio introduced me to Jorge and other men who hung out regularly at "the block," an open-air, Puerto Rican enclave in Springfield, where mostly men gathered each evening to socialize. The block was also a staging ground for the night's drug dealing activities that Jorge organized. I spent two years, from 1996–1998, learning from men on the block.

I had continued to track Fausto's prison experiences during the seven years he was incarcerated. This was not only a period of prison expansion, largely attributable to the War on Drugs, but also an era of getting tough on prisoners. William Weld, the governor of Massachusetts from 1991 to 1997, was a leading public figure in the movement to punish criminals more harshly, and Fausto's story illustrated this. When Fausto was released, he moved to Hartford, Connecticut, to live with his mother. I recorded his efforts to reintegrate into civilian life—particularly his experiences in off-the-books jobs, as well as emerging problems in his family and neighborhood—to document the struggles of community reentry among former prisoners. When reintegration efforts failed, Fausto's life spiraled into crime and drug addiction—another pivotal moment. Fausto moved from robbing drug dealers to counterfeiting money to "boosting" merchandise from large retail stores. He was arrested for shoplifting (larceny) and, with my intervention, ended up in a Salvation Army drug treatment facility—yet another pivotal moment.

After Fausto completed the Salvation Army treatment program, he returned to the streets and alternated between periods of drug relapse and recovery. Meanwhile, his younger brother, Sammy, was living in Hartford, working mostly temporary jobs, living with Maria (his partner and the mother of his youngest child), and managing his drug addiction to heroin. Working a second job, he was driving home late one snowy night when his car slid off the exit ramp and was totaled. Lacking the resources to secure a loan to buy another car, and dependent on the car to get his children to school and himself to work, he returned to Springfield to "double up" his paycheck by selling cocaine. That night, however, he sprinkled cocaine in a marked dollar bill in the bar's bathroom and was arrested. I followed Sammy through the court process, tape-recorded ten hours of his life story, and tracked his life until he was led away in handcuffs for three years of incarceration. At this juncture, my study of the War on Drugs deepened.

If pivotal moments, however, give a study its vitality and its sustenance, then how do we know when it is time to end a study, or to write? There is, of course, no single answer to this question. In my case, my tenure or promotional clock did not bind the study. I saw a narrative running through my fieldwork toward the end of my tenure period and took a sabbatical in 2001, soon after acquiring tenure, to begin writing. However, shortly thereafter, I was pulled back into the field. As I continued writing, the circular processes of writing and doing fieldwork deepened, and both became more focused. The last third of the book was written from this fieldwork, while the fieldwork reorganized and reconceptualized the first two-thirds of the book (Black 2009).

My journey did not end with the publication of *When a Heart Turns Rock Solid*—the relationships continued, especially with the three brothers, as did the occurrence of pivotal moments. In the first few years after the book's release, Julio quit drinking, while he and his wife, Clara, became regular members of a Pentecostal church. Julio ended a seven-year extramarital affair in his efforts to reform his life and devote himself to God and family. Fausto also became a member of the church, although he continued to cycle through drug relapse and recovery. Sammy split up with Maria, quit his job, and returned to the streets, where he made more money and was more highly regarded for his knowledge and skills.

More recently, the matrix changed again. Nearly $100,000 in debt, Julio explored bankruptcy. He owed $46,000 to the company he worked for because of an unpaid lease on a truck he had driven as an "independent operator" for two years, as well as over $50,000 in unpaid federal and state taxes. Blame moved in different directions. Julio blamed himself; his father blamed Julio's wife, while I blamed the trucking company. Financial problems increased pressure on the fault lines in his marriage, which erupted after their daughter moved out of the house into her own apartment.

Meanwhile, Fausto completed a government-funded culinary arts program. As the chef's star pupil, Fausto embraced a new identity. However, his criminal record preempted finding a job, and only through my own networks were we able to secure him an entry-level job at a chain restaurant. In the fifteen months that followed, Fausto made the transition from the streets to sobriety and precarious work. Searching for a new set of routines, identity, and status, Fausto received emotional support from his former street partners; in fact, one asserted how impressed he was by Fausto's courage, a statement reflecting deep divisions that articulate social marginalization.

Finally, Sammy's street activities resulted in his arrest and incarceration. He was videotaped twice selling to a Puerto Rican undercover police officer, who in the second exchange purchased a .45 caliber handgun from Sammy. The district attorney attempted to give Sammy a fifteen-year sentence for the offense, but his attorney threatened to argue an entrapment case at trial that even the DA had to admit had some validity. When Sammy's attorney threatened to subpoena the informant in the case, the DA lowered the plea offer to a four- to seven-year sentence and Sammy was sent upstate to prison.

As I close in on the twenty-fourth year of my relationships with the three Rivera brothers, the journey is hardly complete, and pivotal moments continue to shape the study. My study became a journey as the men I was tracking took me into different social and institutional spaces that were intersecting with their biographies, including bilingual education, street life and the drug trade, the trucking industry, the housing market and predatory lending, prisons and the War on Drugs, drug treatment, and now the Pentecostal church, the food industry, and prison gangs.

The interconnections of these lived spaces, however, tell a larger story. The demise of bilingual education, the changing constellation of the informal and formal labor forces, the growth of the precarious workforce, the increasing role of the criminal justice system in managing the lives of the dispossessed, and the struggle to establish and sustain community, family, and intimacy amid depleted resources, personal vulnerability, social insecurity, and endemic uncertainty provide us with the profile of an era—the era of neoliberalism. Longitudinal ethnography allows us to see these patterns and interconnections over time, and to bear witness to the lived experiences.

Thick Sociological Description and
Long-term Relationships

In qualitative research, writing is the medium through which we explore our
relationships and record our observations, experiences, feelings, and insights.
The relationships are not separable from the field—there is no subject-object
curtain that provides us with clarity or purity of observation. Nor is the time
in the field linear, any more than the experience of aging is linear. Birthdays
mark time in scientific increments, but life itself defies the simplicity of the
measurement; instead, personal change and lived biography are rooted in
experience, and experiences mark time as memories, turning points, pivotal life events, and epiphanies (Denzin 1987, 1997; Erdmans 2007). Writing
occurs within relationships, which, in a sense, make their own time, as connections and disconnections are defined and redefined in the movement of
closeness and distance, and recorded as shared experiences. This becomes the
medium of understanding—naked, vulnerable, ambivalent, and shorn of
grounded certainties.

"We Were So Much Older Then, We're Younger Than That Now"

It is true that if I had written my book soon after I completed my dissertation in 1993, it would have been a very different book. And it is true that I
know more now about the men and women in my book than I did then,
which gives depth to the relationships and to the writing. Even here, however, I would warn against imposing linear criteria. The book I would have
written in 1993 would not have been "wrong," "misguided," "shallow," or
"premature." It would have been different—no less engaged, no less co-
created through the medium or the intensity of relationships, and no less
right or wrong—just different. For instance, the scope of the book would
have been shorter and more focused on the processes that lead adolescent
boys to remain in school or to leave prematurely, and would have examined
the immediate consequences of those decisions. It was a period characterized by much angst, doubt, and confusion for these boys, and the intensity of my relationships with these adolescents was grounded in an effort
to see the organization of the school, the ways in which school authorities
perceived and responded to these boys, and the multiple, and often contradictory, influences that these adolescents were negotiating. In retrospect—
after twenty-four years—this may appear truncated, and even premature,

but it would have been no less rich in detail, emotion, and insight, capturing a moment in time in which an understanding of the social world was co-created through relationships developed in school classrooms and counselors' offices, on basketball courts, and around family dinner tables.

So what then marks the benefits of longitudinal ethnography in the contexts of relationships and understanding? I would suggest that it provides an expanded horizon of possibilities. Slow sociology allows us to write through the webs of relationships as they emerge within varying social and interpersonal contexts. The journey that I sketch above gives us some flavor of the changing contexts of experience, while the interpersonal horizons that are created through a history of shared experiences allow for the material of understanding. Relationships are deeper and thicker, and with more shared history, we can experience the world together through a longer horizon of conversations, memories, and stories, from which our understanding of the present, or the moment, becomes more textured, co-created, biographically interpreted, and hermeneutical (Denzin 1989; Denzin and Lincoln 2008b; Schwandt 2003; Gadamer 1975; Guba and Lincoln 2008; Probyn 1993; Gearing 1995; Lather 2001; Adler and Adler 1987). In fact, it is this process that challenges the idea that understanding is a linear practice—question asked, question answered, analytical construct examined—but is instead a more circular process in which memories, experiences, prior conversations, interpretations, and emotions are woven through a conversation in which meaning is co-created.

A recent example illustrates this point. In the summer of 2012, I drove Fausto to a job interview. He had completed two years of sobriety and had worked at a restaurant for over a year, and was searching for full-time work. Afterward, we walked through a park, sat for more than an hour on a park bench, walked some more, and discussed a range of topics: the complexities of his relationships with both his father and with his live-in partner; the haunting, recurring memories about the tragedies in his past, particularly the deaths of friends, and the guilt he feels for surviving while others did not; the many times that we walked through this same park in the past and how different our conversations were at those times; the ways in which he currently negotiates relationships with former street friends; his work experiences and his strategies for dealing with authority, coworkers who use drugs, and attractions to coworkers; the extreme anxiety and triumph he felt when he planned and drove two hours to a beach for the first time in his life; my move to Cleveland and how the move would affect our relationship; and my fears about moving away from the familiar and how the anxieties of the move were affecting my moods and relationships.

Our conversation illuminated the issue that was preoccupying both of us at the time—transition—and was woven through a tapestry of past conversations, shared histories and memories, intimacy, and trust. These are the benefits of longitudinal ethnography, in which an understanding of the world is acquired through relationships and through the circles of conversations, experiences, memories, and meaning-making. These are the expanded horizons where complexity dwells and sociological insight awaits.

Intimacy or Closeness Is Rooted in Shared Stories

There are of course many shared stories over twenty-four years. Like in any relationship, stories become the emotional glue of the relationship—its articulation, its spoken history. Longitudinal ethnography provides for a history of shared stories through which our relationship is told and is reconstructed to experience the future together. It fosters an "us," and it is through this "us" that similarities and differences are explored and new horizons become possible.

Often the shared stories express humor. They include Julio and Clara's wedding, where the brothers and I wore top hats and tuxedos, rode in a limousine, and participated in the ceremony. There was also the time Julio mistakenly climbed into bed with me after a night of drinking, slapping me on my butt and telling me to move over, thinking I was his wife.

Shared stories articulate special moments of closeness, such as riding in the middle of a small pick-up truck through the mountains of Puerto Rico, sandwiched between Julio and his father, Juan; sitting one evening on the pier in Ponce, watching the sunset and sipping rum; and spending other evenings on Juan's front porch, listening to men from the community tell their stories. There are also the stories of getting drunk together—an age-old remedy for breaking down male emotional dams—and recording the escapades and the moments of embarrassment that ensued, as well as adding to the long list (and photos) of victims of the family's homemade rum recipe.

Shared stories record moments of tragedy and vulnerability (and the support shown during such moments), such as deaths in the family, deaths of friends, arrests, incarcerations, lost jobs, failed opportunities, failed health, victimizations caused by violence, and evictions, to name just some of the types of painful events that dot the landscape and become sewn into the shared history. Perhaps no event is more illustrative of this than when I answered the phone at 4:30 in the morning and heard Julio's trembling voice say that his mother had suffered an aneurysm and was dying; later that day, I sat in a hospital room with Julio, Fausto, Sammy, and Juan as we together made the decision to end her life support.

Long-term ethnography extends a history of shared stories that becomes the articulation of relationships and the ground for intimacy, exploration, and an understanding of human experience.

Managing Closeness and Distance

Longitudinal ethnography may deepen relationships and expand our knowledge of study participants' lives, but is there a risk of becoming too close and thereby sacrificing analytical distance or, in the more antiquated scientific vein, objectivity? Or do closeness and intimacy increase concerns about betrayal that result in a stricter censorship of the material that gets publicly presented?

Regarding the former, it is important to remember that all relationships require the management of closeness and distance—even our most intimate relationships. The strong desire for human connection is tempered by deep-seated fears of self-annihilation, which sets into motion the vicissitudes of closeness and distance within intimate relationships. In the field, our work as ethnographers is to document the processes of closeness and distance—our credibility depends on this. The nature of our closeness with study participants and how this becomes the basis for understanding is a fundamental part of ethnographic description and understanding (Van Maanen 1988). There are obvious benefits—we can examine the internal and external worlds of individuals and ourselves, explore similarities and differences as well as points of connection and disconnection, provide thick description, tell intimate stories, and expose others to worlds with which they may be unfamiliar.

There are obvious benefits to distance as well—it allows us to develop analytical and conceptual frames for understanding, to challenge reified social science categories, and to enhance our critical consciousness about the intersections of individual lives and structural processes. The problem with this formulation really hinges on our positions concerning objectivity. Epistemological and methodological critiques of postpositivism in the last forty years, however, have demonstrated well that it is impossible to observe and write outside of our own historically and culturally situated perspectives, social locations or positions, or interpretive predispositions, let alone stand above and beyond the webs of relationships through which we acquire our understandings of the world (Schwandt 2003; Lather and Smithies 1997; Kamberelis and Dimitridis 2008; Clifford 1988). Even practices of *Verstehen* that promised more objective descriptions of lifeworlds through self-understanding and self-management have been properly disposed of, leaving us with no alternatives but to write within and through relationships rather than outside and above them (Schwandt 2003; Denzin 1997).

The more important issue may concern the ethics of exposure and disclosure of the intimate details of our study participants' lives—or, by extension, our own inclination to censor material in order to protect participants (Fine 1998; Fine et al. 2003; Benmajor 1991). What are our motives for exposing intimate details: To understand the social world? To advance a political agenda? To change public policy? To acquire professional status and prestige? These are difficult questions that affect all ethnography, not just longitudinal ethnography, although they may become more apparent in long-term studies, or in studies in which relationships between the researcher and the researched become more intimate. Authorial power and the power of representation is an important responsibility that cannot be easily dismissed or diminished once we accept the premise that we are writing from within and through relationships—in other words, when the emperor (researcher) no longer has any clothes and is therefore shorn of his or her scientific protocols, we are forced to deal with ourselves as emotional, political, and sentient beings who have a responsibility to those we have become close to in the field (Black 2009; Angrosino 2008). If we have more power via our social locations than those we are studying, this responsibility becomes even greater. Our critical and selective consciousness is central to the processes of constructing knowledge claims, but closeness in the field reminds us of the ethical importance of transparency and requires us to come to terms with our own motives and purposes for doing research.[2]

Very often, distance is not difficult to create in ethnographic relationships—it is structured into the relationship. The researcher is typically different from the study participants. Ethnography attempts to bridge cultural distance, a process that facilitates understanding. Part of the craft of managing closeness and distance is articulating both in the relationship—making (and articulating) connection, while recognizing (and articulating) distance. In my case, maintaining distance was never difficult—I am not Puerto Rican, not street smart, not a fighter, not a drug dealer, not a truck driver, not a prison inmate, and so on. I was never like them—and never tried to act like I was, which would have been pretentious, comical, and unproductive. They are as aware of our differences as I am. There were similarities—gender (male) and sexual identity (heterosexual) with the men in my study—but even these identities are located within intersecting identities of race, ethnicity, class, and age that reconfigure our experiences and understandings of gender and sexual identity, shifting the familiar ground we thought we were standing on. We navigated closeness in a sea of difference. So while getting backstage and betraying intimacy was indeed a risk that I needed to confront honestly, I was more at risk of thinking I knew something that perhaps I didn't, because I wasn't close enough. Long-term ethnography helps us to gain more confidence in what we know, but it doesn't produce certainty—uncertainty remains endemic to the craft. But this brings me to my last point concerning the ethnographic relationship and what we learn.

Exploring Disruptions

The greatest risk to relationships developed in the field occurs when the study is published. The power imbalance is apparent at this point—the authorial voice determines what gets said and how. The longer we know our participants and the more the lines between researcher and participant have been abridged, the more we may feel trepidation as we peck away at the keyboard. Will we offend? Will our perspective, when fully realized, feel like betrayal? Can we rely on sociological jargon to hide our critical, and perhaps personal, observations? Or will sociological language itself offend? There are no easy answers. Julio read a few drafted chapters and commented on them. But he was not on his own turf—the language was mine and he seemed uncomfortable responding to it. He objected to one of my observations. It was not central to my argument so I took it out. But neither Fausto nor Sammy has good reading skills, and neither was interested in reading an advance draft. None of the other men and women in the book saw anything before publication. I wrote with their "presence" in the room and held my breath as the book went to press. In fact, after I made my final comments on the galleys and sent it off, I panicked. Had I revealed too much about the drug trade? Could any of them be traceable? Had I revealed something one of them said to me in confidence about someone else that might result in retribution? I called the people that I had relied on for support through the writing process, and fortunately they reassured me.

Clearly, if study participants are presented in unfavorable ways, strains and tensions may emerge that will have to be managed for the relationships to continue (Lareau 2011). While long-term ethnography may increase our apprehensions as we write, it also makes the restorative work easier: because the relationships have been sustained over time, differences are already more apparent and have been managed with some degree of mutual tolerance—in other words, there's already enough grit in the relationships to absorb tension. Of course, there's no guarantee, and both parties have to be willing to invest the time to work through the tensions. The structured differences in the relationships, along with the end of the study that publication defines, make it easier to part ways at this moment. Nonetheless, long-term ethnography producing long-term relationships provides more incentive to resolve the differences.

One example concerns Julio. Sitting at the table with Julio and his wife, Clara, about five months after the publication of the book, I asked Clara if she had read the book. She said that she had read parts of it and smiled coyly at Julio. Julio had read the book, but at this moment was engrossed in his plate of rice and beans, or so it appeared. After a brief silence, Julio dropped his fork and turned to me and said, "You described me as a *machista* [a male chauvinist]." Clara responded, pointing to the book, "That's because you are, Julio, you are. The book says it, and the book is fact, and that is what it says." Julio look chagrined, but the moment provided an opening for us to talk about his family and others in Villalba, Puerto Rico, where he was born. It allowed us to talk about the role of men and women in their culture and in their families, and how both he and Clara participated in—but were also changing—these roles and traditions. In other words, it allowed us to talk about patriarchy without personalizing it or demonizing Julio. The disruption, in this case, provided an opening for exploration.

Another landscape for eruption was traversed with Sammy. When Sammy was in jail awaiting trial for a drug dealing charge, the book was receiving a lot of press in Springfield—a front-page review in the Sunday paper, a review in a smaller paper, and a series of public talks. Sammy's attorney was aware of the book and Sammy decided to divulge his identity in the book to him. A week or so later, the attorney asked Sammy if he thought that sending a copy of the book to the district attorney might be useful to him in a plea bargain. Sammy asked me about it and I urged caution. "Sammy, the book is about your life. It describes your time in Greenfield and on Franklin Street and on the block [as a drug dealer]. It describes other times in your life too, like when you were working in [a suburb in Hartford], living with Maria, and taking care of children. I want to be helpful, Sam, but I don't want the book to be used against you." I did not mention at the time that I also feared that others might be put in jeopardy if his identity was exposed. Sammy was under a lot of stress, had not read the book, and I could tell was disturbed by my response that the book could work against him. No disruption occurred and Sammy struck a favorable plea agreement.

After Sammy was sent to a state prison, I sent him a copy of the book, and he began reading it. When I visited, Sammy pointed out parts of his story on the streets that I had left out, or, in his perspective, I was unaware of. He did not finish the book, but read enough to develop a critique. Interestingly, while he was awaiting trial, he had worried that the book was not sanitized enough, that I didn't present him in a publicly favorable way, and that it might not be useful to him. However, sitting inside a state prison, he embraced his street identity and identified my incomplete understanding of who he was on the streets.

In both cases, with Julio and Sammy, the book became a medium through which our conversation continued and our relationships deepened. Julio and I ventured into the arena of gender, turning it into an integral part of our conversation and relationship. Sammy and I compared our notes and memories, filled in gaps, discussed my representation of him in the book and how I saw him more generally, and explored different ways of thinking about the streets. In other words, disruptions were absorbed and changed our relationships, deepened our understandings of one another, and provided new horizons through which to move forward together . . . a process attributable to and indicative of longitudinal ethnography.

Macrosocial Forces, Institutional Dynamics, and Individual Lives

One of the strengths of slow sociology is that it allows time to see the interconnections of social and individual changes. That is, both the social world and individuals change over time; the task of the ethnographer is to document the intersections of these changes. Building on the insights of C. Wright Mills, I adopt a narrative strategy, or sociological storytelling (Berger and Quinney 2005; Polletta et al. 2011), to illustrate the connections between the inner lives of individuals and larger social-historical structures. As Mills (1959, 158) wrote: "The biographies of men and women, the kinds of individuals they variously become, cannot be understood without reference to the historical structures in which the milieux of the everyday life are organized."

After twenty-four years, there are numerous examples of this in my study. The period of my ethnography is defined by the early 1990s recession, the longest recovery in U.S. history, the 2001 recession, the subsequent jobless recovery, and now the Great Recession and its aftermath. The era of neoliberalism and mass incarceration is also apparent in the lives of the men and women I have known, illuminating the reductions in public assistance, the privatization of job training, the assault on labor unions, the predominance of precarious work, the use of the criminal justice system to manage the lives of the economically redundant, and the wholly inadequate public efforts to address the health needs of drug addicts among more marginalized populations. These structural forces can be seen running through the lives of the men and women in my study like historical and social streams.

From the Streets to the Workplace

It was not until after a decade of tracking the men in my study that I realized the significance of the 1990s in their lives. The two most prominent social forces of this decade affecting their lives were jobs and prison—jobs because of the tight labor market in the late 1990s, which was associated with a ten-year economic expansion, and prison because of the hyped-up War on Drugs. Looking at this from the streets, some of the men in my study were getting jobs in the late 1990s and leaving the streets, while others were going to prison.

These changing social conditions allowed me to watch men change. A chapter in my book is devoted to transitions men made as they were coming off of the streets and into the workplace, focusing particularly on the barriers to these transitions. Perhaps more important, there were men who left the streets for employment who were immersed in street life—who had adopted dominant street identities. Not only did they take advantage of new opportunities in the late 1990s, but as they did, their identities changed and their perceptions of the streets changed as well.

Mundo is a good example. Mundo was often the center of attention on the block, telling stories and keeping many of us in stitches of laughter well into the wee hours of the morning. He snorted copious amounts of cocaine through the night and shared his brother Jorge's opposition to formal work. Nonetheless, Mundo left the streets in the late 1990s and his identity became organized around fatherhood. Moreover, his perception of the streets changed, as the following quote illustrates:

> Drug money, it ain't shit. Sometimes you got it, other times it's dry out there. . . . You know, you may look good out there, you got clothes and shit, but it don't mean shit, Tim. . . . Who cares? Now that I have a job and a paycheck, I know what's important, and it ain't clothes. But when you out on the streets that's all you care about, looking good and shit. The money comes and it goes. You look good, *but inside you feel like shit.*

Mundo was also fortunate that he was never arrested under drug statutes and given a lengthy prison sentence. He did short bids for small crimes, like driving violations, alcohol-related crimes, failing to show up for court, and failing to comply with probation—crimes of resistance in which he refused to abide by rules about licenses, drinking, and reporting to court and probation. Unlike other men, however, who were apprehended doing the same things that Mundo was doing on the streets, he was able to take advantage of the tight labor market in the 1990s and to become, in his words, the father that his father was not.

Consequences of Prison

I knew several of the men before they went to prison, and then followed them while they were in prison and after their release. Longitudinal ethnography allowed me to see how prison changed them. Two of the Rivera brothers stand out here.

Fausto spent seven years in prison, from ages nineteen to twenty-six. He entered during the era of "getting tough on criminals" and the governor of Massachusetts, William Weld, was a leading proponent of this charge. Fausto was part of a sweep inside the prisons that focused on Latino gangs and was intended to weaken the gangs and break the will of gang leaders. He spent fourteen months in solitary confinement. Fausto was also exposed to and participated in several incidences of brutal violence in prison. Shortly after his release, he was again involved in a crime that was inseparable from his heroin addiction. He was later diagnosed with post-traumatic stress disorder, and was unemployed most of the ten years after his release. Despite periods of immersion in drug dealing and street violence during the ten-year interim, Fausto avoided a second long prison sentence, which gave him the time to make the slow, grinding transition from prison to sobriety and precarious work.

His younger brother, Sammy, is another example of a young man who surprisingly left the streets for the workplace in 1998. Sammy was working for temp agencies, living with the mother of his son, and reorganizing his identity around working and being a father. As described earlier, when he wrecked his car and turned to his resource networks to buy another one, he was arrested and sentenced to three years in prison for dealing cocaine in a bathroom at a local bar. At a time in which Sammy's life appeared to be moving in a different direction, he was incarcerated, and again his street identity became dominant within the prison. He attempted to reclaim his life with his partner, her children, and their son when he was released, but this failed, largely because of the strain that his incarceration had placed on his relationship with his partner. He returned to the streets, and like many former prisoners was again arrested. He is now doing a state bid of four to seven years, has become part of the leadership in one of the prison gangs, and has participated in a series of violent incidents, landing him in the highest-security prison in Massachusetts.

In short, in the process of longitudinal ethnography, I have documented several effects of prison on the lives of Fausto and Sammy, including the effects of violence inside prisons; the hardening of street identities in reaction to prison conditions; the collateral punishment that continues after release, especially in the form of employment discrimination; and the effects that incarceration has on relationships with intimate partners and children.

The Limits to Success

Some of the men who left the streets for the workplace in the 1990s fit Katherine Newman's (2006) description of the "high flyer." They obtained good paying jobs and experienced social mobility, with a few reaching middle-income status. Julio, the oldest Rivera brother, and his wife, Clara, are the best examples. In 2005, Julio had been driving a tractor-trailer truck for ten years, and Clara took a job as a bank teller. The following year, they bought a house that symbolized their success.

As they moved from the streets to middle-income status, their struggles associated with poverty changed to struggles associated with the working class in the new millennium. Several structural constraints on their success and prosperity became apparent. The first was their purchase of a home in Springfield, which has the highest Latino neighborhood segregation of any city in the state.[3] Their neighborhood was a stable West Indian neighborhood (with mostly Jamaican and Puerto Rican residents), but its location on the edge of a poorer neighborhood limited their capacity for building equity in their home over time. A few years after they bought the home, there were several incidents of violence in the adjacent neighborhood that sent their property values spiraling downward. During the 2008 recession, the value of their property bottomed out at what one realtor estimated was half of what they had paid for it.

Second, and related, despite their high income, they were considered high-risk homebuyers because they lacked a credit history, had accumulated debt, and had no savings. The booming but overvalued housing market expanded home-buying opportunities for families like that of Julio and Clara. Take out a subprime loan, they were told, and in five years refinance to a loan with better terms. In three years, the mortgage market imploded and their mortgage interest rate reached 12.9 percent. This, combined with the falling value of their home, pushed them to join the millions of homeowners who were walking away from their mortgages and renting apartments.

Third, the company that Julio works for has engaged in several union-busting practices that have limited Julio's wages. Encouraged to leave the union to become an owner-operator, Julio relinquished this status two years later, returned to the company, and was placed in its nonunion division; the company charged Julio $46,000 for his lease of the truck during the time he was an owner-operator. In addition, the company has closed down the terminal where its union division was housed and moved its operations to a new location, where it is increasing the size of its nonunion divisions.

Looking through one lens, we see that Julio is one of the most successful men from the 1990s block; through another, he is a victim of an overwrought housing market and capitalist duplicity.

OGs and a New Generation of Street Kids

The block looks much different today than it did in the 1990s, when the easy flow of cocaine dominated the trade. Since then, the demand for cocaine has declined, trade connections have been severed, and dealers have gone to prison. However, there is both continuity and discontinuity. Continuity has been maintained through family involvement and control of the drug trade in the area (Duck and Rawls 2012) as well as by old social networks that have persevered despite being reorganized. But discontinuity has also occurred as a new generational cohort reached the streets, as market changes diversified the drug trade, and as the use of armed robbery to secure investment capital increased (Contreras 2013).

One of the markers of both continuity and discontinuity is the presence of OGs. In street parlance, OGs refers to "old gangsters"—men who made money and acquired status from the streets and often were gang involved, but who are part of an aging cohort.[4] Most men age out of the drug trade; they are in it for only short periods of time, and make very little money or acquire little status. Increasingly, however, it has become difficult to age out. With limited job opportunities, increased drug arrests and incarceration, longer prison sentences, and varying forms of collateral punishment, aging street men find themselves in a liminal state. At a point in their life courses in which aging out might be expected, street life provides their only access to revenue and to status and dignity.

There are different ways of responding to these conditions, usually depending on the individual's location within drug and community networks. One OG, for instance, is a member of a family with a long history in the drug trade bridging the island and the mainland. As an aging elder in the family, he is provided for economically but remains largely in the background, occasionally making public appearances to give legitimacy to decisions or changing networks. More commonly, OGs attempt to assert themselves as role models or to teach a new generation "the ropes." They try to create a moral order on the streets, sanctioning violence, facilitating connections, teaching skills and street smarts, and articulating the boundaries of the street code. These efforts are sometimes welcomed and encouraged but at other times rejected by the new generation, who are themselves attempting to establish their own place on the streets.

Finally, some OGs remain in the drug business, adopting a ruthless disposition for staying on top. This has become difficult, however, as the demand for cocaine has declined, trade connections have been lost, and competition has increased (Contreras 2013). One OG who has remained dominant in the drug trade increasingly relies on gun violence to acquire investment capital and to project a reputation that intimidates competitors. On several occasions, he has wooed large buyers (drug dealers) into business exchanges, and then at some point in the relationship robbed them of substantial amounts of money and drugs. This has increased the risk of deadly violence on the block, as well as the presence of guns.

The longevity of my study has allowed me to document these generational changes. Drug raids are now resulting in a new cohort of men and women being led away in handcuffs—men and women whom I recognize as some of the young boys and girls I saw on the block in the 1990s. The drugs being confiscated have changed to a more diverse selection of drugs that includes not only cocaine and heroin but also ecstasy, angel dust, Ritalin, and Percocet. The faces have changed, although several of the OGs are still to be found as well. What has not changed, however, are thwarted job opportunities, a high Puerto Rican school dropout rate, high rates of Puerto Rican residential segregation, and the reliance on the criminal justice system to manage an economically and socially dislocated population. In other words, with longitudinal ethnography, we can see the mechanisms through which social inequality is reproduced.

Conclusion

Longitudinal data sets are highly valued in the social sciences, where a cohort is followed and data collected at regular intervals across time. These data sets comprise the bones from which much meat is cut and theoretically developed in sociology and other disciplines. Longitudinal ethnography is a different animal. Here, the fluidity of self, located within the vagaries of structural conditions, provides the material for a deeper understanding of human experience, the subtle and at times transformative character of personal change, and the mechanisms and dynamics of larger institutional and structural changes.

Not only does longitudinal ethnography pry open spaces for theoretical imagination, it encourages us to get beyond the imposed categories of sociologists that squeeze human experience into oversimplified and static conceptions of human life. For instance, in the study of urban poverty, longitudinal ethnographic description and interpretation exposes monolithic (underclass) or binary (street and decent) characterizations of socially and economically marginalized groups as reductive and vacuous. In contrast, longitudinal ethnography demonstrates that individuals are a complex swirl of tendencies, dispositions, and sensibilities derived from a variety of experiences and influences, often contradictory in meaning, that are located within the spatial configurations of structural dynamics. As such, identities change as different parts of our selves are nourished, shaped, and validated within the social conditions that contextualize our lives, and as these social conditions change, so do we—albeit in often unpredictable ways that defy one-to-one correspondence or, in more standard parlance, co-variation.

This strategy for understanding also requires that we get beyond researcher-respondent duality and postpositivist methodological presumptions. Writing from within and through relationships recognizes that we affect the object of our inquiry the moment that our historically and socially situated selves enter the interpretive field. It places more, not less, responsibility on the researcher to engage himself or herself in the processes of understanding, and to characterize our interpretations within the intersections of relationships, which are themselves historically and socially situated.

Finally, there is much to be said for "taking your time" or, dare I say, committing to a lifetime of relationships. Time adds an invaluable dimension to understanding, and one that is not simply additive or linear, but is also circular, textured, and evocative. Good ethnographic description provides a snapshot of a slice in time, and like a photograph it captures a moment and invites memory, interpretation, and emotional engagement. But a series of snapshots across time allows for different types of analyses. It may be organized as a montage that fractures and splinters while we seek patterns of meaning and coherence. Or it may become a representation of time through which we see not only social and historical change, but also individual change within social and historical streams.

Notes

1. The names used in this paper are the same pseudonyms used in my book (Black 2009).
2. This is a succinct treatment of an issue that needs more elaboration but is outside the scope of this paper.
3. Neighborhood segregation mirrors school segregation. A report issued by Northwestern University's Institute on Urban Health Research in 2010 found that Springfield's primary public schools had the second-highest rate of Hispanic segregation among the one hundred largest metropolitan areas in the United States. Springfield was sandwiched between Los Angeles and New York in the rankings. See McArdle et al. 2010.
4. "OG" refers to other things as well—"old goat," "old moneyman," "old game," or "old generation."

References

Adler, P. A., and P. Adler. 1987. *Membership Roles in Field Research*. Thousand Oaks, CA: Sage.

Angrosino, M. V. 2008. "Recontextualizing Observation: Ethnography, Pedagogy, and the Prospects for a Progressive Political Agenda." In Denzin and Lincoln 2008a, 161–84.

Benmajor, R. 1991. "Testimony, Action Research, and Empowerment: Puerto Rican Women and Popular Education." In *Women's Words: The Feminist Practice of Oral History*, edited by S. B. Gluck and D. Patai, 159–74. New York: Routledge.

Berger, R., and R. Quinney, eds. 2005. *Storytelling Sociology: Narrative as Social Inquiry*. Boulder, CO: Lynne Rienner.

Black, T. 2009. *When a Heart Turns Rock Solid: The Lives of Three Puerto Rican Brothers on and off the Streets*. New York: Pantheon.

Clifford, J. 1988. *The Predicament of Culture: Twentieth-Century Ethnography, Literature and Art*. Cambridge, MA: Harvard University Press.

Contreras, R. 2013. *The Stickup Kids: Race, Drugs, Violence, and the American Dream*. Berkeley: University of California Press.

Denzin, N. K. 1987. *The Recovering Alcoholic*. Thousand Oaks, CA: Sage.

———. 1989. *Interpretive Biography*. Thousand Oaks, CA: Sage.

———. 1997. *Interpretive Ethnography: Ethnographic Practices for the 21st Century*. Thousand Oaks, CA: Sage.

Denzin, N. K., and Y. S. Lincoln, eds. 2008a. *Collecting and Interpreting Qualitative Materials*. Thousand Oaks, CA: Sage.

———. 2008b. "Introduction: The Discipline and Practice of Qualitative Research." In Denzin and Lincoln 2008c, 1–43.

———, eds. 2008c. *The Landscape of Qualitative Research*. Thousand Oaks, CA: Sage.

Duck, W., and A. W. Rawls. 2012. "Interaction Orders of Drug Dealing Spaces: Local Orders of Sensemaking in a Poor Black American Place." *Crime, Law and Social Change* 57 (1): 33–75.

Erdmans, M. P. 2007. "The Personal Is Political, but Is It Academic?" *Journal of American Ethnic History* 26 (4): 7–23.

Fine, M. 1998. "Working the Hyphens: Reinventing Self and Other in Qualitative Research." In Denzin and Lincoln 2008c, 70–82.

Fine, M., L. Weiss, S. Weseen, and L. Wong. 2003. "For Whom? Qualitative Research, Representations and Social Responsibilities." In Denzin and Lincoln 2008c, 167–207.

Gadamer, H.-G. 1975. *Truth and Method*. 2nd rev. ed. Translated by J. Weinscheimer and D. G. Marshall. New York: Seabury Press.

Gearing, J. 1995. "Fear and Loving in the West Indies: Research from the Heart (as well as the head)." In *Taboo: Sex, Identity, and Erotic Subjectivity in Anthropological Fieldwork*, edited by D. Kulick and M. Willson, 141–65. London: Routledge.

Guba, E. G., and Y. S. Lincoln. 2008. "Paradigmatic Controversies, Contradictions, and Emerging Confluences." In Denzin and Lincoln 2008c, 255–86.

Kamberelis, G., and G. Dimitridis. 2008. "Focus Groups: Strategic Articulations of Pedagogy, Politics, and Inquiry." In Denzin and Lincoln, 2008a, 375–402.

Lareau, A. 2011. *Unequal Childhoods: Class, Race, and Family Life*. 2nd ed. Berkeley: University of California Press.

Lather, P. 2001. "Postbook: Working the Ruins of Feminist Ethnography." *Signs: Journal of Women in Culture and Society* 27 (1): 199–227.

Lather, P, and C. Smithies. 1997. *Troubling the Angels: Women Living with HIV/ AIDS*. Boulder, CO: Westview.

McArdle, N., T. Osypuk, and D. Acevedo-Garcia. 2010. *Segregation and Exposure to High-Poverty Schools in Large Metropolitan Areas: 2008–2009*. Boston: Northeastern University, Institute on Urban Health Research. *diversitydata.sph. harvard.edu/Publications/school_segregation_report.pdf.*

Mills, C. W. 1959. *The Sociological Imagination*. New York: Oxford University Press.

Newman, K. S. 2006. *Chutes and Ladders: Navigating the Low-Wage Labor Market*. New York: Russell Sage Foundation; Cambridge, MA: Harvard University Press.

Polletta, F. P., C. B. Chen, B. G. Gardner, and A. Motes. 2011. "The Sociology of Storytelling." *Annual Review of Sociology* 37: 109–30.

Probyn, E. 1993. *Sexing the Self: Gendered Positions in Cultural Studies*. New York: Routledge.

Schwandt, T. A. 2003. "Three Epistemological Stances for Qualitative Inquiry: Interpretivism, Hermeneutics, and Social Constructionism." In Denzin and Lincoln 2008c, 292–331.

Van Maanen, J. 1988. *Tales of the Field: On Writing Ethnography*. Chicago: University of Chicago Press.

2

Conflicted Selves

Trust and Betrayal in Studying
the Hare Krishna

E. Burke Rochford Jr.

As I worried years ago about my insider status, here I am again. I keep thinking, you don't tell secrets on your family. There are rules. There are strong pressures as an insider to avoid revealing dirty laundry in public. To do so raises questions about one's sincerity as an insider. If one is loyal he protects the group from outside attack. This willingness to protect represents a litmus test of membership itself. Yet in writing about child abuse I have brought ISKCON to the front page of the *New York Times*. Some of my devotee friends are likely to feel betrayed. I feel sick about all this.

Fieldnotes, October 10, 1998

Successful field research rests on the ability of the researcher to establish and maintain trust with those under study. Trust opens research opportunities that allow for gaining an understanding of the subjects' ways of life from *their* point of view. This often requires "going slow," given that the social worlds we investigate are almost inevitably complex, multidimensional, and ever changing. But long-term involvement in the field also encompasses more than strategically establishing trust for research purposes. It may also include relationships, including friendships that lead researchers to be seen, and perhaps to see themselves, as insiders within the social worlds they are studying. Given that sociological analysis is often critical, however, trust can readily turn into betrayal.

45

Although establishing trust is important for any research project, it is essential when investigating marginal and deviant people and communities, such as controversial new religious movements, for such groups are often struggling to gain a measure of public acceptance, if not legitimacy. Because scholars write books and articles that may be viewed as reliable sources by the media and the public, members of new religions have legitimate concerns about those who study them. Access to the media, and through it to the public at large, can either bring about sympathetic understanding or further negative stereotypes of the group. Therefore, where a researcher's sympathies lie is an ever-present consideration and, as Howard Becker (1967) noted years ago, those we study often want to know whose side we are on. The answer to this question determines a researcher's access to the setting and shapes the very nature of the research process.

I have spent my entire professional career studying the Hare Krishna movement, known formally as the International Society for Krishna Consciousness (hereafter ISKCON).[1] It has been a life-changing experience for me but also one that has been punctuated by disagreement and even controversy. It has been life-changing because I have been accepted by many ISKCON members as an insider and a devotee of Krishna, something that I have at times embraced over the course of my thirty-five years of research on ISKCON (Rochford 1985, 21–42; 1992; 2001b). But this very insider status, which opened so many research opportunities for me, also produced disappointment and conflict, as some leaders and rank-and-file devotees interpreted portions of my published work as unfairly critical of ISKCON (Rochford 1992). Trust, in these situations, was replaced by feelings of betrayal that challenged my continued presence in the field. This chapter details my efforts to establish trust and how my writings on the movement called into question both my identity as an insider as well as my intentions as a researcher.

Engagement and Establishing Trust

My research on the Hare Krishna movement began in the fall of 1975 as I was beginning graduate study at UCLA. I had enrolled in a course on ethnographic research where I was required to find a setting for an extended research project. Initially, I planned to study political activists, but being new to Los Angeles, I had a difficult time locating an appropriate research site. After I complained about my plight, a longtime friend suggested that

I speak with one of his two brothers who had joined the Hare Krishnas. I had known both brothers from years ago but I was initially steadfast in my refusal. As I said to my friend, "I read the newspapers and the Hare Krishnas are just plain weird as far as I am concerned." Plus, I admitted having little knowledge about or interest in religion. As time grew short and my professor began exerting more pressure, I gave in and called my friend's older brother. At the time, he was living with his wife and two children in the ISKCON community on the west side of Los Angeles. He invited me to his apartment and made arrangements for me to speak with one of the leaders of the community. He also took me to the temple for the evening worship service, and it was there that my interest in conducting a research project on the movement was sparked. The temple was an alien world to me, with images on the altar I knew nothing about and paintings on the walls that were equally mysterious. However, the devotees I observed were young, like me, and as I would learn, most came from backgrounds similar to my own (i.e., they were middle class and had been involved for a time in both the anti-Vietnam War movement and the counterculture).

My initial entrée into the community was largely informal, and while community authorities were aware of my presence and purposes, they never confronted me directly about my research. In large part their disinterest grew from a greater reality that would define my presence in the field over the months ahead: I was seen by virtually everyone I met in the community as a potential convert rather than as a researcher. This was my greatest fear in starting the project and I was subject to ongoing conversion attempts by the devotees. Most quickly turned aside my explanation of being a student researcher by responding, "Yes, *prabhu*, we all have our stories but we understand why you are *really* here."[2] Whether I knew it or not, Krishna had sent me. Such statements only intensified my discomfort, as I had hoped my research role would serve as a protective shield against the devotees' conversion attempts. During my first weeks in the field, I desperately sought to establish myself as a strict observer. Participation, I was convinced, would suggest to the devotees that I had a personal interest in Krishna Consciousness and ISKCON. Yet, as I was soon to learn, participation was a requirement for everyone in the setting, and I was expected to demonstrate growing commitment to Krishna Consciousness. During these formative years of ISKCON's development, one was judged either as a "devotee" or, to use the colorful language of the 1970s, a "demon" or a "karmie." Securing any degree of acceptance would depend on my willingness to actively participate in the religious life of the community. From the moment of my first foray into the Los Angeles community, the devotees asked me repeatedly if I chanted the Hare Krishna mantra. Although sometimes I answered affirmatively to avoid an uncomfortable situation, I still refused to chant among the devotees in the temple. Chanting, I thought, was appropriate for someone becoming a devotee, but not a researcher, or at least not *this* researcher.

A few weeks into my research, a critical situation arose that would reshape my project and my relationship with community members. It occurred early in the morning (3:30 a.m.), when devotees chant individually before the first worship service (*arati*) of the day. As I wrote in my fieldnotes:

> [As] all the devotees were chanting their rounds in the temple, I refrained from doing so. It was very uncomfortable to be among all the devotees while they chanted. I observed for a while, but then realized that I was being observed more than I was observing. I could see that all the devotees were noticing that I wasn't chanting. I felt that I was being avoided (looked down upon) because of my refusal to take part in the chanting. . . . I had visions of the study coming apart at the seams. Several devotees stopped and suggested that I try chanting the mantras. I continued to refuse. (Rochford 1976)

As I contemplated the end of my project, the younger brother of my friend came into the temple. Seeing that I was not chanting, he came over and asked if I had *japa* beads (a string of 108 beads used for individual chanting).[3] When I replied that I didn't, he offered me an extra string of beads and suggested I try chanting.

> At this point I felt I had better take the beads and try chanting. I succumbed to the pressure. I knew that by chanting, the devotees would be pleased and the pressures I was feeling would subside. Soon after I began chanting, things started to happen. First, a devotee came over to me and put a flower garland around my neck (flowers that had previously been on the altar and thus were very special to the devotees). He welcomed me to Krishna Consciousness. A few minutes later, another devotee stopped and showed me the correct way to hold the beads while chanting. Immediately after that still another devotee came

over and asked if I wanted to water the spiritual plant *Tulasi Devi*. We went over to the plant and he showed me the proper way to "offer" the water to *Tulasi*. (Rochford 1976)

Although I had given in to the devotees' expectations, I continued to interpret my actions in terms of my researcher role. As I wrote in my fieldnotes following this incident, "I felt that I was surrendering more to the thought that if I didn't show my interest (as a potential convert) my relationship with the devotees would suffer, and my research would also. I sense I am getting into a bind. I've got to think this out some" (Rochford 1976).

During the months that followed, I slowly became more comfortable with the role of potential convert, in large part because I realized that researching recruitment and conversion were the only topics available for study. As time went on, however, I began to participate more frequently and with less hesitation in the ceremonial life of Krishna Consciousness. Doing so provided access to a wider range of community members. To my surprise, I also gained personal satisfaction from worshiping in the temple and began attending temple functions as much for my own spiritual purposes as for my research (Rochford 1985, 26).

Although early on in the research process, building trust was largely a product of my willingness to participate in the rituals and practices of Krishna Consciousness, my role changed over time as I became more involved in the life of the community. In 1979 and 1980, as I was conducting my dissertation research, I began working in the community school, where my job was to take young boys aged five to eight years to a nearby park, or to the beach a short drive from the community (Rochford 2011). I also began expressing my views about issues in the Los Angeles ISKCON community, as well my views about issues in the movement more generally, especially about the leadership controversies that emerged following the death of ISKCON's founder, Prabhupada, in 1977. These actions signaled both to myself and to the devotees my commitment to ISKCON and its well-being.

My membership status grew further during the years that followed. Beginning in the early 1990s, I served as a member of ISKCON's North American Board of Education and was an advocate for children in that role. As controversy grew about ISKCON's leadership in the 1980s and 1990s, I was asked to serve on a committee investigating the appointment of ISKCON's successor gurus following Prabhupada's death. In the early 1990s,

I agreed at the leadership's invitation to conduct a survey of ISKCON's worldwide membership as part of the centennial celebration of Prabhupada's birth (see Rochford 1999). During these years, I also contributed a number of scholarly articles to the *ISKCON Communications Journal* about family development, child abuse, and leadership (Rochford 1997, 1998a, 1998b, 1999, 2000, 2001a).[4]

Insider Knowledge, Sociological Analysis, and Betrayal

Ethnographers face a variety of challenges in the field that may call into question or potentially rupture the trust established with their informants. In the extreme, a loss of trust may push researchers out of the field or otherwise render them so marginal that research opportunities become sharply reduced (see, for example, Leatham 2001).

During my early months in the field, I made a number of mistakes that raised questions about my trustworthiness. Yet the occasions where my identity became a topic of critical scrutiny by ISKCON members occurred after the publication of my two books on ISKCON (Rochford 1985, 2007) and especially following the publication of my article on child abuse in the movement's boarding schools (Rochford 1998a). These publications produced highly charged situations where some ISKCON members saw reason to reassess my identity and motives. Was I a devotee after all, or even a "well-wisher" of ISKCON? Several powerful and influential ISKCON leaders and members believed my writings were proof of my outsider status because of the controversial issues I chose to explore using the language and perspectives of the social sciences. As one devotee critic stated after reading portions of my manuscript *Hare Krishna in America* prior to its publication: "I am convinced that there is a serious objectivity problem in your work. A sociologist reading your work won't see it. What you have written may be seen as good sociology but the movement [ISKCON] is not depicted accurately. . . . You have a lack of understanding of your own bias" (March, 1983). Another devotee leader challenged my argument that ISKCON's missionary goals had been displaced because of an increased emphasis on economic gain in the devotees' distribution of religious literature in public places. He countered my analysis by asserting that as a nondevotee, I lacked an understanding of the thinking and motives of the devotees distributing Prabhupada's books: "It's really hard to separate the missionary desire, or motivation, from practically any element of our [ISKCON] society. That philosophical con-nection is there for devotees. Every activity is a preaching activity. That is not perceivable by an *outsider*. Or even—[*pause*]—it takes a while to get used to that principle" (March, 1983; my emphasis).[5]Convinced that my writing was one-sided and biased, several ISKCON leaders mobilized a campaign to discredit me and my work among scholars of new religious movements. In 1983, the organizer of a conference on new religions informed me that he had been asked by another ISKCON scholar to reconsider my invitation to participate. The scholar protested my involvement based on a source within ISKCON who suggested that my work was "biased" and "unscientific." The organizer of the conference, however, reaffirmed my invitation and I attended the gathering.

In 1985, within months of the publication of my book *Hare Krishna in America*, ISKCON held a scholarly conference on the movement at its West Virginia farm community (New Vrindaban). During the previous year, I had been in conversation with the devotee organizing the conference and had expressed a willingness to help in any way I could. The devotee in ques-tion was one of those who had previously criticized my book manuscript. I was dismayed when another scholar sent me the program for the upcoming conference. He expressed his own surprise at my not being invited to the conference. I phoned the devotee organizer and expressed my displeasure at his decision to leave me out of the conference. At one point in our conver-sation he remarked, "I don't want to promote you as a scholar of the Hare Krishna movement. . . . You have allowed yourself to develop a biased view [of ISKCON]. I don't think you would make a useful contribution to the conference."[6] After this conversation, I gave up any hope of continuing my research on ISKCON and moved on to another research project unrelated to new religions.

Four years later, however, another research opportunity presented itself in the form of a longtime devotee friend who had risen to a position of influence within ISKCON. I had been thinking for some time about the fate of the devotee children I had worked with in the Los Angeles ISKCON community years earlier. In conversation with my friend-turned-leader, he suggested that I might be able to start a research project on ISKCON's sec-ond generation. It became clear from our conversation that I was no longer a controversial figure as, unbeknownst to me, a reform movement had grown within ISKCON as my book was being published. The reform movement successfully changed the controversial guru system that had been instituted after Prabhupada's death (Rochford 1998c). The writings that had pushed me out of ISKCON years earlier were no longer controversial to most ISKCON leaders and members.[7]

Reporting on Child Abuse

In the summer of 1989, I began a study of ISKCON's second generation by interviewing seventy parents affiliated with four ISKCON communities in the United States. I had been warned that many of the young people who had grown up in the movement would likely be hesitant to speak with me. At the time, no one told me why, and I assumed it was because my age placed me with their parents' generation and that ISKCON was experiencing some degree of generational conflict. Because of this, I decided to begin my research by interviewing parents about their children's experiences. Almost immediately after beginning my interviews, I learned something unexpected: several parents mentioned that some of the children had been sexually molested and/or physically abused in the movement's boarding schools (*ashram-gurukulas*). At first, I did not know how to interpret what I was hearing, as it remained unclear whether these were rare occurrences or something more substantial. Subsequent interviews with parents, *gurukula* teachers, and several adolescent devotees confirmed that the abuse was more than isolated. Over the next several years, accounts of abuse circulated widely throughout the movement as young people and their parents began detailing the experiences of the children in ISKCON's boarding schools (Rochford 2007, 41–44). By the early 1990s, few devotees remained unaware of the abuse allegations.

Once I had accepted that the abuse was commonplace, I was unsure what to do with the information I had. How would I integrate child abuse into my emerging analysis of family life and ISKCON's second generation? What harm would this information do to ISKCON should the abuse allegations be made public through my writing? I wrestled with these and related questions over several years. Then, in 1997, the editor of the *ISKCON Communications Journal* asked me to write an article on the child abuse that occurred in ISKCON's schools. He suggested that since the allegations of child abuse were widely acknowledged within ISKCON, the time was right to take on the issue. He also emphasized that I was the only person who could do this. I expressed to him my worry that such an article would likely prove controversial within ISKCON. On the other hand, although I did not say as much to him, I believed the article might offer support to the young people struggling to heal from the abuse and/or mistreatment they had suffered in ISKCON's schools. Even so, I remained anxious and conflicted about writing the article.

I wrote a draft of the article and sent it to a number of first- and second-generation devotee friends for comment. The responses I received varied (see Rochford 2001b) but one longtime friend in a position of leadership wrote: "I do have a visceral reaction to protecting the institution seeing ISKCON as the extension of Srila Prabhupada's will and vision. While we may serve well as lab rats for some social research study, what will be the effect on ISKCON's reputation?" (January 20, 1998; quoted in Rochford 2001b, 163–64). I was dumbfounded by his reference to "lab rats" and wrote back:

> If you use it [reference to lab rats] simply as a defensive strategy, well okay. I don't like it but okay. If you actually believe this is the way that I see you and the many devotees I have known over the past twenty odd years I have to say you are wrong, very wrong. There is more I might say here but I won't, only because it is so off the mark and it reveals something that concerns me greatly about how you must view me as a person. I respect your honesty on this, but not much else. . . . This doesn't make me a "demon," or someone who sees other human beings as mere "lab rats," although you and others may think so. I have a deep respect for ISKCON and all those devotees who have committed themselves to Prabhupada and Krishna. But understand also that I am a social scientist. I see no reason to apologize for this. (January 20, 1998)

In response, he wrote, "If it [the abuse article] blows up, I can see the worst happening. You are labeled a turncoat, mole, or the more colorful terms of ISKCON-ese; someone who has used his confidences to stab ISKCON in the back" (January 21, 1998; quoted in Rochford 2001b, 157).

These and similar responses made me want to withdraw the article from publication in the journal and I expressed my reservations to the editor. He reassured me that publishing the article was the right thing to do and I reluctantly went along.[8] I came to regret my decision when my article became the basis of a front-page story in the *New York Times* (Goodstein 1998).

Thereafter, newspapers and media outlets throughout the world reported on the Hare Krishna child abuse allegations. I was devastated by what was happening and was especially concerned about the reactions of my devotee friends. Several wrote me after the *Times* article appeared and I sought out others for their reaction. One devotee teacher with whom I had worked on educational issues ended her message with, "Thank you so much for all your friendship and clear vision" (November 5, 1998). These simple words meant so much to me at the time. Another wrote, "Don't worry. In the ultimate issue, it is not your fault. I am thinking of that old line, 'Don't shoot me I am just the piano player.' This is karma coming home to rest for us. . . . Don't worry, we are still friends. We are both trying to fight the good fight here" (October 18, 1998; quoted in Rochford 2001b, 171).

On June 12, 2000, a lawsuit was filed in Dallas, Texas, on behalf of forty-four young men and women who alleged that they had been subjected to "sexual, emotional, mental and physical abuse and exploitation" while minors in ISKCON's boarding schools (Children of ISKCON et al. vs. the International Society for Krishna Consciousness et al., 2000). The plaintiffs sought $400 million—$200 million in actual damages and $200 million in punitive damages. Not surprisingly, the lawsuit resulted in considerable discussion and debate among devotees throughout the movement. Many, in and outside of ISKCON, expressed anger at the leaders, who were seen as ultimately responsible for the abuse that occurred. Others directed their anger at the plaintiffs because the legal complaint had directly implicated ISKCON's founder, Prabhupada, in the abuse that occurred. The claim that Prabhupada had concealed or had otherwise tacitly allowed the abuse drew me directly into the controversy. An extreme but vocal minority viewed my child abuse article as the basis for the allegations against Prabhupada. As one wrote in a newsletter he circulated: "Prabhupada was defamed and blasphemed in Oct., of 1998 where HDG's [Srila Prabhupada's] teachings were given as the cause (by E. Jerk Rogueford) for all the egregious attacks these monster, child swallowers perpetuated on all the demigod-children of Srila Prabhupada. . . . Another point about Mr. E. Jerk Rogueford is that unless you expose this rascal you will be supporting his envious conclusions by this Turley [lawyer representing the plaintiffs] case" (S. Dasa 2000). Two devotees, including the one quoted above, made death threats against me because they believed I had implicated Prabhupada in the abuse of ISKCON's children.[9]

In the final analysis, the lawsuit and my role in the child abuse controversy left me torn. On the one hand, I believed that the lawsuit was a proper means for those abused to gain justice. Yet I continued to feel guilty about my role in bringing ISKCON to the edge of financial ruin and possible destruction. As one ISKCON official told me, "If we lose the suit it will set us back twenty years."[10] Although I expected to be a target of the leaders' ire, surprisingly little criticism came my way. One member of ISKCON's governing body whom I had known for many years wrote: "Actually I have not heard any negative comments about you from the GBC [ISKCON's Governing Body Commission]. I think most GBC's recognize that you have presented the facts, the only criticism was from one GBC on the wisdom of publishing it at all without consulting the GBC. But even that comment, directed at the publishers, received little comment" (October 15, 1998).

Hare Krishna Transformed

In 2007, my book *Hare Krishna Transformed* was published. It focused primarily on how the growth of family life changed ISKCON in profound ways. It also detailed the politics surrounding marriage and family and how ISKCON's renunciate leadership sought to limit both in an effort to preserve the movement's traditional goals of literature distribution and the recruitment of new members. The book also discussed child abuse and the abuse and neglect of women, as well as how the organization struggled to survive in the face of a mass exodus of householders and their families after book distribution revenues declined dramatically and ISKCON's North American communities faced serious economic problems. In order to stay afloat financially, ISKCON undertook a campaign to recruit Indian immigrants and their families into its temple communities. While successful, ISKCON's religious culture underwent a process of Hinduization and the organization moved ever closer to becoming a Hindu sect catering to the spiritual and social needs of its growing Indian congregation.

Like my first book, *Hare Krishna Transformed* received criticism from within ISKCON. Unlike the previous book, however, it was reviewed by two devotee academics for religion journals. Both offered a combination of praise and criticism of the book (Greene 2011; Gressett 2008). More consequential for me and my research was the objection of a small number of ISKCON leaders to my participation on an ISKCON committee.

The committee had been preparing for several surveys of ISKCON's worldwide membership as part of ISKCON's long-term strategic planning initiative. In 2008, I was asked to join the committee to help construct the necessary questionnaires and to help establish a research methodology. After several months of work, the committee completed a near-final draft of the first questionnaire. We sent a copy of the questionnaire to several ISKCON leaders to get their feedback and their approval to go forward. Shortly there-after, committee members became aware of disagreement among some of the leaders reviewing the questionnaire about the wisdom of conducting the survey. At issue was that the questionnaire included a number of sensitive questions about the movement's leadership. Because my book dealt with sev-eral controversial issues affecting ISKCON's development—including the failures of the leadership—three influential leaders challenged my presence on the survey committee. To address their concerns, I was asked to attend a meeting in New York City to meet with the leaders critical of my book. Any decision about the survey and my continued membership on the committee would come only after this meeting.

I went to New York in August of 2008. An experienced devotee media-tor led the meeting, but the leaders who had expressed concern about my writings on ISKCON failed to attend. The two leaders who did were both longtime friends who were largely, but not entirely, sympathetic toward the book. As the summary of the meeting prepared by the mediator concluded:

> The group described their reservations about shortcomings in the
> presentation of data. Key constituents were not included, particularly
> children of immigrant devotees and younger, more recent ISKCON
> members. Data was not the most up-to-date and did not reflect
> maturation which may have occurred among leaders in recent years.
> In places the book projects a narrow vision of ISKCON's scope and
> breadth, giving readers an incomplete impression of the [ISKCON]
> Society's goals and how well they may or may not have been achieved.
> Burke reminded the group that this was a book about ISKCON's
> history, presented from a sociologist's perspective. (August 18, 2008)

The report also concluded, "There was a general agreement that Burke is uniquely qualified to analyze the data from these [planned] research projects, but that to do so requires an understanding among ISKCON leaders that he is fair. That understanding is not uniform across ISKCON's leadership currently and needs to be improved."

At the conclusion of the meeting, I was asked to make contact with an ISKCON leader who was especially critical of both my book and my involvement with the survey committee. I already had a strained relationship with this devotee because of an article I had published about the ISKCON community (New Vrindaban) where he served as the temple president (Rochford and Bailey 2006). I e-mailed him shortly after returning from New York and suggested that we discuss his concerns. He failed to respond to my invitation, however, and I concluded that he had no real interest in talking with me. Rather, he simply wanted me to step down from the committee.[11] Several weeks later, I received a phone call from the devotee responsible for overseeing ISKCON's strategic planning initiative. He stated in very clear terms that the leaders would not support the planned survey any time soon, and perhaps not at all.

I was upset by the turn of events not only because of the criticism directed toward me and my inability to obtain face time with my critics, but also because participating on the survey committee had been both a productive and enjoyable experience. After some thought, however, I decided to withdraw from the survey committee, given the distraction I had become. Several members of the committee asked me to reconsider, but by then I had decided to disengage from my ISKCON research altogether.[12] As I wrote to the members of the committee and to the two leaders present at the New York meeting:

> Before the New York meeting I spent a good amount of time reflecting on what it would mean if the leaders decided to wash their hands of me and my research efforts. I decided that while I hoped this wouldn't happen that I could live with it. And I can. So I think it is time for me to move on and let ISKCON, and all my devotee friends, get on with their lives and duties without my involvement. I am not bitter. I am really at peace with this. (September 5, 2008)

Only later did I realize that I was far from being at peace with my decision. Put simply, I recognized that disengaging from my research meant losing contact with the many friends I had gained over the years. No longer would there be research trips where I could catch up with my devotee friends and their families. Nor would I be able to worship at a temple on these trips. The depth of my despair was revealed to me only when a dear devotee friend and ISKCON leader phoned to talk about my decision. To my utter surprise, in the midst of our conversation I choked up and tears filled my eyes. At that very moment, I realized how emotionally attached I was to my many devotee friends and to the Krishna Consciousness that remained within.

Disengagement Hangover

Exiting the field includes both physical separation and emotional disengagement (Berg 2009, 236–37). For short-term research projects, or where researcher and researched have little or no direct involvement with one another (as in survey research), leaving the field involves separation without the need for emotional work. But, as my case shows, slow sociology is fundamentally about building and sustaining meaningful relationships over time. As with all friendships, these relationships are inevitably built on intimacy and trust. Exiting the field, therefore, inevitably challenges the mutual emotional attachments between research subjects and the ethnographer. It may also communicate to those studied that the exiting researcher has been disingenuous and that self-interest rather than genuine friendship formed the basis of the relationship. This very possibility leaves the researcher with what amounts to an "ethical hangover" born of a persistent sense of guilt about betraying the people studied, especially those who have become friends as part of the research process (Lofland et al. 2006, 30). As I wrote to a devotee friend, "This is not easy for me. I have never gone through a divorce but that is the analogy I have in mind" (September 8, 2008). Today, I have occasional contact with a limited number of devotee friends and monitor several devotee websites on a daily basis to keep up with some of what is happening in the movement. But the hangover persists. As one of my devotee friends commented, "This is the 'blue boy' [Krishna] factor at work, Burke. Krishna won't let loose of you" (October 13, 2008). Perhaps, but for me it feels more like some of Krishna's followers won't let loose of my heartstrings.

Notes

1. ISKCON's historical roots have been traced to Bengal, India, in the sixteenth century. The Krishna Consciousness practiced by ISKCON members is part of the Krishna Bhakti movement of Caitanya Mahaprabhu (1486–1533). A

distinctive feature of the Gaudiya Vaisnava tradition to which ISKCON belongs is the belief that Caitanya is an incarnation of Krishna. The movement was brought to the United States in 1965 by A. C. Bhaktivedanta Swami Prabhupada (or Srila Prabhupada, as he came to be called by his disciples and followers). ISKCON was incorporated as a religious organization in New York City in 1966 and is dedicated to spreading Krishna Consciousness, with temple communities and preaching centers throughout the world. The aim of the Krishna devotee is to become self-realized by chanting Hare Krishna and living an austere lifestyle that requires avoiding meat, intoxicants, illicit sex, and gambling. While young Westerners were drawn to the movement in the 1960s and 1970s, today the largest portion of ISKCON's North American and Western European membership comprises immigrant Indian-Hindus and their families (see Rochford 2007, 181–200). For discussions of the movement's growth and development in North America, see Judah 1974; Rochford 1985, 2006, 2007; Rochford and Bailey 2006; Shinn 1987; and Squarcini and Fizzotti 2004.

2. *Prabhu* is a Sanskrit word that means "master" or "the Supreme Lord." ISKCON devotees often use the term when addressing one another as a form of respect.

3. Initiated devotees are required to chant sixteen rounds of the Hare Krishna mantra on their japa beads each day: Hare Krishna Hare Krishna, Krishna Krishna, Hare Hare, Hare Rama Hare Rama, Rama Rama, Hare Hare.

4. Although my personal relationship with ISKCON and Krishna Consciousness changed during these years, changes also took place within the movement that facilitated my taking on a membership role. During the late 1970s and early 1980s, ISKCON became a congregational movement as its communal structure collapsed because of dwindling revenues from book distribution (Rochford 1985, 175–76; 2007, 63–64). As a result, less committed people gradually gained recognition as devotees and ISKCON members.

5. This and the previous quote are based on two face-to-face conversations with three devotee leaders who read and critiqued several chapters of my book manuscript prior to its publication. These conversations were tape recorded. My effort at bringing findings back to the field is detailed in Rochford 1992.

6. The challenge to my analysis was framed largely in terms of the discourse of social science. My critics complained that the interview data I presented were not representative and that I tended to overgeneralize my findings, given that the majority of my ISKCON research had been carried out in Los Angeles. In addition, my objectivity was called into question because of my research involvement with a group of dissident devotees in Los Angeles who had defected from ISKCON and began the Kirtan Hall as an alternative to ISKCON (see Rochford 1989). My critics believed that I had been unduly influenced by their negative views in my writings on ISKCON.

7. It is likely that *Hare Krishna in America* was controversial to a limited number of ISKCON members—mostly leaders who wanted to protect their positions and standing within ISKCON. Although many devotees know of me and my ISKCON research, it seems that few have actually taken the time to read my writings on the movement. Of course, it only takes a few powerful leaders to limit or deny research access, as the discussion in this chapter makes clear.

8. Months later, the editor admitted that asking me to write the child abuse article had been politically motivated in part. As he said, "Someone has to be a leader, even if it is someone small like myself. Someone has to take the responsibility for leading the movement" (Rochford 2001b, 173).

9. Despite these claims, I did not directly implicate Prabhupada in the abuse that occurred, although some second-generation devotees did. In my article, I quoted a young man who stated that Prabhupada was aware that he had been subject to corporal punishment while a student in the Dallas gurukula during the early 1970s but failed to intervene on his behalf. Some second-generation devotees implicated Prabhupada because, as head of the institution, he had failed to protect vulnerable children from abuse by some of his disciples. Virtually all of Prabhupada's disciples rejected the very notion that Prabhupada had any role in the child abuse that occurred. My own research indicates Prabhupada was aware of several incidents of corporal punishment and had intervened in a number of those cases, but that he remained unaware of any sexual abuse within ISKCON's schools.

10. After several ISKCON communities named in the lawsuit filed for Chapter 11 bankruptcy protection, the case was resolved in May 2005 by U.S. bankruptcy courts in West Virginia and California. During the lead-up to the final settlement, hundreds of additional claimants were added, for a total of 535, and each received compensation ranging between $2,500 and $50,000 from the $9.5 million settlement (A. Dasa 2005). For more details on the abuse that occurred and the resulting lawsuit, see Rochford 2007, 74–96).

11. I did finally hear from the leader in question after other devotees alerted him about my dissatisfaction with his refusal to contact me. By mutual agreement, we decided not to meet.

12. I should add that my decision was also influenced by family health issues that would have made travel for research purposes extremely difficult.

References

Becker, H. S. 1967. "Whose Side Are We On." *Social Problems* 14 (3): 239–47.

Berg, B. L. 2009. *Qualitative Research Methods for the Social Sciences*. Boston: Allyn and Bacon.

Bromley, D. G., and L. F. Carter. 2001. *Toward Reflexive Ethnography: Participating, Observing, Narrating.* New York: JAI Press.

Children of ISKCON et al. vs. the International Society for Krishna Consciousness (ISKCON) et al. 2000. Filed in U.S. District Court, Dallas, Texas, June 12. *www.culteducation.com/reference/krishna/complaint0606.pdf* (accessed November 2013).

Dasa, A. 2005. "Press Release: Courts Confirms Hare Krishna Chapter 11 Reorganization." Accessed at *www.iskcon.com/press/index.htm* (no longer available).

Dasa, S. 2000. *Kick on His Face* (e-mail newsletter), June 20.

Goodstein, L. 1998. "Hare Krishna Movement Details Abuse at Its Boarding Schools." *New York Times*, October 9. *www.nytimes.com.*

Greene, J. M. 2011. Review of Rochford 2007. *Journal of Vaishnava Studies* 20: 1.

Gressett, M. J. 2008. Review of Rochford 2007. *Journal of the American Academy of Religion* 76 (1): 189–92.

Judah, S. 1974. *Hare Krishna and the Counterculture.* New York: Wiley.

Leatham, M. C. 2001. "Ambiguous Self-Identity in Ethnological Fieldwork on a Mexican Millenarian Colony." In Bromley and Carter, 77–92.

Lofland, J., D. Snow, L. Anderson, and L. H. Lofland. 2006. *Analyzing Social Settings: A Guide to Qualitative Observation and Analysis.* Belmont, CA: Wadsworth/Thomson.

Rochford, E. B., Jr. 1976. "Worldview Resocialization: Commitment Building Processes and the Hare Krishna Movement." MA thesis, University of California, Los Angeles.

———. 1985. *Hare Krishna in America.* New Brunswick, NJ: Rutgers University Press.

———. 1989. "Factionalism, Group Defection, and Schism in the Hare Krishna Movement." *Journal for the Scientific Study of Religion* 28 (2): 162–79.

———. 1992. "On the Politics of Member Validation: Taking Findings Back to Hare Krishna." In *Perspectives on Social Problems*, vol. 3, edited by G. Miller and J. Holstein, 99–116. Greenwich, CT: JAI Press.

———. 1997. "Family Formation, Culture and Change in the Hare Krsna Movement." *ISKCON Communications Journal* 5 (2): 61–82. *content.iskcon.org.* ("Krsna" is a spelling used within ISKCON.)

———. 1998a. "Child Abuse in the Hare Krishna Movement: 1971–1986." With J. Heinlein. *ISKCON Communications Journal* 6 (1): 43–69. *content.iskcon.org.*

———. 1998b. "A Response to Child Abuse in the Hare Krishna Movement: 1971–1986." *ISKCON Communications Journal* 6 (2): 64–67. *content.iskcon.org.*

———. 1998c. "Reactions of Hare Krishna Devotees to Scandals of Leaders' Misconduct." In *Wolves within the Fold*, edited by A. Shupe, 101–17. New Brunswick, NJ: Rutgers University Press.

————. 1999. "Prabhupada Centennial Survey: A Summary of the Final Report." *ISKCON Communications Journal* 7 (1): 11–26. *content.iskcon.org.*

————. 2000. "Analyzing ISKCON for Twenty-Five Years: A Personal Reflection." *ISKCON Communications Journal* 8 (1): 33–36. *content.iskcon.org.*

————. 2001a. "The Changing Face of ISKCON: Family, Congregationalism, and Privatisation." *ISKCON Communications Journal* 9 (1): 1–11. *content.iskcon.org.*

————. 2001b. "Accounting for Child Abuse in the Hare Krishna: Ethnographic Dilemmas and Reflections." In Bromley and Carter 2001, 157–79.

————. 2006. "The Hare Krishna Movement: Beginnings, Change, and Transformation." In *Introduction to New and Alternative Religions in America*, vol. 4, edited by E. V. Gallagher and W. M. Ashcraft, 21–46. Westport, CT: Greenwood Press.

————. 2007. *Hare Krishna Transformed.* New York: New York University Press.

————. 2011. "Boundary and Identity Work among Hare Krishna Children." In *Children and Religion: A Methods Handbook*, edited by S. B. Ridgely, 95–107. New York: New York University Press.

Rochford, E. B., Jr., and K. Bailey. 2006. "Almost Heaven: Leadership, Decline and the Transformation of New Vrindaban." *Nova Religio* 9 (3): 6–23.

Shinn, L. 1987. *The Dark Lord: Cult Images and the Hare Krishnas in America.* Philadelphia: Westminster Press.

Squarcini, F., and E. Fizzotti. 2004. *Hare Krishna.* Salt Lake City, UT: Signature Books.

3

Returns

Joanna Dreby

The city looks different. I cannot tell how much my own perspective has changed and how much the city itself has. I am particularly conscious of my own movement; when I first made the trek across Route 80, to a new home in northeast Ohio in 2007, seeing so many blond-haired children in my son Temo's kindergarten class surprised me. The return trips to New Jersey, starting just a few months later and continuing over the next three years, shook me just as much. As we drove by so many people walking on the sidewalks—an uncommon sight where we lived in Ohio—Temo asked from the back of the car, "Mom, why are there so many brown people here?"

We have come a long way since. After living in Ohio for three and a half years (2007–2010), we moved back to New Jersey for six months (January to July 2011) before relocating up Route 87 to Albany, New York, in the summer of 2011. Now when we visit, it is my younger son, Dylan, who asks about the "brown people." Temo, at age ten, is a bit more sophisticated. As we cross the city to our friend's house, we pass the hub of Latino businesses: all the signs are in Spanish, and *ranchera* music sounds from the store with an iconic towel of the Virgen de Guadalupe displayed on the open glass door. Temo breathes in deeply and says, "I love the smell of it here." I smile. I smell a mixture of corn oil and purple Fabuloso floor cleaner. A few minutes later, Temo asks a bit more seriously, "Why have so many Mexicans come to live in this place?"

I should have a ready-made answer. I teach about immigration. I have interviewed hundreds of members of Mexican families in this particular site for two projects. My first project, on Mexican transnational families, involved work with parents in New Jersey and children in Oaxaca, Mexico (2003–2006).[1] More recently, my study of children growing up in Mexican families draws on interviews and fieldwork in Ohio and New Jersey (2009–2012).[2] I also lived in the city, beginning work with the Mexican community in 1999 before I started formal research in 2003. But I cannot think of how to answer. "I'll tell you later."

Every return to this place is a self-reflective exercise—in contemplating how I have changed as a mother and a woman, how my relationships have changed, and how my children have grown across these movements through time and place. Returns are highly personal. They involve influential characters in my formative years; the memories tug at my insides for reasons I cannot explain. They are difficult to write. So I've put this off, waiting for just the right moment to make the intellectual return and to explain how profoundly returns have shaped my perspective as a scholar seeking to understand how migration alters family relationships, especially in the experiences of women and children—women and children like myself and my boys, who have also moved around, but under entirely different circumstances.

To write on these scholarly returns is to focus on one particular period: the first six months of 2011, when I moved back to New Jersey for fieldwork and interviews in the Mexican community. Temo was a third grader, and Dylan, at four, attended preschool. Not teaching that semester, I set myself a difficult task: to interview the children and parents in forty families, and to do school observations and home visits with six children. (I had completed the same amount of fieldwork in Ohio over a span of two years.) I did the logical thing and reconnected with as many people as I could. I met new families—recommendations from friends or friends of friends. I interviewed a few of those closest to me—people whose houses I had stayed at and who had visited me during my tenure in Ohio—who agreed to help. I took such care not to step on toes or ask too much that my discomfort shrouded these interviews. And, I reconnected with those I knew more marginally from times past, including a family I had interviewed in my first study, a friend from back when I was married whose baby shower I had attended, a woman whose husband I had visited when he was in jail, and a former ESL student whose son had gone to preschool with Temo.

The six months in New Jersey, although hard for me emotionally, imparted methodological, theoretical, and empirical insights. They allowed me to compare my work in this familiar (or not so familiar) site in central

New Jersey to another time (when I lived there from 1999 to 2007) and to another place (my time in Ohio from 2007 to 2010). I learned that perhaps the best role in terms of access is that of the reconnected family friend, like the people from the past whom you find on Facebook. I confirmed some of my prior findings on the consequences of family separation for children, and achieved greater insight into how separation affects relationships over time. And, I learned that illegality, once a terrible inconvenience, had become a more divisive issue now threatening to fracture families and communities—the elephant in the room that can no longer be ignored.

On Access: The Reconnected Family Friend

Andrea squints. She appears to be holding in tears. I had just asked the ten-year-old if she knows what an immigrant is. "Yeah, it is when someone is illegal in this country and police-ICE comes to look for them to send them back to their country." She then tells me her parents are immigrants, which seems to have provoked the emotion. I try for a positive spin, asking if she isn't proud that her parents are immigrants. She says no. "Do you ever feel scared that they are immigrants?" I continue. "Yeah," she says, chin quivering. "What scares you?" I ask. "When the police-ICE comes, they will take them."

Andrea is exceptionally shy, her mother, Leticia, tells me. I had noticed this myself when I attended a *quinceñera* party Andrea was at with her cousins, whom I also knew and interviewed. Andrea smiled sweetly, and often, but only spoke when whispering into her cousin's ear with a hand over her mouth. Leticia tells me Andrea hates to go to dances because she worries that gang members may be present: "*Es muy miedosa*" (She is very fearful). She is the type of child whom I would expect to be difficult to interview—the type I have interviewed before without any sort of emotional confessions. Why did Andrea talk so candidly to me?

When I present my work on interviews with children—which I have done in Mexico, Ohio, and New Jersey—to professional colleagues, I am often asked, "How do you get children to talk to you?" Two things are essential, I think. First, when I feel comfortable talking to children, they seem fairly comfortable talking to me. This means formulating questions that are easy to ask and to answer, which is not so intuitive for adults and worse for those of us accustomed to academic-speak. I also jump from topic to topic so that interviews don't build into too serious a direction; I want the stakes to remain low and for children not to feel any pressure. So a child and I may end up talking about his favorite video games or TV shows, and I'll get play-by-plays that I can barely follow—"I hit the last goomba with a koopa shell and then Bowser comes out of nowhere! He throws a fiery breath at me, but I jump out of the way." Then I'll ask something a bit more serious, like how often he talks to his father on the phone—that is, the father he doesn't live with: the one who was deported to Mexico.

Second, children seem to talk to me more easily when they know that I know their parents, and that I am a part of their parents' world. I typically interview the parents first, so that the children see me at their house before I ever try to sit down and talk to them. This is because university human subjects review boards require researchers to gain the parents' formal consent to interview children, in addition to minor children's assent. In my experience, young children have no interest in and little understanding of this paperwork or the formal procedures. What they want to know, and quite crucially *see*, is that their parent or guardian sanctions my presence and likes and trusts me. The more they see me around, the better. Then, they talk.

My returns to New Jersey proved that a third strategy may be the best of all: children seemed to like talking to me when they view me as family friend who has been away and is reconnecting. Andrea does not remember me; she tells me as much when I meet her at the door to the second-floor, three-room apartment where she waits for me. As I walk up the icy sidewalks to the house, I immediately recognize her—a grown-up version of the four-year-old I last remembered seeing. I greet Andrea warmly, and she smiles shyly. As she leads me up the stairs to the overheated, sparsely furnished apartment to her mother, Leticia, she says that she doesn't know me but that her mom told her about me. In fact, I had been at the baby shower for Andrea—or rather, for Leticia—and still have the photograph of me measuring Leticia's round belly with sheets of toilet paper. Leticia and I spent a lot of time together back when I was married and Leticia was still with Andrea's father, when we were both young mothers. After the year I spent in Mexico, I became absorbed with dissertation writing; although we were still friendly, we stopped seeking each other out. Then I moved to Ohio, and completely lost touch.

I spend the next hour catching up with and interviewing Leticia. Andrea sits in, listening, perched on the edge of a twin bed covered by a matted, once fuzzy black blanket etched with a bright green lion face, while I sit on the other full-sized bed in the room. Leticia holds her newborn son, feeding him and rocking him in a chair. I ask if Andrea ever speaks to her biological father, whom I knew before he and Leticia split up and he went back to Mexico. Leticia directs the question to Andrea: "When did your dad last talk to you? When did your aunt call him?" Andrea doesn't answer, so Leticia directs her comments back to me: "Her aunt calls him. But he hardly calls. Very little." And then back to Andrea: "Joanna knows your grandmother."

Andrea smiles. "Yes, I met your grandmother," I add. "My mother and my grandmother," says Leticia. We go on to recall the visit I made to Leticia's hometown, a place that Andrea has never visited but had often heard stories about, like this one.

By the time I interview Andrea, Leticia has given me three white tank tops, a green and black striped T-shirt, and a thick brown hoodie, all drawn from a large clear plastic bag she brings out from her closet—clothes she had been given at the last factory she worked at. "I have so many," she says. "Take them, they are new. They are nice." I accept the gifts. Leticia warns that Andrea is shy, and then leaves to warm up food in the kitchen. Andrea proceeds to tell me, with no shyness intervening, about the kids in her school, her best friends, what she thinks Mexico is like, and—most importantly—the confession at the end of her fears about her mother's immigration status.

Andrea is not the only one. I interviewed eleven-year-old Edward, whose younger brother was in my son Temo's preschool class. Years earlier, I had taught English to his father, Mauro, when Mauro was just eighteen and I was not much older at twenty-one. At the time, Mauro had been in New Jersey for two years: he had left his school on the coast of Oaxaca at sixteen to come work here. Young and bright, Mauro had placed into the highest-level class. He dreamed of college. Now, having spent half his life in New Jersey, Mauro held onto aspirations only for his children. "I wanted to be someone in life: to be a professional. I could not do it. So I would like my children to be someone."

Edward, like Andrea, opened up to me about the sensitive topic of immigration, unlike many of the children I had interviewed in Ohio, who had mentioned their fears, but usually uncomfortably, in passing, without elaboration. Edward said he preferred that the other kids at school not know that his parents were immigrants from Mexico, "'Cause then everybody gets everything spread around the whole school. Then they start making rumors." For Edward, the fact that his parents are Mexican immigrants was a private affair. "'Cause I don't really like to tell what happened—like, what has happened in—like, in our life." I asked Edward if he knew what an immi-grant was and what it was like to be an immigrant. "Weird," he told me.

"In what way is it weird?" I asked.

"That, um, people think . . . like, the people that are not from here . . . that, um, they're not supposed to be here."

Then there was twelve-year-old Osvelia, whose mother I had known for years. In the past, we had frequented picnics and parties together; once we went on a camping trip overnight. Osvelia was three years older than my son Temo. Back when I was interviewing transnational mothers, her mother, who had never been separated from Osvelia, told me stories of others from her small rural town in Oaxaca who had moved to Mexico City without their children to work as domestics. Her own mother was the town midwife; stories of the strong black coffee and herbs her mother used during deliveries entranced me. However, like with Leticia, I had lost touch.

During my visit, Osvelia made tacos for us for dinner while I sat at the kitchen table interviewing her mother. When Osvelia finished serving us all, and we had eaten, she sat down and told me about her aspirations to be a cook and what it was like to change to a new middle school, where most of the other kids were White and not-Latino, after having attended a nearly all-Hispanic elementary school. Like Andrea and Edward, Osvelia felt comfort-able enough to talk about these difficult things. When I asked if she wanted people to know about her parents' undocumented status, she wavered some: "I really don't—like, um, I want some people to know."

I pushed a little, probing. "So which people would you feel okay knowing?"

"My friends that I feel like keep secrets well."

I interviewed a few children in New Jersey, and some in Ohio, who spoke openly about immigration issues and whose parents I had not known before. Yet my returns to New Jersey proved that the best sort of access, especially with children, is achieved somewhat serendipitously.

In the two years I worked in Ohio, I planned repeated contact with fami-lies, and cultivated relationships with women and children, as part of data collection. Of course, this has benefits. Because I was able to observe chil-dren over time, I learned more about their daily routines and the changes in these routines each year, as they grew. But the return to New Jersey yielded much more candid interviews with children whose parents I had known for a long time. Significantly, these are not the interviews I did with the closest people in my network; they are not my best friends. I interviewed a couple of my closest friends quite uncomfortably; their children trusted me, but knew me a bit too well. My maternal role—as the mother of their friends and someone who had occasionally watched them—trumped our interactions. The best interviews occurred with the children whose parents had *once* been my friends, or my students, or fellow parents of young children. One can plan out long-term commitments in a research site with longitudinal designs, but I achieved the best type of access through embedded personal relationships that had not been developed solely for the purposes of research. These were with people who share a history with me, but with whom I am not so close that my role as researcher causes confusion. Returns to New Jersey taught me that perhaps the best interviews result from the role of the reconnected family friend who happens to be a social science researcher.

On Theoretical Returns: Outcomes over Time

I cry during my short conversation with Candida. I listen to the transcript now, trying to remember what sets me off. Candida, who is nineteen—but who looks and acts older than her years—sits at the glass dining-room table in the first-floor apartment with her mother, Antonia, whom I have been interviewing. Before Candida joins us, I have already learned from Antonia that Candida spent two years living in Mexico City with Antonia's mother when Antonia, her husband, and their younger daughter first migrated. Candida was eleven at the time, and thirteen when she joined her parents and her sister in New Jersey. That Candida remained in Mexico for two years without her parents was, in part, due to economics: Antonia and her husband could not borrow enough to afford the crossing of both girls. But other motivations prompted the decision. Antonia explains that "it seemed to us to be very difficult to arrive here with two daughters. One at age eleven, almost twelve; it seemed too complicated to bring her here, without [us] having work. And we didn't know what complications we would find on the way—they tell many stories, of bad things that happen [to young girls crossing the border]. We were always thinking about our oldest daughter."

Candida arrives from the bus, having just come from her classes at the community college. Her simple pair of jeans and grey and black striped T-shirt downplay the full, curvaceous figure so different from that of her tall and lanky eleven-year-old sister. While I talk with Antonia, the sister has been watching TV and ignoring my son Dylan, who tries to watch with her. Candida, in contrast, immediately joins us at the table and, when she finishes her conversation with us, pulls out a Candyland game from the closet to play with Dylan. Her thoughtfulness reminds me of sixteen-year-old Cindy, whom I interviewed in 2005 in Mexico while her mother lived in the United States; Cindy always played so cheerfully with my son Temo while plaintively complaining about her mother's absence (Dreby 2010, chapter 10).

"It was really hard, at the beginning," Candida explains in telling me about that time of her life. "I didn't have the same kind of *confianza* [trust] with my grandmother as I did with my mother." Later she specifies, "To a parent you can say, [*in a childish voice*] 'No, I don't want to eat this.' And with your grandmother it's, 'No, you have to eat this.'"

Antonia tears up while Candida talks about the time in Mexico without her:

> I remember that my grandmother and all my aunts and uncles worked. So I remember that I had to go to school all by myself. I was maybe ten . . . no, eleven years old at that time. So at that age I had to take public transportation alone and go all over the place. So I remember I had to go one and a half hours before school started. But the school where I went wasn't far from the house where I used to live with my mother, it was just like ten minutes walking. I remember I would go over there, before school started, and I would just sit outside there, the house where we used to live with my other grandmother [with whom they lived with before Antonia migrated]. I would just sit there, thinking. Remembering.

Candida's voice breaks. My eyes water. There is something about the image of a young girl sitting alone and remembering her parents that is so reminiscent of the stories of the more than sixty children I interviewed in Mexico living without their U.S. migrant parents. How often have I heard this refrain: a grandmother is not the same as a mother (Dreby 2007, 2010).

Antonia too is upset. "It's what I told you about earlier," she explains. "All that we went through and how we had no money [when they first arrived in New Jersey]. When [Candida] got here, everything was settled." She offers this justification for the heartache. Antonia suffered as a new migrant, and had protected Candida from this hardship. She reasoned that the temporary separation was best for all. It avoided the dangerous crossing for a preteen girl. It allowed Antonia and her husband to stabilize their economic situation before bringing Candida into the world of undocumented immigrant life in New Jersey. But Antonia had not been able to protect her daughter from the hardship she experienced in Mexico resulting from her mother's absence.

Antonia and Candida's account returns me to the many stories—from both parents and children—I listened to that were wrought with pent-up sadness: the sadness of parents who did not want to leave their children but saw no other way, and the sadness of children seeking ways to express their feelings of powerlessness in their families' migratory process. It is only now, in hearing Candida cry, that the sterility that so often shrouded the renditions of heartache in those earlier stories stands out. In my earlier study, I purposively interviewed families currently experiencing separations—that is, mothers and fathers living without their children in New Jersey, and children living in Mexico without their parents. I intended to study separations while they occurred. My interviews focused on how parents, children, and caregivers coped with separation while apart.

Listening to Antonia and Candida cry openly, together, reminded me of how dry the interviews in Mexico with children had been: they had recounted their resentment at feeling left behind with bitter detachment. Like Candida, they had told me about feeling sad without their parents and how they wanted their parents to come back. But only two out of the sixty had grown emotional during our interviews. They had *talked* about being upset during their parents' absences, but they rarely *expressed* this emotion. In retrospect, the emotional detachment seems to have been a defense mechanism.

My visit with Candida and her mother affirmed prior research findings, reiterating many of my key findings about the impact of parent-child separations on family members. But it was at once different; it could be different because Candida had now lived with her parents for six years in the United States. The pain lingered, but Candida—and Antonia—could now talk about it, feel the emotion, and express the emotion, because the period of physical separation was over. As I left, Antonia confessed, "We have never spoken about that time like this before."

My new work does not specifically focus on parent-child separations, although I included in my sample in a handful of transnational families. Yet I stumbled across stories like this one, about previous periods of separation, embedded in the others that I sought about the impact of legal status on growing up and on childrearing. In doing so, I found answers to some of the nagging questions my book *Divided by Borders* had introduced; namely, what happens over time to children who have experienced family separations? I followed a small number of families in the earlier research and learned that the separations typically turned out to be, as for Candida, relatively short-lived. No one intended them to be permanent arrangements, although they often dragged on much longer than expected. But I had limited data about how children had fared after reunifications with parents. Reunions, I suspected, rarely panned out as everyone hoped; the heartache seemed to continue and expectations remained unmet, at least for the time immediately following reunification. Ultimately, though, I could say little about the long-term consequences of separation. The question has been asked of me again and again: does family separation, as a migration strategy, work out over the long run, for both parents and their children? Are separations ultimately worthwhile?

In *Divided by Borders* I left this question unanswered, letting readers decide for themselves based on the stories I presented. I am still inclined to do so. Families differ, as does each child. No true experiment can compare the experiences of a child who remains in Mexico while a parent goes north with the experiences of another version of the same child who migrates with a parent and those of a third version of the child who stays in Mexico with a parent. The sacrifice may be worthwhile for some children, and in some family situations, but not in others. Yet returns to New Jersey, and conversations like the one with Candida and Antonia, convince me that patterns exist.

Children separated from their parents for short periods of time while they are young seem to recover from the period of separation fairly seamlessly. Jasmine is a case in point. I interviewed Jasmine's parents as part of my first study (they were members of the only family I interviewed for both projects). At the age of one and a half, Jasmine had stayed in Mexico with her maternal grandmother when her mother, Jacinta, joined her father in New Jersey. Jacinta knew she would not be able to carry the toddler across the border but had grown severely depressed without her husband and wanted to reunite the family in the United States. Three years later, after the birth of their second child in New Jersey, Jacinta sent for Jasmine. I first met Jasmine when she was four, soon after her arrival. For the first few months, she hid in her parents' room anytime I visited, clinging to her father; her parents explained that he looked like an uncle Jasmine knew back in Mexico. Jasmine also did not speak. She was born with developmental problems and used hand signals to communicate. The move initially traumatized the little girl. The immediate aftermath proved difficult.

I talked to Jasmine—now age fourteen—upon my return to New Jersey. Her younger sister, Ana, is eleven; she also now has another U.S.-born sibling who is five years old. Jasmine speaks clearly enough to be tape-recorded, although with some noticeable speech difficulties. For this reason, I interviewed Jasmine together with Ana. Jasmine is in a regular eighth-grade classroom, but she also continues to receive therapy in school, although not as often as her mother would like. According to Jacinta, "she doesn't remember Mexico, because I don't talk with her about it." But Jasmine and Ana are aware of the legal status differences between them. When I ask the girls about what it's like to have parents who are immigrants, Ana explains, "I'm scared that our parents are going to get separated."

"How about you? Do you feel scared?" I ask Jasmine.

"Yes," she answers.

"How come?"

"I feel scared we might be apart. I've seen on TV that happened."

Ana adds, "I think the people from America, me and my [younger] brother, will go to another family. And Jasmine and my parents will go back to Mexico."

But Jacinta and her husband have not made any plans to return to Mexico. Later that year, in the spring, they throw Jasmine an elaborate *quinceñera* party, her father explaining that even though it was expensive, he wanted to give this one thing to her, her dream, because of all that she has been through. Jacinta explains that she would go back to Mexico for herself, but there is no future for her children there—no special services in the schools to meet Jasmine's special needs. Of course, it is impossible to know how Jasmine would have fared in Mexico had she not migrated, but it is easy to imagine that she would not have received the same attention to her speech difficulties. In this case, the sacrifice Jacinta made to be separated from Jasmine seems to have paid off: the trauma of reunification subsided before Jasmine entered school, and she has now adjusted well to life in New Jersey. It seems likely that the services Jasmine has received in New Jersey have enabled her to learn to speak and provided access to an education alongside other children her age.

Children separated from their parents at older ages, and for longer periods of time, may fare worse over time because of periods of separation. The experiences of Carlos and Milagros' family exemplify this. Carlos met Milagros, a mother to two young children (ages one and four), in Mexico. They moved in together, and then after a few years Carlos came to New

Jersey to work. Within a year, Carlos saved enough money to send for Milagros. For four years, their two children (Rebecca and Silvio, ages five and eight when their mother left) lived with an aunt and uncle in Mexico and their four cousins.

In New Jersey, Carlos and Milagros had a son, and then, when he was three, in 2006, they sent for the two older children. "At first they didn't want to come," Milagros tells me, "but then they decided to because the older one began to complain that I wasn't there." They also wanted to meet their little brother. But the reunion was not easy. "We didn't recognize each other," Rebecca explains in describing her arrival to New Jersey. "I remember just standing there and looking at them because I remembered that when my mom left them she was all skinny and then she got a little fat here. It took about a month to get used to living with them again."

Up until this point, the story sounded familiar, like those of children I have met before. But the father, Carlos, tells me more: how difficult it was for Silvio—at age twelve—to adapt to life in New Jersey. "For two or three months he cried almost every night, uncontrollably." Silvio was resentful, feeling like he had been left behind in Mexico by his mother, who had gone on to have another child without him. "We didn't know what to do," Carlos says. "He even had suicidal thoughts. He said he was going to get a knife and cut himself and hurt himself and his siblings."

In school, Silvio's performance fluctuated. Milagros said, "Sometimes he would do badly. When he was mad at me, he would say, 'I am going to get all Fs.' And, he would get all Fs. Then he would say, 'Don't worry, mommy, I am going to get good grades now.' And he would get good grades, all As and Bs. They gave him a special recognition, because he is very intelligent." The account suggests that emotional issues directly affected Silvio's schooling.

When I interview the family five years after their reunion, Carlos says that things had gotten much better, but Silvio's life had taken a different path than his mother, who had been a schoolteacher in Mexico, had originally hoped. When Silvio was sixteen, his younger girlfriend got pregnant. She moved in with Carlos and Milagros, who supported the teenage parents so they could finish high school. But neither did. Silvio opted out, leaving school to work full time. According to Milagros, "Now that he is working he says, 'If I had the opportunity to get my papers, it would be easier to find a better job.' In one place he was working, they wanted to keep him, but they asked for his papers."

Silvio's prospects, in fact, do not look all that much different from those of his parents, who have worked without papers for so many years in the United States to provide a better future for their children. In spite of his aptitude, it seems that Milagros and Carlos' intention of providing Silvio with a better future, through the sacrifice of unauthorized migration and the separation it entailed, did not pay off. For Silvio, the four years apart from his parents came at such a critical moment in his lifespan that the emotional aftermath of the separation deeply affected his schooling. The temporary family separation had not borne out well for Silvio, at least in the sense that Milagros and Carlos's sacrifice did not yield the intended results.

As difficult as it is to make predictions, my returns suggest that for some children, like Jasmine, whose two years in Mexico without her parents is a time she can no longer remember, the sacrifice can be worthwhile, while for other children the emotional wake of a separation has more long-standing effects, provoking, as the case of Silvio suggests, a spiral downward when the separation falls during a critical period of a child's life. The differences are in the age of the child at the time of separation and reunification, with younger children experiencing the least trauma, and the length of time parents and children live apart, with the shorter periods of separation having lesser long-term impacts.

For still others, like Candida, the end result is less clear. The emotional wake of the separation—which was short, but fell at a critical time in Candida's life—appears to have had some long-standing effects (such as Candida's memories of the period still provoking tears), although it has not derailed her from a desirable path. Although she is still unauthorized, Candida graduated from high school and is studying at the community college, hoping to become a nurse. The Dream Act was not passed as Candida had hoped, but since my meeting with her, the Deferred Action program for unauthorized youth has gone into effect and she will surely qualify for employment authorization. Silvio, however, will not, because he had already dropped out of school as of June 2012; the long-lasting burden of separation will continue to mark his life chances.

On Contexts: Changes Wrought by Illegality

"I don't think he will come. If one could cross [the border], then yes, I would want to go and then come back again [with him]. But the way it is now, I am too afraid." This is Yessenia talking about her twelve-year-old son, who lives with her mother in Mexico. Based on my conclusions above, one might deduce that leaving children while young is the best strategy. But Yessenia had left her son ten years earlier. Circumstances have prevented their reunification, and she has not seen him since.

In *Divided by Borders*, I wrote: "In leaving their children, migrant parents are both thoughtful and proactive. They take advantage of their available resources to move to a place where they can earn more for their labor. They weigh the costs and benefits of migration and decide that leaving their children temporarily is sensible, even if heart-wrenching. They consider this difficult decision a sacrifice. They hope to make the most of their sacrifices by working hard in the United States" (Dreby 2010, 203).

Yessenia's story confirms my earlier assertion. When Yessenia finished sixth grade, at the age of fourteen, she moved in with her boyfriend and they married. At age fifteen, Yessenia had her first baby. At the time, Yessenia's own father already worked in New Jersey. He offered to help Yessenia's young husband migrate so he could work and support Yessenia and the baby. After a year in New Jersey, Yessenia's husband stopped sending money and left Yessenia to be a single mother. "The truth is I did not want to come [to the United States]," she explains. "My mom told me to come so that I could buy things for my baby. So I could give him a better life." Yessenia left her son at the age of two and a half with her mother, in Mexico. The decision to leave still troubles Yessenia ten years later; her voice falters in telling me the story. But at the time she left, a temporary separation seemed like the only viable choice for the teenage mother.

In *Divided by Borders*, I also wrote about how the costs and benefits equation changes during periods of separation. Parents' lives evolve during the time they live in the United States. They have new children, and, at times, new partners. They become invested in a lifestyle of hard work and low-wage labor, attempting to achieve a sense of stability that will enable them to reunite their families. Meanwhile, children in Mexico also change. They become emotionally close to their caregivers; their resentment at their parents for leaving them builds. Children may resist parents' efforts at reunification. Separations become increasingly difficult the longer parents and children live apart.

Again, Yessenia's experiences confirm this. In New Jersey, Yessenia works as a temporary worker at a local factory that hires many Mexican women, including her sister. Periodically, she gets laid off and collects unemployment, and then is later rehired by the same company. This way they avoid taking her on as permanent worker with benefits. For Yessenia, securing stable, steady employment has proved difficult. Her family circumstances have also changed during her time in the United States. Originally single, Yessenia met a man whom she moved in with, and the new couple had two children, ages six and four, when I met her. Yessenia's economic problems persist as she struggles to support herself and her children.

Yessenia has wanted to send for her son for the past seven years. Money has been an issue, but not a prohibitive one. In fact, she recently found a way to send $2,000 for braces to fix his teeth since children at school were making fun of him. A few years back, Yessenia tried to bring him. "My dad came and so I tried to bring him over here. But he didn't want to come. He refused."

"Did he say why?" I ask. "Did he give you an explanation?"

"He said that he doesn't like it. That here it is very ugly, he knows because he sees it on TV. That over there it is much prettier, that they are free, that they can go to the river. They go to school, they jump and play. Here they [kids] are all stuck inside."

Yessenia's son has changed during the time they lived apart, just as Yessenia had. Like so many of the children in Mexico I interviewed, he resisted reunification, which prolonged the separation of mother and son. "I feel bad about my son in Mexico. Sometimes sadness overcomes me, and I feel like crying. I have my two children here, but it isn't the same." Yessenia goes on to explain:

> He never throws it in my face, thank God. He understands. I tell him, "Do you remember when I was there and you wanted something, I couldn't buy it for you? My mom gave me something, but it wasn't enough. I had to work to buy you things. . . . He [her son] has never told these things to me [over the phone]. But at school he writes poems. My aunt said she found them. My mom said she found the papers from May 10th [Mother's Day], from the Day of the Child, [and he writes] that he feels sad, and alone. That sometimes he wants to tell his mom that he feels alone, that he loves her very much. But when I talk to him, he doesn't tell me this.

I did not interview Yessenia's son, but if I had—based on the interviews I did do with children in Mexico—I expect that he would have expressed some dry resentment at having been left by his mother, and that it was fueling his

resistance to a reunion. I also might expect that at some point this resentment will start to fade, and that Yessenia's son will look to her to bring him
to the United States to work, just as Yessenia's own father had done for her
when things did not work out for her in Mexico. So I pressed Yessenia on
the point.

> Joanna: How long have you been trying to get him to come?
>
> Yessenia: Since he was five years old.
>
> Joanna: And what would happen if today or tomorrow he started to
> say that he wants to?
>
> Yessenia: Sometimes I talk to him about it. But he says no.
>
> Joanna: You know, that could change. Many kids, when they get to
> be fourteen or fifteen, all their friends begin to come north . . .
>
> Yessenia: But now the crossing is difficult. Not anymore.
>
> Joanna: People aren't coming anymore?
>
> Yessenia: They say no. Haven't you seen the wall they put up over
> there [on the border]? Then they kill people. It isn't like it was
> before. One used to leave home and be here after a week.
>
> Joanna: If he asked now, would you send for him?
>
> Yessenia: I'd be too afraid. . . . There are so many bad people. They
> kill them.

Yessenia's story affirms patterns I wrote about before regarding the change
in family dynamics during separation—specifically that of children's
increasing influence on the parents' decision-making processes, resulting
from the guilt parents experience. But Yessenia's story also introduces a
new calculus, one I did not fully account for before: the political context
of illegality. Since the time I did my first interviews with parents living
without their children, three main changes to the legal context in which
the unauthorized live have occurred, altering the legal landscape under
which separations occur.

First, the border has become ever more dangerous. This is in part due to
the U.S. militarization of the border—the wall that Yessenia references—
and greater levels of funding for border control (Cornelius 2001; Eschbach
et al. 1999). This is also due to the drug cartels taking over much of the
smuggling operations, putting individual migrants at greater risk (Slack
and Whiteford 2011). One woman I interviewed, for example, said that the

coyote from her town who used to take people across the border has gone out of business because he is too afraid to work with the drug cartels to bring people across the border.

Second, there has been no form of immigration reform that will allow the unauthorized to regularize their status. When I interviewed families for *Divided by Borders*, many parents planned to return to Mexico after saving enough money to support their children in Mexico. Rather than return to Mexico, many—like Yessenia—feel they must hunker down, waiting until some sort of relief is passed; after all, they have their U.S.-citizen children to think about. As of 2010, with no reform having been passed, the result has been a dramatic number of people, estimated at nine million, living in mixed-status families—that is, families in which at least one parent is unauthorized and one child is a U.S.-born citizen (Taylor et al. 2011). Parents now have even deeper ties to the United States, like Yessenia does via her citizen children, without any options for legalization.

Third, the number of deportations has risen drastically, from close to 190,000 deportations in 2001 to close to 400,000 each year between 2009 and 2012 (Preston 2012; U.S. Department of Homeland Security Office of Immigration Statistics, 2011). The threat of these enforcement policies has had deep impacts at the local level. Parents worry about deportation and know that if it happens, they will not be able to get back across the border. Moreover, if they are deported, they will be unable to regularize their status if comprehensive immigration reform is in fact ever passed. Children, as the accounts in this chapter resoundingly express, fear separation from their parents and from their siblings. They fear the police. (For more on children's fears, see Dreby 2012 and Dreby 2013.)

Consequently, legal conditions have altered the cost/benefit calculus of separation for mothers like Yessenia. Once she gained a foothold in New Jersey, although ever so tenuous, she wanted to bring her son, but he was unwilling to come. Now if he decides he wants to migrate—like so many children I interviewed did when he comes of age—he will be unable to because Yessenia deems the border crossing now to be much too dangerous, and her return to Mexico ever less likely. In this case, the changing legal context seems to be leading to a permanent separation. The decisions to separate that I wrote about in *Divided by Borders* also resulted from immigration policy that did not allow parents to migrate legally with their children, and required them, because of their ongoing unauthorized status, to take low-wage jobs. But the changing legal landscape now means that the temporary separations parents expected to endure are ever more likely to become permanent.

Final Thoughts: On the Legacy of Illegality

My returns to New Jersey gave me methodological and theoretical insight. But, by far, the shifting legal context dominates all the stories I have told in this chapter. Legal status was on everyone's mind when I returned to New Jersey. Andrea trusted me—as a long-lost family friend—enough to relate her fears about her mother's legal status, as did Osvelia and Edward, who confided in me because they knew my connections to their parents. Candida, Jasmine, and Silvio's prospects are tied—in part—to their continuing lack of a legal status. Candida, attending community college, likely still waits anxiously for the Dream Act to pass so she can finish a degree in nursing and work in the field permanently. Jasmine fears that she and her parents will have to return to Mexico while her sister and her brother, U.S. citizens, remain here. At the age of eighteen, Silvio now faces the same economic fate of his parents—a life of low-paid, undocumented labor. And Yessenia predicts that she will be permanently separated from her son in Mexico because of the changing legal context, which has made the unauthorized crossing of the border more dangerous and expensive than she ever originally imagined.

When I first lived and worked in New Jersey, legal status created significant barriers, for sure. It prevented those I knew from getting driver's licenses. People worked in low-wage jobs when they were qualified for better positions because they lacked the necessary paperwork for better-paying positions with benefits. Mexican immigrant families I knew faced barriers to mental health services, and health care more broadly, because they lacked a social security number. These obstacles kept them from reuniting with their children in Mexico, but just for a time. Legal barriers significantly shaped families' lives, but with some creativity and hard work, they were somewhat negotiable. At that time, it was still a number—a missing paper.

My returns to New Jersey have shown me just how significant the changing legal context has become over a relatively short period. The meaning of illegality has changed dramatically across a five-year span. The children I interviewed upon my returns, and their parents, described palpable fears about legal status. For example, I asked a six-year-old—one whose family

I had not known before—if she ever feels scared that her parents are immigrants. She said yes, "because if I am here and my mom goes to Mexico I am going to be sad because I would miss her." And a twelve-year-old boy told me he is scared his parents are immigrants because "we might be apart." These increased fears result from changes in enforcement practices over the past few years, and they trickle down into the daily lived experiences of children and their families, affecting the relationships between spouses, parents, children, and siblings. My returns have taught me that in the absence of comprehensive immigration reform, illegality becomes a status imbued with social meaning. My returns have shown me just how important this elephant in the room, illegality, has become.

New Jersey continues to feel different for me every time I go back. At times, I so long for my connections to people back there. When the loneliness at being the new girl on the block (now in Albany, but also when I lived in Ohio) gnaws at my insides, I cling to memories of my friendships when I was younger—those people who in my twenties replaced my own parents, aunts, uncles, cousins, and sibling as my most significant others. My longings for home also hit me in my role as a researcher. Interviewing families in Ohio, for example, I quickly learned to be uniquely aware of my status as a community outsider and as a woman—a single woman, at that. Originally I thought I would interview mothers and fathers for the new project; I dropped this as soon as it became clear that as a single mother and a White woman, formally interviewing men in Ohio crossed over some line previously invisible to me; it was too risqué. I desperately missed my town in New Jersey where, whether it was because I had worked as a volunteer teaching ESL or because many people knew my ex-husband, a Mexican, I had little trouble interviewing men. Back in New Jersey in 2011, I spoke with many men about my study, and interviewed quite a few along with their wives—and even a few separately. And then there were my observations of children in 2011 at a school where, in 2000, I had spent time working, attending meetings, and participating in community events. The smells of the hallways and the brightly colored murals comforted me. My return liberated me from of the burden of being the stranger.

Yet at other times in New Jersey, shifting tides alienate me, turning me into a stranger once again. Eventually, friendships need new life and new memories; with some, the connections continue to grow, but with others, experiences cause us to drift apart. The built landscape that looks at once so familiar also feels strangely foreign. New businesses have opened, a new parking garage and a shopping center erected where there previously was none, and the roadways in and out of the city have been revamped. Change sticks to every place I used to habituate, challenging my assumptions from the past. When I accompany one woman I interviewed to the ER, for example, it takes all afternoon for me to realize I am out of place. I anticipate having to translate, as I had done many times in the past at that same emergency room. Now, however, the receptionist brushes me aside, not needing the help to communicate. The doctor looks straight into the patient's eye, ignoring me completely, speaking in an abrupt and awkward, yet functional, Spanish. No longer needed as a resource, I save my interviewee the taxi fare and give her something to do while waiting. Times have changed.

As I too have changed, and continue to change with every return. In New Jersey, I was always a student, relatively poor. Medicaid insured my children; I used WIC during both pregnancies. I shared every room in my house to make ends meet—to get through grad school as a young mother. In New York, and Ohio previously, I am a professional, making a decent salary. I am a homeowner driving (cringe) a Prius. Now I am the mother of older children who do not tag along quite so easily on interviews, which I cannot work in and around the winter hockey schedule. My Spanish falters, and my children are no longer bilingual. My perspective, like the physical space, has evolved considerably.

To me, New Jersey will always be a special place—a place with more heart than anywhere I have known. But it is also a place that is not really city or country, where one municipality bleeds into another; the older historical sites have town centers, but it is mostly shopping centers and strip malls that define the start of one place and end of the next. New Jersey, now, seems to me to be traffic, and congestion, and endless commerce. There we cherish the smallest plots of earth and trees because there are no others. I used to scoff at the ignorance of the "which exit in New Jersey" jokes, which miss everything: when I moved away from New Jersey, I missed the diversity of the state, the ability to find great food from all parts of the world without the grit of New York City, and the people who knew me, with whom I felt at home. But now, living a few hours upstate, the openness relieves me. I still live in a small city, not too different from the one I know in New Jersey. But here a nearby small farm delivers fresh milk in old-style glass bottles with blue tops every Tuesday to my door, along with fresh eggs. I can drive in fifteen minutes in any direction to see snow glistening in trees, or picture-card-perfect farms stocked with red barns and, yes, bales of hay. Driving just a bit further, I can see graceful hills transform into stunning landscapes: to the north, the wild, high peaks of the Adirondacks; to the east, the Petersburgh Pass into the rock fences of the Berkshires; and to the south, the heights and grooves of the Catskills and the Hudson Valley.

I now have my own New Jersey joke. When I am driving us south, the boys always ask, "Are we in New Jersey yet? Are we almost there?"

"Look outside," I say. "Is it still beautiful?"

"Yes," they nod.

"Then we are still in New York."

Returns mark so much change. They have taught me about changes in the structures that shape our daily lives, be they the legal structures that mark the lives of the children I have interviewed or the class structures that shape my life and the lives of my children. The returns have brought with them methodological benefits, theoretical insight, and greater self-awareness of my own evolution. They have brought with them new perspectives and new appreciations of what I have already learned about transnational family life, and about what I love, and hate, about the places I think of as home.

Notes

1. See Dreby 2010 for details on the study and methodology.
2. See Dreby 2012 and Dreby and Schmalzbauer 2013 for more details on the study and methodology.

References

Cornelius, W. 2001. "Death at the Border: Efficacy and Unintended Consequences of U.S. Immigration Control Policy." *Population and Development Review* 27: 661–85.

Eschbach, K., J. Hagan, N. Rodriguez, R. Hernandez-Leon, and S. Bailey. 1999. "Death at the Border." *International Migration Review* 33: 430–54.

Dreby, J. 2007. "Children and Power in Mexican Transnational Families." *Journal of Marriage and Family* 69: 1050–64.

———. 2010. *Divided by Borders: Mexican Migrants and Their Children.* Berkeley: University of California Press.

———. 2012. "The Burden of Deportation on Children in Mexican Immigrant Families." *Journal of Marriage and Family* 74: 829–45.

———. 2013. "The Modern Deportation Regime and Mexican Families: The Indirect Consequences for Children in New Destination Communities." In *Constructing Immigrant "Illegality": Critiques, Experiences and Responses*, edited by C. Menjívar and D. Kanstroom, 181–202. New York: Cambridge University Press.

Dreby, J., and L. Schmalzbauer. 2013. "The Relational Contexts of Migration: Mexican Women in New Destination Sites." *Sociological Forum* 28 (1): 1–26.

Preston, J. 2012. "Record Number of Foreigners Were Deported in 2011, Officials Say." *New York Times*, September 7. *www.nytimes.com*.

Slack, J., and S. Whiteford. 2011. "Violence and Migration on the Arizona-Sonora Border." *Human Organization* 70: 11–21.

Taylor, P., M. H. Lopez, J. Passel, and S. Motel. 2011. *Unauthorized Immigrants: Length of Residency, Patterns of Parenthood*. Washington, DC: Pew Hispanic Center. *www.pewhispanic.org*.

U.S. Department of Homeland Security Office of Immigration Statistics. 2011. *Immigration Enforcement Actions: 2010* (annual report). *www.dhs.gov/xlibrary/assets/statistics/publications/enforcement-ar-2010.pdf*.

4

Studying My Hometown

Albert Hunter

While living on the South Side of Chicago in Hyde Park during graduate school, my wife and kids and I used to return home to the North Shore suburb of Evanston almost every weekend for Sunday dinner with my parents, who still lived in the house in which I grew up. Evanston became a "natural" place for me to turn to as I looked to make my mark as a Chicago School urban sociologist; indeed, returning home as a townie gave me a unique vantage point as a researcher. Moreover, my moves around this town at different points in my life exposed me firsthand to Evanston's diversity: I grew up in the upper-middle-class part of town and while in high school I first met several of the people who would figure into my later research. When I returned to Evanston in midlife to assume a job at Northwestern as an associate professor, I moved around town several times, living in various neighborhoods that reflected my personal life stages. A large single-family home near the lakefront in an upper-middle-class neighborhood gave way, after a divorce, to an apartment and then a small house in a working-class, racially integrated neighborhood. Later, after my remarriage, I moved to another, larger Victorian home in a middle-class, racially integrated neighborhood where I am (still) raising my second family.

So I grew up in Evanston and then after a hiatus of more than a decade in the East I returned and reconnected with people I knew from high school. For example, the daughter of the police chief had been one of my classmates; she was now the successful owner of an upscale imported food emporium and a travel agency, and a leader in the community. Another grade school friend was now associate dean of admissions at Northwestern.

This essay focuses on how these social ties and my deep knowledge of the community both facilitated and at times impeded research on it. I also consider how over time the politics of space and place had elements of continuity and discontinuity; some things remained the same, some changed. More particularly, I reflect on disruptions in the research that emerged from different stages in my personal career coupled with shifting fads and fashions of sociological inquiry as they became refracted though different theoretical and methodological lenses of the discipline over the decades. Different questions were posed at different times although the subject, broadly construed as urban and community sociology, and the object, the City of Evanston, remained the same even as it too underwent profound changes. Throughout my research, the focus remained on the social life of the residents of my hometown at both the personal network level and the collective institutional level. The community's social life and social ties are both the subject of these studies, and perhaps most significantly for this analysis they are the intertwined means of investigation. As a researcher I was directly tied into the social life I was studying. The result was a slowly evolving and gradually enriched understanding of a variety of different facets of the community.

I first briefly outline in chronological order the sequence of over half a century of discrete pieces of research on my hometown. I then outline the types of social ties and networks I had established in the community over the years. Finally, I show in more detail the many ways in which these research topics and social ties were interrelated.

Research Topics

The first research project in which Evanston figured was my MA thesis at the University of Chicago, which focused on community politics, using Evanston as a case study. I explored the question of the relationship between a community's economic base and the nature of the community's power structure. More specifically, I studied the building of one of the first shopping malls in a neighboring suburb and how this had led to the decimation of the retail base of Evanston as a satellite commercial city. This type of "economic base analysis" was prevalent in the ecological studies of the 1950s and 1960s (Pfouts 1960). For data, I conducted interviews with local elites such as the mayor and the city manager, the heads of corporations, and local voluntary associations; some of these were people my parents knew. I also drew on archival and census data. The research question echoed the central question my grandfather would often pose as we drove around various local communities in the industrial mill towns of Western Pennsylvania: "What kind of works are in this town?" From the answer, he would infer various community characteristics, such as the race and ethnicity of its residents and its relative prosperity and class structure.

I began my second piece of research involving Evanston a decade later in the 1970s (after a hiatus that included a dissertation and its publication). It was a comparative study of community politics in four suburbs (one of which was Evanston), looking at how their power structures and political issues varied depending on their social class and ecological position as smaller dormitories or larger satellites within a metropolitan hierarchy of communities. This research relied on observations at council meetings, interviews, and a survey of elites to elicit through block modeling analysis the varying power structures in the suburbs. I conducted this research during the period when "community power" studies in political science and sociology focused on a central debate as to whether a single pyramidal power elite or pluralist elites best characterized local community power structures (Polsby 1980). Although in this research I clearly drew on my earlier MA thesis, I now expanded it to a more systematic comparative study of communities and used the latest quantitative analytic techniques (Hunter 1984; Hunter and Fritz 1985; White et al. 1976).

My third study of Evanston, begun in the late 1980s, was a comparative study of how three neighborhoods in Evanston (White, Black, and integrated) varied in their responses to a local gang problem. The focus on urban street crime had been a national issue in the 1970s, and after participating in a major multicity, multiyear national study of "the fear of crime" (Skogan and Maxfield 1981), I returned to the gang question in Evanston first as a neighborhood actor and then as a researcher. I was interested in exploring how the racial and class composition of neighborhoods influenced residents' varying perceptions of the gang problem and organized collective responses to it. This research relied on participant observation, surveys, interviews, and archival and census data. This research has continued over the decades as gangs unfortunately have remained an enduring problem to the present day (Hagedorn 2008).

A fourth research project involving Evanston was a series of studies that grew out of my participatory role as chair of the Evanston Plan Commission. Like the previous research on neighborhoods and gangs, this research did not begin as a set of academic disciplinary questions; rather, it was connected to applied planning questions that included neighborhood plans and surveys of Evanston residents' cognitive mapping of their neighborhoods. The research gradually evolved into sociological questions about volunteer participation in local government, and it drew on participant observation through my official duties, meetings with residents of various neighborhoods, informal conversations, and the use of archives and records.

Subsequently, the research morphed into what was, at the time, my reemerging theoretical and empirical interest in "civil society" and the role of the voluntary "third sector" in social life (Ehrenberg 1999; Milofsky 1988). This research certainly had a base in my familiarity with prior research on local communities, but it grew more directly from a curiosity about the actual application and participation in the governing process itself as a "public intellectual"—a role that has been increasingly emphasized in sociology since the 1990s (Burawoy 2005; Etzioni and Bowditch, 2006). The understanding of the Evanston community and its politics gained from my prior research certainly informed my participation in this role, and perhaps equally significant data gleaned from this participant/observer role has fed back into and continued to inform all three of the prior studies, further elaborating and revising them over time. For example, the West Side neighborhood planning process in the Black community of Evanston informed me about residents' concerns with crime and gangs, just as my prior gang research led me to understand where the neighbors were coming from in our neighborhood meetings.

A fifth (though perhaps not final) piece of research involved a historical analysis of the factors that led Evanston, after more than a century of prohibition since its founding, to become a "wet" community permitting the sale of alcohol, a project I explain more fully below. This research was based on archives, in-depth interviews, and personal recall.

Although the research projects above are listed in their sequential and linear temporal order, in reality they mutually informed one another throughout the decades. One might feed directly into another, and still another be put on hold for a time, only to be further developed by insights from a later research project that circled back and informed the prior research in a nonlinear fashion. In short, these varying projects illustrate that you can come back to the same place because it can constantly be made new, through changes in the subject itself as well as changes in the frameworks at hand.

Types of Ties

As a long-term resident of Evanston—a townie—I am embedded in a number of different types of ties and networks that have had direct implications for the progress (or lack thereof) of my research over the years. These ties and networks may be thought of as multiplex, or (in the language of Robert Merton's [1968] older role theory) as a complex "status set" and "role set." Briefly, the types include the dominant status of researcher—ties made doing various research projects in the community; family ties—links to both my family of origin and families of procreation; youthful ties—links to my peers and others based on having grown up in the community; professional ties—links based on my academic position as a professor at Northwestern University; neighborhood ties—links to my immediate neighbors, fellow members of "Nichols Neighbors"; and community ties—connections exemplified by those reflecting my position as a member of the city plan commission.

As I interact with this or that individual in the community, I am sometimes operating simultaneously in multiple statuses, or overlapping networks, though at any given moment the exigencies of the situation may dictate the predominance of one status over the others. For example, in one case I had to recuse myself from the plan commission's discussion of a new development by a long-term care facility for the elderly because my mother was a resident of the facility.

In what follows, I focus on those situations where my dominant status was that of sociological researcher and I show how the complexity of the multiplex relationships affected the research, at times positively and at other times negatively. Of course, I also reflexively take into account the reverse causal impact and reflect on how my sociological research may have affected the ties as well.

Familiarity Has the Cost of Oversight

Oversights occur as a result of overfamiliarity—the "taken for granted" stance that does not see a sociological problem worthy of investigation and explanation. Being familiar has its costs. This was the case, for example, with Evanston's long history as a dry town and its shift to a wet town when it legalized the sale of alcohol, an event I noticed early on in my research career but failed to analyze in depth. For me, the community being dry was a taken-for-granted fact; it was, in the words of Robert Merton (1968), "noticed" but not "noted." In my first piece of research in my MA thesis, the vote to go wet in the 1960s was simply "noticed" as one among a number of strategies pursued by the local elite to try and promote downtown economic growth in the face of declining retail sales and tax revenues due to competition from new shopping centers constructed in neighboring suburbs. When permission to sell alcohol was granted to two hotels in the community, the visible impact on the long-cultivated conservative prohibitionist image of Evanston was minimal. Evanston, after all, was the home of the Women's Christian Temperance Union founded by Frances E. Willard. My "oversight" was not corrected until some fifty years later, when one of my students, through fresh eyes, "noted" the same phenomenon and we pursued it in greater depth. He conducted a longer-term historical analysis that looked at a sequence of votes on the question of prohibition in the community over the past century and framed the issue as a "moral" political and cultural question.

This new perspective, the shift from "noticing" to "noting," was facilitated by the emergence of new theoretical and substantive questions in the field. I had framed the movement from dry to wet in terms of a community economic development question, an issue that was more central to the discipline at that time; my student framed the issue as a politics of "morality" question that reflects the more current cultural symbolic turn in contemporary sociology (Beisel 1997; Swidler 2003). New eyes and a new perspective meant that what was previously "taken for granted" was now the focus of analysis.[1]

Continuities would usually suggest an absence of change and an acceptance of "the way things are"—for example, the fact that the intersection of Church Street and Dodge Avenue in Evanston has always been a "troubled corner" in the Black neighborhood for over more than half a century. I accepted and never interrogated this corner, already knowing its meaning from my youth.

Familiarity Has the Benefit of Insight

Even if occasionally I have "overlooked" issues of importance, to a great extent the ties I have developed over the years have been the source of astoundingly rich data. To take one example, as a resident of an integrated community, I was familiar with various forms of informal neighborhood organization within that community. These included a twelve-family pot-luck dinner and rehearsal for Chicago's "Do-It-Yourself Messiah" (a gathering of thousands at Orchestra Hall in the Loop); an annual Saturday alley clean-up in the spring, organized by all the neighbors whose houses back onto the common alley; and a "deck raising" where my son and I recruited about eight neighbors to collectively help raise to chest height a deck we had built on the ground in our backyard. Beers were the payment in kind.

When a flyer showed up on my doorstep calling for a neighborhood gathering to address two events—a recent drive-by gang shooting in the playground at Nichols Middle School across from my house, and an altercation between two White youth and a group of Black youth as the former walked home from the high school to their homes in the integrated neighborhood—I went as part of the neighborhood. I expected a small neighborhood gathering and was surprised to see a line forming out the front door, down the steps, and onto the sidewalk. Over one hundred neighbors had shown up, including three fellow sociologists as well as two professors of criminology. Out of the discussion, a decision was made to form an organization. Five leaders were selected to organize it, and a name was sought for the group. After a number of ideas had been considered, I suggested that since the middle school was the central institution in the neighborhood, we name the group after the school. "Nichols Neighbors" was born, and has now become a symbolic name of the community (Hunter 1974). In that case, I was acting as a full participant, and only after involvement in the organization as a resident did I turn my familiarity with this voluntary form of civil society into a research project on neighborhood responses to gangs, a project for which my insider knowledge led to both fuller understanding and deeper access.

Subjective Empathy and Objective Distance

A central concern in ethnography is the enduring dilemma of maintaining a balance between subjective empathy and objective distance. Coming into a social setting as an outsider and gaining entry is a topic that has been thoroughly discussed as a key concern in the literature (Emerson 2001). I often had the *opposite* problem of being an insider who had to establish distance, a task that often proved equally difficult. I was "burdened" with deep biographical knowledge of many of the people I was studying and also with their prior knowledge of me. I could observe firsthand the continuity and change in individuals shaped by life experiences, including my own, and this had direct implications for the research.

Many of the people who would enter into my research as subjects were the same individuals I had known in my youth, yet they were now different people. World events had changed and shaped us. Vietnam affected one as a fighter pilot, and another as a Navy SEAL mine demolition diffuser; a third, an Annapolis grad, became a rescue helicopter pilot, and another a Navy Swift Boat captain serving alongside John Kerry. Others joined the Peace Corps in Colombia or participated in mobilizing antiwar rallies; one dropped out of Harvard to participate in civil rights voter registration drives in the South, later publishing a novel about it. Over the ensuing years, I would discuss with them political and local issues of the day, such as the civil rights movement of the 1960s and the antiwar movement of the 1970s, on up to more contemporary issues of gun violence and gangs, as well as liberal versus neoconservative issues of government versus market priorities in land use and local development.

These autobiographical and political conversations took place in such venues as a Fourth of July garden party and a local bar after meetings of the plan commission. What they did was provide not only information on general motives, attitudes, and ideologies, but a greater understanding of specific attitudes and behaviors that had to do with the subject matters I was studying. One of these "old high school buddies," the fighter pilot, was elected to the school board for a term of six years, after which he then served on the plan commission with me. When he subsequently unsuccessfully campaigned for mayor, I served as an informal consultant to him, and during the same municipal election I organized a joint undergraduate seminar with a journalism professor titled (borrowing from former Speaker of the House Tip O'Neill) "All Politics Is Local."

Mixed within this mélange of social ties were old high school personal ties, community actor ties, and professional ties as a teacher at the university. I have remained a participant/observer researcher of the local community's politics, and more recently of the voluntary sector of civil society. Because I was a sociology professor, I was asked to conduct three surveys of my high school graduating class over the decades. Besides the usual mundane questions about marriages, divorces, and kids, I asked some questions about political attitudes and behaviors. I was surprised to learn that the majority of my classmates were much more conservative than myself in supporting the Vietnam War and in opposing class and racial neighborhood integration and diversity. The research and subsequent conversations made me realize that I too had changed and that my friendship circles and personal ties in the community had shifted over time. For one, I had consciously moved into a diverse, racially integrated neighborhood with greater class heterogeneity, whereas many of those surveyed were rather steadfast supporters of class segregation and exclusion. One item also suggested a different interpretation of "commitment" to the local community, in that the men were much more likely to remain local while the women had moved away from the area. In my write-up I interpreted this finding: "The males were less adventurous and either remained or returned to the area, while the women became liberated and more cosmopolitan." One of my female classmates responded, with perhaps even more sense, "No, Al, we were dragged away through marriage!"

C. Wright Mills ([1959] 2000) suggests that a deep knowledge of how the biographies of these individuals intersected with history heightens the sociological imagination and leads to an understanding of the forces that shaped their particular attitudes, opinions, beliefs, and behaviors, and their roles in the community as adults. In my experience, he is right. But there has been more to it than that. All of these personal insights into attitudes, motives, behaviors, and beliefs also made me particularly hypersensitive to the interpretations that I might place on my data, since I fully realized that the publication of my research would not only reflect on many of these people in my personal networks but likely be read by them. As I agonized over numerous drafts and varying ways of framing the results, I reflexively anticipated their reactions to it. Some of these data have been written up and published or presented as papers in very objectified and abstract academic formats and outlets. Much, however, remains to be analyzed and slowly integrated as I have struggled with the implications of these results on people with whom I have enduring local ties. One thinks of the aging Charles Darwin in his study at Down House, pondering for decades the mass of data gathered on his world cruise on the *Beagle* in his youth, slowly ordering the evidence, and crafting the argument for his theory of evolution by natural selection; some have suggested that his personal tie with his deeply religious wife delayed his publication, since he was concerned about the impact his theory would have on her cherished biblical beliefs (Quammen 2006).

These concerns with the impact of publication are not unfounded or merely hypothetical. This was pointedly brought out to me one evening when I was chairing a plan commission meeting. A local attorney representing a local developer was making his summation to the commission prior to our final vote for approval, and in response to local citizens who had opposed the development he began quoting from an article by an "urban expert" in support of his position. By the second sentence the words began to sound familiar and I slowly realized he was quoting from one of my own published articles. As he concluded he looked up with a sly smile on his face, which I acknowledged with my own smile and a complimentary nod: he had indeed "done his homework." He then announced the author, and all my fellow commissioners and assembled citizens turned and looked at me. I felt compelled to give a short exegesis on the distinction between "rational exchange value" of developers versus "subjective use value" of residents over contested land use for the benefit of all present to explain the basis of my quoted comments (Hunter 1979).

Personal Aspects of Local Family Ties and Local Research

Over the years, I had had other job offers and inquiries from other universities, which I turned down in large part because I had "family obligations" in the area. These included responsibility for two aging parents who still lived in the same house in which I had grown up, and after a divorce a new kind of responsibility for my two children, who remained in the town with their mother. At several points over the years my son lived with me full time and I was actively involved with both of the children. These responsibilities took their toll in disrupting the time available to devote to research—especially on weekends, which were often a prime time for participant observation and interviewing in the local communities I was studying.

For the first sixteen years of my career, my research and writing time had been privileged in the family's time budgeting. I had been the sole breadwinner ever since my undergraduate days. With two kids and a wife to support, I had hard-charged though grad school in three years. After the divorce and subsequent related changes, I suddenly had more direct child care responsibilities as well as more everyday time commitments (such as shopping, cooking, doing laundry, and being the master of the family dog, not to mention dating). Now less routinized, smaller blocks of time for research and writing were all that was available. In addition, over the next ten years three moves took me to three separate neighborhoods.

Remarrying and establishing a second family with three children (one of whom was adopted from Guatemala in a lengthy and time-consuming process over a two-year period) required a second round of soccer and softball practices, music lessons, and band concerts; I also served as a Cub Scout den leader, a Daisy Dad in Girl Scouts, and a chaperone on Indian Guide and Indian Princess camping trips through the local YMCA. To be sure, these activities are routine for any dutiful dad, but for me this was the second time around. While many professional peers my age were rediscovering new hours in the day and weeks and months to devote to their research and writing as their kids left the nest, I was once again engaged in nesting. A colleague who also has five children through two families once wryly observed, "I figure each kid has cost me at least one book."

Although family ties slow research, they are not without their benefits. My parents' networks with a number of community leaders very clearly opened some of the doors with people I interviewed for my MA thesis research. The networks of my children drew me into an entirely new set of networks and created new insights into the local community. Tales from the local high school about race relations and gang activities were relayed by my kids in informal family conversations over the dinner table. I also had more direct experiences with gang issues in Evanston. One morning my son returned within ten minutes of having departed for his walk to the high school. I asked, "What's wrong, did you forget something?" He responded, "No, I just wore the wrong clothes—I accidently had on gang colors and got yelled at by some older guys I don't know. Thought I better come home and change." On another occasion, the data literally came to my doorstep. One evening, I answered the ring of the doorbell and opened the door to an adolescent Black male who anxiously kept looking over his shoulder. He asked, "Mr. Hunter, I am a friend of your son Andy from a few years back, and I was wondering if I could come in for a few minutes?" I invited him in and explained that Andy wasn't home. He said that was okay but wondered if he could "hang out" for a few minutes because guys from a rival gang were after him; he had seen the light on at my house and run to it for safety. As we talked about his gang involvement and the particulars of the situation he was in, he kept going to the window to peer out. After about half an hour, he thanked me politely, said to say "hi" to Andy, and left.

Family activities carried out at the neighborhood and community level helped me establish a range of network associations. My children's soccer and camping networks connected me to members of a predominantly White middle-class neighborhood that became a focus of my research on neighborhood responses to gangs. I drew on these ties and gleaned knowledge from informal conversations with these residents of the neighborhood as they discussed, for example, the establishment of a private school that would further remove them from the effects of racial, ethnic, and class diversity, as well as related social problems prevalent in the wider community. This additional knowledge confirmed and gave increased validity to survey and interview data previously collected in the neighborhood.

Trust, Access, and Legitimation

"Where do you live?" and "How long have you lived here?" are two central questions for establishing one's "local community status." Responses are often dichotomized as those of "newcomer" versus "native," or in the case of many academic settings, member of the university community versus "townie" (Brown-Saracino 2010; Kasarda and Janowitz 1974). I often let people know how long I had lived in the community as I attempted to gain their trust and legitimate my standing. As a plan commissioner, I also heard this issue raised routinely when local residents rose to make public comments: after giving their name and address as required, they invariably added, "I am a [xx]-year resident of Evanston." Sometimes in meetings this took an almost humorous form, with residents engaging in an escalating competitive bidding war that occasionally spilled over into multigenerational claims. Such claims of legitimacy could be linked to institutional affiliation as well when adults would mention they were members of the high school class of this or that year, local grammar schools they had attended, or youth club memberships in the "Y" or local churches.

As one might expect, being identified as a local was usually beneficial in establishing a quick rapport with subjects. However, as with many social ties there was a certain ambiguity: sometimes being identified as a local made me suspect as to possibly having a biased personal agenda. This concern by people we are studying is perhaps more readily deflected by one doing research from an "outsider" perspective—a neutral stranger who can more readily dip "in to" and "out of" of a field setting. Though the literature highlights the problematic nature of "gaining entry" and "exiting gracefully" as ethnographic issues, it gives scant attention to the problems associated with studying one's own social milieu (Emerson 2001). Formally, concern about distinctive and potentially questionable interests is exemplified in the conflict of interest disclosure statements that I was required to fill out with the Cook County clerk as a governmental office holder on the Evanston Plan Commission. Informally, as a "known" local I had to be wary about being overidentified with this or that neighborhood or social group and set of networks. (Interestingly, given the many town/gown issues in the community, the university was concerned as well about my foray into local politics and I had to sign the university's own conflict of interest statements.)

At times, my professional affiliation gave me a degree of legitimation as a knowledgeable expert; equally often, it seemed to impede the research, calling into question my commitment to the subjects of the research over and against the interests of the university or my professional career interests. There was always a lingering sense that there was an ulterior motive beyond the welfare of the subjects, which indeed there was. As Sudhir Venkatesh (2008) put it in his book *Gang Leader for a Day*, as defined by one of the gang members, research is a "hustle."

This suspicion was aroused in different neighborhoods for different reasons. In the Black community, there was a growing concern with "encroachment" of the university, especially as students expanded their search for off-campus housing into the bordering fringes of the Black community. Uneasiness was also manifest in the reaction to the instituting of patrols by the campus police and its later expansion in size and territorial jurisdiction, which came to be seen by some in the Black community as a means of controlling their movement, especially that of young Blacks in the boundary areas. The patrols seemed in part to be a response to increasing numbers of street robberies and confrontations on or near campus.

In the White neighborhood, I at times had to face a different suspicion: that I was a "liberal" sociologist likely to be advocating certain social changes, and that my research might be used as an exposé to advance policies detrimental to my subjects' interests. This was especially true with respect to the sensitive issue of race, as well as housing and land use that might affect property values. In short, I often had to disabuse my subjects of their suspicions as to my understanding of their concerns and that I was not merely an outsider—"the professor," an ivory tower academic—asking for cooperation but offering few direct benefits in return.

"Giving Back" and *Noblesse Oblige*

As a long-term resident, the idea that I would "give back" to the community was an especially strong normative expectation among both current neighbors and among high school peers who themselves were doing the same. Many of those I knew in high school were now very consciously "giving back" to the community in which they were raised and educated. They occupied such positions as school board members, head of the local chamber of commerce, board members of the local "Y," and leaders of other philanthropic and voluntary institutions in the community. To an outsider they had become part of the local community elite, but as an insider I personally felt the same sense of commitment toward volunteering time and energy for the collective good.

A vice president of the university complimented me at one point for my degree of "local engagement" and referred to my services on the plan commission as an act of "*noblesse oblige.*" This compliment was in spite of the fact that the plan commission was often in land use and property zoning conflicts with the university. To many of my university colleagues, time spent in such "local" activities was seen as counterproductive to one's career and beneath their more "cosmopolitan" national and international orientations. To me, the story is not quite so simple. The small-scale, unfunded local studies of Evanston were fit in here and there over the years, interspersed between other larger projects involving grants and national comparative research, and the local and cosmopolitan research mutually informed each other. Many of these pieces of research on the local community permitted me to simultaneously help my community—and become what today is called a "public intellectual"—and engage in academic research that could in fact also further my career through publication.

Notes

1. The symbolic continuity of the prohibitionist image of Evanston is now celebrated ironically in the many cafés and bars that dot the downtown, as part of a strategic branding of Evanston's image as a destination restaurant center promoted by research and policies of the plan commission. The full irony is seen in the name of the first boutique distillery established as part of this economic development: F. E. W.—the initials of Frances E. Willard.

References

Beisel, N. 1997. *Imperiled Innocents: Anthony Comstock and Family Reproduction in Victorian America.* Princeton, NJ: Princeton University Press.
Brown-Saracino, J. 2010. *A Neighborhood That Never Changes.* Chicago: University of Chicago Press.
Burawoy, M. 2005. "For Public Sociology." *American Sociological Review* 70 (1): 4–28.

Ehrenberg, J. 1999. *Civil Society: The Critical History of an Idea*. New York: New York University Press.

Emerson, R. M. 2001: *Contemporary Field Research*. Long Grove, IL: Waveland Press.

Etzioni, A., and A. Bowditch, eds. 2006. *Public Intellectuals: An Endangered Species?* Lanham, MD: Rowman and Littlefield.

Hagedorn, J. M. 2008. *A World of Gangs: Armed Young Men and Gangsta Culture*. Minneapolis: University of Minnesota Press.

Hunter, A. 1974. *Symbolic Communities*. Chicago: University of Chicago Press.

———. 1979. "The Urban Neighborhood." *Urban Affairs Quarterly* 14 (7): 267–88.

———. 1984. "Suburban Autonomy/Dependency: Elite Perceptions." *Social Science Quarterly* 65 (March): 181–89.

Hunter, A., and R. Fritz. 1985. "Class, Status, and Power Structures of Community Elites: A Comparative Case Study." *Social Science Quarterly* 66 (3): 602–16.

Kasarda, J. D., and M. Janowitz. 1974. "Community Attachment in Mass Society." *American Sociological Review* 39 (June): 328–39.

Merton, R. K. 1968. *Social Theory and Social Structure*. New York, NY: Free Press.

Mills, C. W. (1959) 2000. *The Sociological Imagination*. New York: Oxford University Press.

Milofsky, C. 1988. *Community Organizations*. New York: Oxford University Press.

Pfouts, R. W. 1960. *Techniques of Urban Economic Analysis*. West Trenton, NJ: Chandler-Davis.

Polsby, N. 1980. *Community Power and Political Theory*. 1980. Berkeley, CA: Institute of Governmental Studies Press.

Quammen, D. 2006. *The Reluctant Mr. Darwin*. New York: Norton.

Skogan, W. G., and M. G. Maxfield. 1981. *Coping with Crime*. Beverly Hills, CA: Sage.

Swidler, A. 2003. *Talk of Love: How Culture Matters*. Chicago: University of Chicago Press.

Venkatesh, S. 2008. *Gang Leader for a Day*. New York: Penguin.

White, H. C., S. A. Borman, and R. L. Breiger. 1976. "Social Structure from Multiple Networks: 1. Block Models of Roles and Positions." *American Journal of Sociology* 81 (January): 730–80.

5

Breaching Boundaries and Dowsing for Stories on the Great Plains

Karen V. Hansen

As I drove out to the Spirit Lake Dakota Indian Reservation for the first time, I was filled with trepidation. I had never been on an Indian reservation before, and I was searching for the spot where my Norwegian grandmother had settled in North America—a place she told me her mother had stolen from Native people. Who could possibly welcome my intrusion?

I was struck by the beauty of the prairies and the astonishing bird life coursing down the North American flyway. But nothing was familiar, and I knew no one. A gravel road headed to the Sheyenne River marked a border of my great-grandmother's homestead: as I drove on it, after talking to local history keepers, I realized she had not been the only Norwegian living there. Nor was she the only woman landowner. The curious juxtaposition of Scandinavian homesteaders with Dakota Indians intrigued me and provoked me to ask: How did it happen? With what consequences? Having just gotten tenure, I could ask these questions and contemplate a research project outside of my geographic and temporal areas of expertise, one that might take a while.

Could I, with integrity and equivalence, interrogate relationships between Scandinavians and the Dakota people they dispossessed? My feminist hesitation was grounded in a critique of ethnocentrism and academic voyeurism. A long history of antagonism between anthropologists and Native Americans has created a climate of mistrust, misunderstanding, and a well-grounded fear of appropriation. Not just social scientists, but photographers, tourists, and others have set out to observe—and even steal—secret rituals and objects, and in the process treat Indian people disrespectfully. They have sought in Native American culture a way to make themselves whole by absconding with something—a point of view, a prayer, an affirmation—absent in their own lives. What right did I have to intrude on cultures so distant from my own?

By breaching disciplinary and social boundaries, I commenced to study an uneasy coexistence between two peoples who were complete strangers to each other. In the wake of the U.S.-Dakota War of 1862 and U.S. military and legislative action to dispossess Native people, Congress created the conditions for White homesteaders to take land on Indian reservations. How did Dakotas, who had been promised territorial integrity, respond to the incursion of the flood of homesteaders, most of whom were Scandinavian? What are the communal consequences when one group's acquisition of land is predicated on the dispossession of the other?

I now understand that stretch of sixteen years since I first visited the reservation as an evolution—a necessary condition for the viability of my project, *Encounter on the Great Plains* (Hansen 2013). Through doggedly returning year after year, piecing together small discoveries and new understandings, I was able to make sense of the reservation's curious configuration and social relationships, and to overcome my initial reluctance. Importantly, through grappling with insights and insults, over time I embraced ownership of the project with greater confidence.

It was not the historical sources that changed over this decade (although they were hard to find), but rather my relation to the living, and hence to the dead. As I kept returning to Spirit Lake, people on the reservation became less reserved and more open; they seemed to understand that I was not casually passing through simply to glean surface understandings. In various ways they let me know that they not only felt fine about my project, they wanted to be interviewed; they wanted to show me their treasures; they wanted me to write my book. My persistent search for sources yielded many dead ends, but also long-ignored documents. My extended time in the field coincided with theoretical developments that enabled me to frame the project more squarely as a case of settler colonialism in an "entangled history."

A Stranger in the Field

Norwegian homesteaders who began claiming land in 1904 were not the only strangers to the reservation. A few years after I launched a full-scale research project on the Spirit Lake Nation, I was interviewing a respected elder, Agnes Greene, when her son arrived to have coffee and inspect me.

He greeted me: "Good morning."

"Hi, I'm Karen Hansen, visiting from Boston."

"Oh, a stranger, in other words."

Yes. I'm a stranger. I am foreign to these people—Dakota and Norwegian alike. I'm a female professor teaching at an elite eastern university. I talk fast. I travel thousands of miles with a university grant to pay for my rental car, my hotel, and the fancy equipment I use to record interviews. I've never been a farmer or a farmer's daughter. I don't speak Norwegian or Dakota. I had never been to a powwow or to a 17th of May celebration of the Norwegian Constitution. Before 1995, I had never been to North Dakota. As a result of my stranger status, some people simply denied me access. I have had people hang up the phone on me, not answer my letters or e-mail, and even threaten to beat me up.

A confluence of additional challenges made this research difficult, and perhaps even foolhardy. With institutional support for travel, I began making local contacts; reading multiple literatures; searching for letters, diaries, and other historical records; and learning all I could about Dakota history, Norwegian farming practices, and federal immigration and Indian policy. I was studying a remote past (1890–1930) that was not well documented, in a distant site—a three-hour drive from Fargo—while I lived in Boston. I quickly discovered that poor people in the Midwest were much less likely to keep diaries than their counterparts in New England, and that archives in Norway and the United States collected letters primarily from the nineteenth century, not the twentieth.

I began working with historical plat maps, which invitingly documented the jagged mosaic of racial-ethnic coexistence on the reservation. I assembled a large database of the names, ethnicity, and gender of property owners in 1910 and 1929 that allowed me to analyze patterns of landownership over time. But it could not give voice to the texture of daily life or the human face of coexistence after landtaking and dispossession. I read historical newspapers in microfilm, but they were notoriously unreliable, biased in favor of the Yankee landowning class, and unapologetically prejudiced against Native Americans.

I would go to North Dakota for one week at a time—the most I felt I could be away from teaching responsibilities and my home with two small children. While each visit generated more answers, the data would seem tangential, oblique, and frustratingly vague. I kept struggling because the evidence simply did not answer my set of questions. My colleagues and members of my writing group urged me on, believing in me and recognizing the power of this unusual scholarly quest. As the years stretched into more than a decade, as my children grew up, and as I published a completely unrelated monograph and two anthologies, my thirteen trips to North Dakota generated a pile of interviews, observational data, insights, and sustained relationships with people living on the reservation.

Social science values doing fieldwork from an outsider status; it is a basic premise of ethnography in sociology and anthropology. But people in the field do not embrace strangers, nor do they immediately trust them. From the North Dakotan perspective, the only thing that gave me traction— any kind of legitimacy—was my grandmother. My Norwegian great-grandmother had homesteaded there. My grandmother grew up on the reservation. My quest to understand my grandmother's life stemmed from genuine curiosity and a desire to grapple with the moral dilemmas precipitated by her journey. In the field, it was not my academic credentials but my genealogical connection that prompted people to open their doors to me.

The absence of first-person primary sources led me to seek contemporary accounts of the past: memoirs, family histories, and oral narratives. Thankfully, in the 1960s and 1970s oral histories had been collected by the State Historical Society of North Dakota and the American Indian Research Project in South Dakota. Because those archived interviews only rarely spoke to my questions about land and coexistence, I decided to conduct interviews of my own.

When I first approached local scholars about the prickly coresidence of Dakotas and Scandinavians, they were a bit surprised, but encouraging. One professor at the University of North Dakota told me that only an outsider could ask these contentious questions and dare attempt to answer them. Diving into the middle of ancient hostilities fraught with racism and resentment necessitated breaking a taboo. History is alive, and of course, controversial.

Iterative Fieldwork

For historical sociologists, fieldwork typically means going to the archives. But a savvy anthropologist advised me early on that to understand the past, I had to comprehend the present. He recommended spending time hanging out on the reservation. He was right. Those years intermittently in the field were *not* a series of delays or explorations of tangents, but a time for establishing relationships with people, understanding their unique history, finding new sources, and deepening my ability to interpret the evidence. Although my focus centers on the pre-Depression era at the Spirit Lake Dakota Reservation, the descendants of those early landowners still live there.

I had been skeptical of using government records, though abundant, because they had been kept with the intention of monitoring, subduing, and ruling over Indian people. Fortunately, they allowed for multiple readings. For example, letters and annual reports from Indian superintendents to the Indian Office in Washington, DC, revealed the officials' irritation at the persistent requests by Dakotas. I found this significant not because the superintendents were annoyed, but because it showed that Dakotas advocated for themselves and relentlessly insisted that the government abide by treaty obligations as well as verbal promises. When I rummaged through the Great Plains Regional repository of the National Archives and Records Administration (NARA), I discovered a batch of daily reports from 1913 to 1915 by the field matron, Carrie Pohl, hired to promote housekeeping and sanitation on the reservation. Her handwritten notes were still held together in clusters by slightly rusted straight pins that had never been removed. While Pohl's accounts of her visits to Dakota households reflected her harsh racial judgments, they revealed more. It was possible to read Dakota women's resistance to Pohl's admonishments and observe over time how they softened in response to her increasing empathy and efforts to provide resources like building materials and medicine.

After doing research at NARA, I was once again reminded of the potential chasm between historical evidence and current assumptions. My interest in women as landowners is but one example of how a contemporary vision of the past can be distorted through a gendered and racialized lens. I entered the "blue building," as it is called, on the reservation, where tribal offices are housed and local allotment records are kept. I asked the clerk in the land office to show me the files of several Dakota women who had purchased land. She told me Indian women did not buy land. Excited about my recent discovery, I gleefully reported that I had just been looking at Indian Office records of bids to buy reservation land in the 1910s and 1920s, and Dakota women's names appeared among the bidders. I thought I had brought a gift of good news, but thereafter silence greeted my correspondence and queries. My requests for more information and copies of files went unanswered.

I set out to be reflexive, or "rigorously self-aware," as Judy Stacey (1991) puts it. I tried to understand the ways that my "partial perspective" (Haraway 1988) has been shaped by my disciplinary training; my community of orientation; who was willing to be interviewed—what they remembered and what they forgot; my ancestry—Norwegian and Danish—and its cultural mythology; and my kinship ties to Norwegian homesteaders on the reservation. I grew up with stories about my grandmother's ruggedness—how else could she have homesteaded three different times over the course of her life?—and admiration for what we called her pioneer spirit. But I possessed little knowledge about the life and family she left in Norway or awareness that her landtaking activities had concrete consequences for Native peoples. However well intentioned, I did not always know what I did not know.

Working outside my field meant that I was not swimming in the concepts and literature relevant to my encounter project, another boundary I breached. The huge disparity between my daily university work (which included teaching contemporary sociology) and my new research questions and academic networks gave me scholarly whiplash. I felt intellectually misplaced.

Yet coming from outside the discipline facilitated an inductive approach. I was familiar with the hazards of generalizing from the literature, just as anyone who goes into the field and does not want to be biased by preconceptions. I knew that what held true for Dakotas or Scandinavians nationally might not apply to the local situation. My extended time in the field allowed me to learn the particularities of how Spirit Lake Dakotas interpret and appropriate national symbols and holidays. For example, coming from Massachusetts, the birthplace of alliances between Wampanoag people and English colonialists, I was sensitive to the politics of history and commemoration. Here Thanksgiving is a day of resistance to protest U.S. mythmaking and dispossession of Native peoples, and I assumed the same would be true at Spirit Lake. So when I asked Louis Garcia, the honorary tribal historian, how Thanksgiving was being observed, I was in for another shock. He told me that the tribe worked hard to put a turkey on every table, and people were counting their blessings.

Near the end of my data collection and deep into final revisions on my manuscript, I thought I had finally nailed my analysis of the differences in political activism engaged by Dakotas and Norwegian immigrants. I had mapped the legal dimensions of their contrasting citizenship status, read the national literature on indigenous activism, and interwoven evidence of farmers' socialist electoral activism into my narrative. Cleverly, I argued that Dakotas had channeled their political activism through the federal courts and Norwegians through the ballot box. My writing group loved the neat parallelism and thought the chapter was brilliant.

Then I read a nonacademic book that led me to an article on November 20, 1892, in the *Grand Forks Herald*; it reported that hundreds of Dakotas showed up to vote at the Fort Totten precinct on the reservation (Diedrich 2009, 68). Startled, I had to rethink my analysis. Across the country, suffrage was not a major issue for indigenous activists. Unbeknownst to me and invisible in the federal records, Spirit Lake Dakotas had interpreted the allotment of land as granting them full citizenship. With their allotment certified just one week before the election of 1892, they immediately acted on their interpretation of that entitlement. My tidy analysis fell apart. It was only my persistent search for sources, even when I thought I was "done," that yielded this more complex narrative.

My repeated visits to the field have been riddled with ambivalence. Sometimes flooded with a sense of affirmation after a particularly incisive interview, I would renew my commitment to the project. At other times, overwhelmed by simmering conflict between the two groups and frustrated by insufficient evidence, I would vow to abandon it. Nonetheless, something kept drawing me back: the kindnesses of a few, the intrigue of the puzzle, my unreasonable determination. Stories give shape to history, to the incomprehensible chaos of life—to my life as well as the lives of those I interview. Unquestionably this research project offered a means for me to come to terms with the controversial processes that drew my grandmother and her mother to North America and landed them in the middle of a colonial project.

Even with the roadblocks and my occasional dispiritedness, I now think that returning year after year cumulatively had a positive impact. My iterative time in the field made me more sensitive to the Sisseton-Wahpeton Dakotas' complicated relationship to the U.S.–Dakota War of 1862. I came to understand the particularities of place and that the lives of marginal Scandinavian farmers did not represent a "promise fulfilled" as some scholars have suggested (Lovoll 1998). Through returning, I conveyed to people that my intentions were enduring and I was committed, not just episodically intrigued. Over time, local residents became familiar with me; some even developed a cautious trust.

Reciprocity and the Oral Tradition

Oral history interviews that reach back to a narrator's childhood, or a time before she or he was born, dovetail with an oral tradition common to both Dakotas and Scandinavians. As I learned, both rely on reciprocity.

The oral tradition requires at least two people—a storyteller and a listener. Listening is fundamental to historical memory. Without asking, a person cannot learn and cannot hope to know. Some members of the tribe profoundly understood the principle. Ambrose Littleghost, pipe carrier for the tribe, told me of how he would stay up late and listen to stories being told by his grandparents when Canadian relatives came to visit. Perfectly illustrating this process, Dakota elder Grace Lambert told me, "I was a great listener when I was a kid." She relayed an example: "My grandma used to tell me stories. One time she was telling me that they crossed the [river]. I said, 'How did they take the kids across?' I said, 'Did they swim with them on their back? Or what?' She said, 'No no, that's not the way'" (Lambert 1999). And then her grandmother proceeded to explain that swimming horses would pull a floating travois with children across the Missouri River. Grace Lambert actively listened. She would hear a story and then clarify aspects of it, asking questions, experimenting with theories about how things worked, and trying on the cultural logic for herself.

Old medicine men would not pass on knowledge to just any younger person, according to Louis Garcia, chronicler of Spirit Lake Dakotas. The person had to be worthy. The person had to *want* to know and had to offer a gift in exchange for learning. In the 1960s, when Garcia first came to the reservation, he witnessed a history in the process of being lost. While young people had a responsibility to listen, they had stopped being interested. So he made it his job to learn, to listen, to record. When I came to the reservation, I entered with a desire to know the past and a genuine interest in and respect for the people who lived there. But there was no question that potential narrators had to be convinced of that—I had to prove myself worthy.

Louis Garcia opened doors for me when I first arrived. He and his wife, Hilda Garcia, a Dakota tribal member, introduced me to Marcy Young

McKay, the director of the Senior Meals program on the reservation. After vetting my proposal with the tribal council, she connected me with some of the tribe's most respected elders. She invited me to the Elder's Day luncheon that honored veterans and aged members of the tribe, and generally facilitated my entry into the field. I understood the power of her sanction, and that of those who agreed to be interviewed.

One morning in 1999, my tape recorder jammed just as I was testing it before going to interview Grace Lambert, one of the most astute and highly respected history keepers in the tribe. In an utter panic, unwilling to disappoint a ninety-year-old woman and forego an opportunity to talk to her, my mind raced. Where could I possibly find a replacement recording device in time for my appointment? The casino-hotel where I was staying did not have one. The clerk suggested that perhaps the radio station KABU, "The Heart Beat of the Spirit Lake Nation," might have one. I raced upstairs. Needless to say, they did. More amazing was that they lent their expensive equipment to a stranger, with nothing but my business card as collateral. After two stunningly illuminating sessions with Mrs. Lambert, I realized the power of her consent to be interviewed. Surely the generosity shown by the people at KABU radiated from the halo of her agreement. It was not until fourteen years later, however—as I was putting the finishing touches on the manuscript—that it completely hit me: Grace Lambert had decided, for whatever set of reasons, that I was worthy.

Anthropologists have long understood the gift exchange as fundamental to doing fieldwork. Social scientists debate what researchers should give subjects in return for their participation. Some think that listening is sufficient because the act validates the life of the storyteller. They worry that giving money can be a thinly veiled form of expropriation—dollars for answers. What if stories are tailored to monetary value, corrupted by the process of profits to be made from the opportunity?

In fact, paying respondents was the price of doing business on the reservation, as Louis Garcia had advised. I arrived bearing tokens of appreciation—calculators, flashlights, penknives, and small amounts of cash—to give narrators. But I was disconcerted by how clearly payment was expected in an exchange with Marcy Young McKay's brother, Phillip John Young. One day as I was driving with him to a quiet coffee shop where we could conduct a formal oral history, he told me how delighted his friend had been to learn that Phillip John was being interviewed. Curious, I asked why. He rubbed his fingers together, intimating a cash payment. Startled, I took a deep breath.

While I had expected to pay him, I had not realized that nabbing a visiting social scientist was so commonly seen as a chance to make a quick twenty bucks. For six years, Phillip John had been a willing informant; he had escorted me to the site of my great-grandmother's homestead, maintained jovial relations, and introduced me to the pipe carrier of the tribe. As one of a minority of tribal members who had earned his BA, and a strong supporter of education, he found me an interesting curiosity and expressed admiration for my having earned a PhD.

Never before had he mentioned money. I often hung out with Phillip John during my visits—we would eat lunch in Devils Lake or at the casino, and I would give him small gifts, like the petrified buffalo tooth given to me by my uncle. I thought of myself as a professional, dowsing for stories. But this was the first time I would formally interview him, and it radically altered our dynamic. I had to wonder, was I the one being taken for a ride? Phillip John was the informant who had volunteered himself. As ethnographers caution, it is important to understand why some people want to talk to you and what makes them marginal in their own right.

Then Phillip John assured me that he did not want the money for himself—that he wanted me to give it to a scholarship fund established in honor of his sister Marcy, at the Cankdeska Cikana Community College on the reservation. At that point, I relaxed. That was something I believed in and would have done in any event. But formally interviewing him laid bare the terms of exchange and turned the table in ways I had not expected.

Some scholars argue that the researcher should give back more than money. They insist that one should help mobilize resources for political ends, teach skills, or provide services. And some feminists go so far as to argue that you should give something of yourself—friendship or empathy—to equalize the relationship, to diminish the potentially lopsided gift giving. I sought that middle ground of respect and appreciation, but the sticky tentacles of encompassing fieldwork do not observe clear boundaries. My ability to give back has been hobbled by my stranger status and my acute awareness of the fine line I walk as someone interested in Native American history as well as Scandinavian immigrant sagas.

Double Epiphany

After being in the field several years, I had my first epiphany as my responsibility in the reciprocal exchange became clearer to me. I had been worried—about appropriation, hostility, getting things wrong. I realized that my calling was to publish the narratives I was being told—these were my stories to tell.

As Agnes Greene had pointed out during our exchange, the interview was mine, not hers. Ending the interview, I had asked her a final question: "Is there anything [else] I should know?" She retorted, "Ask me. You're the one who wants to know. Ask me. If I know it I'll tell you" (Greene 1999).

I bristled at her sharp reply. In the moment, I didn't know how to respond. But her clarity gave me a lot to ponder. I was not "giving her voice," as some recovery projects claim to do. Ultimately, the interviews were mine. I directed the conversation; I asked the questions; I was motivated to publish. My challenge was to ask the right questions. But I should not make the mistake of thinking the story I was telling was hers. In the retelling, the accounts became my stories, reframed through my prism of interest.

Several years later, when Phillip John Young anointed me an "apostle," I again became deeply uncomfortable. He called on me, as he put it, to "teach the other people what they don't know" (Young 2005). The invaluable gifts he gave me—not just the star quilt, or the intricate feather powwow fan, but the stories—obliged me not to give up. But I did not want to preach; nor did I want to deliver his version of history, packaged and unquestioned. As Agnes Greene had seen clearly, the narrative was mine, constructed around my intellectual interests and my family history. Phillip John was reminding me that I had an obligation to convey what I had discovered.

The second epiphany came from my community of reference—academics. As I explored ways to interpret my observations, I quickly ran up against the limitations of theoretical models situated in colonialism. Although Europeans did colonize North America, the twentieth-century environment I was studying simply did not fit the assumptions or the time period. Racialization (à la Omi and Winant 1994) explained one aspect of the process of dispossession, but much more was simultaneously unfolding. I was interested in everyday practices: interactions, mutuality, collaboration, and coalition building, as well as prejudice, rejection, community divisions, and how people enacted racial hierarchies.

Settler colonialism, a developing perspective applied via illuminating international comparisons, opened a new theoretical door. Settler colonists relocated to find a place to make home, not to extend the power of the nation–state. They, like Scandinavians at Spirit Lake, intended to make farms and families and live on the land (Hoxie 2008; Wolfe 2006). As good theory is supposed to do, this emergent frame clarified the intersections of economic structural processes and micro everyday practices.

One particular event crystallized the importance of what I had set out to do. I discovered that my research sat on the leading edge of a new field that Gunlög Fur (2014), a Swedish scholar of seventeenth- and eighteenth-century North America, calls "entangled histories." In no other moment in my academic life was I more aware of the power of my interdisciplinary approach. Fur had organized a workshop titled "Immigrants and Indians" that brought together scholars from multiple disciplines. Her vision theoretically and empirically brought immigration history and Indian studies scholarship into sustained dialogue. My time in the field chronicling and interpreting interactions on the land coincided with this new theoretical development. In that workshop, I suddenly saw that my struggle to balance perspectives and multiple literatures was precisely what the group was urging. While not the first to study encounters of this kind (see, for example, Calloway 1991; Fur 2009; Jensen 2006), I nonetheless came to understand more fully how my case illuminates interactions between White settlers and Native people more broadly. Mine was not an obscure, irrelevant, or idiosyncratic case, as I had originally feared.

On Interruptions and Long Gestations

My colleagues and students complain that historical sociology takes too long. Digging in dusty archives and searching for evidence that may not exist (in contrast to asking live people specific questions) can be frustrating, and dangerously delay one's professional progress. Like all ethnographic projects, slow sociology requires time for understanding a social context, observing deeply, and letting data percolate. It demands piecing together awkwardly shaped, incomplete puzzles—in my case, historical maps, photographs, census data, and oral histories. It necessitates creatively improvising, using multiple methods, triangulating sources, and listening for silences. I have discovered through revisiting, rereading, rethinking, and reviewing that being open to disruption makes for good historical sociology.

I spent years searching for sources that simply do not exist. The evidence I do have is lopsided, weighted toward the more thoroughly documented Scandinavians. Persistence yielded more data, but never parity. Nonetheless, taking time to hunt, ponder, engage, and discover has made it possible to see the global in the particular, to link micro interactions to macro processes, and to observe social structure in a handwritten name on a plat map. Sensitive that the tools of social science act in tension with postcolonial taboos, I was able over time to meld them respectfully and effectively. Embracing the fullness of my family history simultaneously with my scholarly position enables me to indeed be a messenger. I am still an outsider, although I am no longer a stranger in the same way.

The new field of entangled histories invites a breach of disciplinary and social boundaries. Entanglements are necessarily interactional, multifaceted, and just plain complicated. Listening involves more than hearing words. It requires remembering. It obliges one to respect and honor secrets, tragedies, triumphs, humor, and miracles, and to recognize the humanity of everyone's struggles.

Note

My heartfelt thanks to Anita Ilta Garey for her inspiration and her commitment to the foundational idea of this book. Conversation and debate with her contributed to my insights at each stage of this long journey through the encounter. Rosanna Hertz and Peggy Nelson are remarkable not just as creative editors but as energetic people who make projects happen and friendship fun as well as meaningful. Debra Osnowitz and Mignon Duffy continue to see diamonds in the rough, and for that and their friendship I am forever grateful.

References

Calloway, C. G., ed. 1991. *Dawnland Encounters: Indians and Europeans in Northern New England*. Hanover, NH: University Press of New England.

Diedrich, M. 2009. *Little Fish: Head Chief of the Dakota on the Fort Totten Reservation*. With K. Garcia. Rochester, MN: Coyote Books.

Fur, G. 2009. *A Nation of Women: Gender and Colonial Encounters among the Delaware Indians*. Philadelphia: University of Pennsylvania Press.

———. 2014. "Indians and Immigrants—Entangled Histories." *Journal of American Ethnic History* 33 (Spring): 55–76.

Greene, A. 1999. Interview by author. Audio recording. Fort Totten, ND.

Hansen, K. V. 2013. *Encounter on the Great Plains: Scandinavian Settlers and the Dispossession of Dakota Indians, 1890–1930*. New York: Oxford University Press.

Haraway, D. 1988. "Situated Knowledges: The Science Question in Feminism and the Privilege of Partial Perspective." *Feminist Studies* 14 (Autumn): 575–99.

Hoxie, F. E. 2008. "Retrieving the Red Continent: Settler Colonialism and the History of American Indians in the U.S." *Ethnic and Racial Studies* 31: 1153–67.

Jensen, J. M. 2006. *Calling This Place Home: Women on the Wisconsin Frontier, 1850–1925*. St. Paul: Minnesota Historical Society Press.

Lambert, G. 1999. Interview by author. Audio recording. Fort Totten, ND.

Lovoll, O. S. 1998. *The Promise Fulfilled: A Portrait of Norwegian Americans Today*. Minneapolis: University of Minnesota Press.

Omi, M., and H. Winant. 1994. *Racial Formation in the United States: From the 1960s to the 1990s*. New York: Routledge.

Stacey, J. 1991. "Can There Be a Feminist Ethnography?" In *Women's Words: The Feminist Practice of Oral History*, edited by S. B. Gluck and D. Patai, 111–19. New York: Routledge.

U.S. Bureau of the Census. 1921. *Statistical Abstract of the United States, 1920*. Washington, DC: Government Printing Office.

Wolfe, P. 2006. "Settler Colonialism and the Elimination of the Native." *Journal of Genocide Research* 8 (December): 387–409.

Young, Phillip John. 2005. Interview by author. Audio recording. Devils Lake, ND.

PART II

Changing Methods, Changing Frameworks

Themes raised in earlier essays are amplified here, especially the themes of how during a long time spent "in the field" both appropriate methods and appropriate analytic frameworks underwent profound changes. These changes, in turn, created opportunities for the development of new concepts and new intellectual approaches to research begun within different sets of understandings.

Susan Bell traces the ways in which the "changing epistemologies in various fields of social science" are reflected in her book about the women known as "DES daughters," a book that she wrote over a period of almost thirty years. These changes include different methodologies (resulting in the inclusion of visual and performative evidence in her manuscript), different understandings of social activism (what she refers to as an "embodied health movement"), different ways of conceptualizing the experiences of DES daughters (from "stress and coping" to narrative analysis), and different ways of being a scholar (with the emergence of feminist studies). In a later portion of her essay, Bell writes about "life's vicissitudes," the personal events in her own life that "disrupted"—even as they enriched—her own scholarly journey. This theme is picked up again in the final section of the collection.

In her chapter, **Mary Romero** writes about the two decades she spent interviewing Olivia, the daughter of a "live-in domestic worker in a gated Los Angeles community." From the start, Olivia took control of each interview session, telling her complex narrative in her own terms for however long she felt like going on. Romero was savvy enough to allow Olivia to lead: Romero wrote up notes and asked for clarification, but mainly took a passive role. While many social scientists, especially sociologists and anthropologists, have shifted the interviewing process from a hierarchical one to one in which the interviewer and the interviewee together craft a narrative, Romero has led the way in a new direction. In her essay, she explores how she was able to take Olivia's narratives, with their multiple twists and turns, and understand Olivia's story through a life stages approach. Romero locates Olivia as an individual embedded in a changing, broader social and economic milieu.

The other chapters also raise the issue of changing understandings. **Will C. van den Hoonaard** thought he understood cartography but, when he came back to explore issues of gender in that field after a hiatus of about thirty years, he realized he could not approach it with his traditional ethnographic tools. To be sure, he found gender everywhere, including behind the markings on maps and in the spatial distribution of exhibitors at cartography conferences. He also discovered that his knowledge of cartography had to be brought up to date and that it would take both international travel and the adoption of an interdisciplinary approach to make a meaningful contribution to the field. Van den Hoonaard mentions, as do others, how women's work might be perceived as being trivial and might even be made invisible.

Linda Burton and **Carol Stack** offer a complex look at their relationships with each other, with the African American boys and men who constitute the focus of their essay, and with the theoretical concept of "kinscripts," which they developed in a 1993 publication by that name. Most significantly, their essay develops the notions of changing frameworks and how the politics of science impeded their own awareness of, and ability to present data on, what it was they were observing—especially the invisible contributions of teenage boys and young men to their families—as they studied low-income, African American families. In the final section of their paper, they note that because times have changed, new scholars who have picked up the kinscripts gauntlet and applied it to studies of adolescent fathers have met with a far better reception than their own initial foray into the topic. Indeed, in a personal communication they mentioned that rather than accusing such scholars of "making up stories about deviant Black boys to make them look like they care about their families," as a senior White male professor did with Burton in 1989, the academy now welcomes discussions of the engagement of Black males in family life.

Changing frameworks can occur at two levels: outside the academy (as shifts in political, social, and economic realities) and inside the academy (as shifts in academic or theoretical frameworks). Hunter's essay deals with both as he writes about a lifetime of involvement in Evanston and the changes in that community itself as well as in the intellectual concepts with which he assessed those changes.

In a way, **Pamela Stone**'s essay also embraces both meanings. The topic she is writing about—what is called "opting out"—achieves prominence in the national media while she is working on her own analysis; inside the academy, the issue is considered unimportant until that media attention focuses on it and Stone is able to locate it within a distinctive analytic framework. The heightened media attention is also reason for anxious concern: a careful scholar becomes a perhaps more cautious one, as she works through the complexities of a new methodological approach and reflects on the representativeness of her sample and the accuracy of her conclusions. And, as she discusses these concerns, she is open and honest about issues of self-doubt and the complexities of crafting a meaningful career.

6

Disrupting Scholarship

Susan E. Bell

When Susan Bell first interviewed DES daughters in 1982, could she possibly have imagined the book she eventually wrote? It is not necessarily a recommendation for a book to be 30 years in the making, but *DES Daughters* is a remarkably seamless weaving of older and more recent approaches to studying health and illness.

Arthur Frank (2010, 817)

I admit to blushing when I read the first two sentences of Frank's review of my book, not because of the praise he heaps on it but because of the date range he names in it: 1982–2009 is indeed a very long time for a book—not quite thirty years, but so long that it demands explanation. For many years I would not name the starting date, hoping to avoid the stigma of being so slow and preferring to pass as a "normal" scholar, one who managed to publish at least one article or book chapter per year. Even now I find myself start to sweat as I write these words and that is a signal that this chapter places the body at its center.

I was a postdoctoral fellow when I began my study of DES daughters. I then started a tenure-track job at Bowdoin College. I adopted a son and gave birth to a daughter within an eleven-month stretch of time before I was tenured, and completed the book when they were both in college. "Disrupting Scholarship" is about the ways in which my commitment to activism and raising my children interrupted my scholarship, the ways in which feminist and narrative scholars disrupted standard ways of doing sociology in the 1980s, and the ways my activist and family life disrupted and is interwoven into the thirty years it took me to complete *DES Daughters: Embodied Knowledge and the Transformation of Women's Health Politics.* I begin by briefly describing the book. I then trace tensions in my work between feminist scholarship and women's health activism, describe changing epistemologies in various fields of social science, and explore how these changing epistemologies are reflected in the development of the book. I demonstrate my openness to learning about them and to working with them to expand my thinking, change my research strategy, and transform my writing. Following my discussions of these disruptions, I provide another context for understanding my version of slow sociology by focusing on how my personal struggle to balance my life with my work over the course of the project illustrates the need for long-term social structural and cultural changes.

My book tells a story about women who attained legendary status in the annals of medicine. They were exposed prenatally to a medication promoted as a wonder drug that would prevent miscarriage. In 1971, the *New England Journal of Medicine* published an article about DES (diethylstilbestrol) that announced what is now recognized as a watershed in medicine (Herbst, Ulfelder, and Poskanzer 1971). The authors of the study, physicians at Massachusetts General Hospital (MGH), reported an association between DES and vaginal cancer in women who were just fifteen to twenty-two years old. From the 1940s to the 1970s, between five and ten million women had taken DES during pregnancy. When their daughters became teenagers and some of them developed reproductive tract cancer, the MGH physicians identified DES as the first transplacental carcinogen and the daughters took on the new identity of "DES daughters." When DES daughters had trouble becoming pregnant and giving birth to healthy babies, DES was connected to miscarriage and other problems during pregnancy. These characteristics—crossing the placenta, disrupting the developing fetus, and affecting the bodies of DES daughters in multiple ways that often do not appear for many years—are those that identify DES as the first endocrine disruptor. After 1971, DES daughters and their mothers began to participate collectively as well as individually in DES regimes of practice, and in so doing they reconfigured the political landscape, with consequences for DES daughters, the doing of science, and the practice of medicine. Joining together to found the grassroots organizations DES Action (1975) and the DES Cancer Network (1982), activists challenged existing medical and scientific knowledge about DES. They also developed alliances with medical scientists to pursue funding and support for DES research, screening, and treatment programs.

My book argues that the DES story is about more than a tragedy that occurred to a population in the mid-twentieth century and more than a humbling experience for medicine. It shows that the DES story is also about a women's health movement that questioned whether doctors always know best. These women were among the first to judge science based on their intimate, firsthand knowledge of their own bodies, and to join together in collective action for social change. DES daughters used what they had and created a different kind of social movement, one that actively contributed to the development of transformed relationships of power and knowledge, not only in the history of DES and care for DES daughters but also in the politics of women's health more generally. *DES Daughters* connects three frameworks—feminist health scholarship, embodied health movements, and narrative—and weaves them together to tell a story about embodied knowledge and the transformation of women's health politics.

I simply couldn't have written the book I eventually completed if I had finished it twenty years ago, or even ten years ago. It would have been much more narrowly focused on interview material, would have excluded the analysis of visual and performative evidence, would not have given attention to how science can be "undone," and would not have shown how DES daughters created an embodied health movement. I would have been less visible in the text.

Connecting Activism and Scholarship

Before becoming a sociologist, I worked in feminist health centers on the East Coast and West Coast of the United States in the early 1970s to transform how women's health care and knowledge about women's health and health care are developed and taught. I chose a dissertation topic—a study of the science of DES from the time it was synthesized in 1938 to its release for sale in 1941—while I was working in feminist health centers, because I wanted to combine my activist and scholarly commitments (Bell 1987, 1995). I stopped working in women's health centers before I became a full-time faculty member at Bowdoin College, and from the early 1980s to the late 1990s I combined feminist critique with women's health information by writing chapters in what has been called the "bible" of feminist health, *Our Bodies, Ourselves* (*OBOS*); I authored the birth control chapter in the 1984, 1992, and 1998 editions of *OBOS*. As an untenured professor, I was advised to clearly distinguish these activist and scholarly strands of work—to list them in two different categories on my CV—and to focus on the scholarly category of publications. That said, doing the research and writing for each version of "Birth Control" became my primary task for roughly nine months (the equivalent of a semester and summer—and the length of a pregnancy) in each instance, and thus privileged activist writing for large chunks of time.

In "Birth Control," my work consisted of reviewing the scientific and medical literature about current and possible future birth control methods, reviewing national and international policies about the development and distribution of birth control, talking with scientists and clinicians about their research, distilling these materials, and translating them into a text that people without any specialized scientific knowledge could understand and use. In "Birth Control," I connected the world inside the academy to the world outside of it. For me, the stakes were high: I wanted the text to be accurate and accessible. I wanted it to reflect a range of scientific views, and I wanted it to provide a critical perspective on this knowledge. I wanted to provide all of this for readers who were thinking about using birth control because they didn't want to get pregnant.[1]

Despite the periodic activist disruptions to my scholarly output when I wrote "Birth Control," I successfully turned work on the 1992 and 1998 editions of *Our Bodies, Ourselves* into scholarly publications, and in each of them I reflected on the feminist and reproductive science of birth control. After I read and taught Emily Martin's *The Woman in the Body* (1987), I incorporated her critique into the language of the 1992 edition of "Birth Control" (see Bell 1994). When I reviewed the literature about potential future methods of birth control for the 1998 version of "Birth Control," I learned about a partnership between women's health activists (Women's Health Advocates on Microbicides) and reproductive scientists (at the Population Council) to produce vaginal microbicides to prevent transmission of HIV and other sexually transmitted diseases. I relegated the partnership to a long footnote in *OBOS* but later turned to a more sustained examination of this transformation in women's health politics (Bell 2000, 2003).

To put it simply, for two decades I published two lines of work: one was activist and the other was scholarly, and although each drew inspiration and evidence from the other, I viewed them as distinct and I viewed myself as doing either one or the other. Eventually, my ongoing commitment to joining activism and scholarship found its way into *DES Daughters*, in my investigation of the emergence and effects of DES as an "embodied health movement" based on a different conception of identity. I could see practices and identities differently in light of feminist and postmodern scholarship (e.g., Foucault 1978; Scott 1991; Haraway 1988, 1991). Haraway (1991, 181) questioned the possibility of an "identity" in which "we" can be clearly demarcated from "they" and argued that giving up the search for bounded individuals with distinct statuses or a universal totalizing theory could open up the possibility of heteroglossia and of taking seriously partiality and fluidity. Similarly, Scott (1991, 780) argued that "it is not individuals who have experience but subjects who are constituted through experience." These ways of understanding selves and identities gave me a framework for seeing how my activism and scholarship could be intimately connected—and indeed that ignoring this connection could be problematic. As I discuss below, this scholarship also gave credence to empathy, connection, and responsibility as sound research strategies (Reinharz 1992). Many of these scholars included themselves in the analysis (e.g., Behar 1993), and thereby provided models for engaged research.

As I write in my book, young women who have become known as DES daughters have taken actions on their own behalf that have contributed to transformations in ways of knowing, investigating, and monitoring their hybrid bodies' combination of natural and synthetic estrogens. Cultural discourses shaped their individual responses, and their collective responses created new pathways, transformed relations of power and knowledge, and contributed to making new spaces and conversations. Additionally, their organized actions, emanating from the groups they formed (DES Action and the DES Cancer Network), led to interdisciplinary, international conferences about DES in 1992 and 1999 where they worked to "undo science as usual" (Bell 2009) by introducing subjective knowledges into the conference discourses; their organized actions also led to funding and legislation favorable to research that continue to this day. These lines of research and practice have transformed the doing of science by incorporating activists in the conceptualization and conduct of DES science.

The DES daughters themselves (not the book) produced an embodied health movement. Embodied health movements frame their organizing efforts and critiques of the system through personal awareness and understanding of individuals' experiences. They also challenge science by forming alliances with scientists to secure funding and legislation and by collaborating with scientists in the doing of scientific research itself. The politicized collective work of embodied health movements transforms illness experiences, critiques medicine's treatment of patients, and turns attention away from individual bodies as sites of risk to the risky environments in which they live.

The concept of "embodied health movement" was first proposed by Phil Brown and his colleagues (2004). It was given depth by Maren Klawiter (2008) in her study of breast cancer and Steve Epstein (2000) in his study of HIV/AIDS. Individually and collectively, DES daughters drew from cultural resources and put "together in novel ways bits and pieces of what they found at hand" (Layne 2003, 236–37) to create new knowledges, institutions, and practices. One of these new knowledges was rooted in their embodied experiences of worrying about having cancer, having cancer, becoming and not becoming mothers, and living with the lifelong effects of endocrine-disrupted, synthetic chemical–infused bodies. The DES embodied health movement embraces fluid collectivities. Its past reflects the ways in which illness, suffering, and uncertainty can become opportunities for making social change. Its lessons include the value of embodied knowledges as integral elements in doing meaningful science.

Disrupting Scholarship: From a Study of Stress and Coping to a Narrative Analysis

In a memo dated September 16, 1982, I wrote:

> If you examine the assumptions (theoretical framework) underlying concepts of "coping" "stress" [and] "social support," you run into familiar terrain—a structural/functional understanding of the world. This has implications both for the formulation of these concepts and their study, as well as for analyses of them (e.g., Coelho, Hamburg & Adams [1974]; and Pearlin & Schooler [1978]). This perspective limits what can possibly be discovered as ways of coping, for example, or as relationships between individual and "social support." . . . As Thoits [1982] and a few others point out, these relationships may not always be supportive—or I might add elements of them may not be supportive. The theories of stress, coping and social supports stem from (at least the sociological ones do) [Walter B.] Cannon's and [René J.] Dubos' notion of homeostasis. This notion has already been criticized by Marxists. Also, the methodology involved in studying ways in which people cope, whether or not they're successful, etc., limits what can be discovered

about this. Using (or developing) scales predetermines what people are allowed to say, and how they'll describe themselves. And experimental designs decontextualize them further.

If, on the other hand, you create another "open" theory, contextualize the study, and use a more flexible methodology, you can begin to understand both the concepts and the strategies people use and the outcome much more comprehensively. That's what I propose to do.

My postdoctoral project was designed to enlarge and deepen our understanding of how people respond to and cope with exposure to synthetic hazardous substances—an exposure that increases the risk of serious illness. In my application for the postdoc, I wrote that I wanted to trace the emotional and physical impact of DES on a person's life and that "a prerequisite to this is understanding the ways in which the psychological component of experience can be described and assessed." Thus, I proposed to study the field of stress, coping, and social support. By the end of the postdoctoral fellowship, I was discouraged by the limits of this field, but nonetheless I designed and began the empirical portion of the research based on its epistemology.

The field of stress, coping, and social supports was a hugely influential field in medical sociology at the time.[2] It offered a theoretical framework and empirical approach to understanding the health of individuals by attending to the effect of life events and ongoing circumstances on their health, as well as to their responses to these events, circumstances, and outcomes. Theories of stress and coping examine pressures in the larger social environment to which people react protectively. After a year of studying the literature and trying to understand what I heard in my pilot interviews with DES daughters, I became increasingly discouraged by its potential for explaining the emotional and physical impact of DES on a person's life and for explaining how DES daughters lived with risk.

As I wrote in a series of memos from that period (which I unearthed for writing this chapter), I identified three major problems in this field of research. First, the concepts used in these theories and studies—stress, coping and adaptation, social supports—were loosely defined. Furthermore, while the analysts argued in theory that people interact with their environments, they treated people as passive individuals who must adapt to changes in their environments, seeking only to return to a state of equilibrium, or homeostasis, in the face of threats. Second, research in stress and coping did not investigate how people's responses help reproduce a stressful environment or, alternatively, help change it. The literature also decontextualized events and did not take historical circumstances into account. Third, most analyses of stress and coping at that time used quantitative measures and methods of aggregate statistical analyses.

I concluded that key aspects of DES daughters' experiences fell beyond the theoretical and methodological framework of the stress and coping literature. For example, the range of strategies DES daughters adopted in response to threats they faced could not be characterized as solely passive and defensive. They broadened the potential range of choices for young adult women in their roles as patients, consumers, and political actors.

In the analysis of pilot interviews, I saw stories emerging in response to the question with which I began: "How did you find out you were a DES daughter and what was it like?" (Bell 1988). Although I did not ask the women to tell stories, they often answered my opening question and subsequent questions by telling stories. Seeing stories in the interviews tapped into and reflected what is now referred to as the narrative turn in the social sciences. At the time, a number of scholars, including my mentor at Harvard, Elliot Mishler (1986), argued that because interviewers and respondents jointly construct interviews, respondents will recall and report some material in the form of stories if interviewers allow them to. This depends on how they negotiate their dual and shifting roles as interviewer/listener-to-a-story and respondent/narrator during the course of the interview. During interviews with DES daughters, I listened carefully without interrupting, allowed the women to direct the flow of the interview (pace, topics, topic shifts), and remained noncommittal. Although I had not intended it to, my interview approach created space for DES daughters to tell stories to tie together significant events and important relationships in their lives, and to make sense of their experiences.

Social scientists had begun to draw inspiration from literary scholars (e.g., Mitchell 1981) and had begun to consider how the form and content of stories told during interviews could shed light on the experiences of individuals (e.g., Labov 1972; Paget 1982, 1983; Mishler 1986), including illness experiences (Williams 1984; Kleinman 1988). Today, "narrative" is a term used ubiquitously in social science discourse, and there are different—competing—strands of narrative research (Riessman 2008; Andrews, Squire, and Tamboukou 2008; Polletta et al. 2011). At the time I made my turn, there were few guideposts for what "narrative" means or what would constitute "narrative analysis."

Building on the work of Labov and Waletzky (1967), I defined narrative as a sequence of ordered events that are constructed in a meaningful way for a particular audience in order to make sense of the world or people's experiences in it (Hinchman and Hinchman 1997). More than a list or chronicle, a narrative adds up to "something." A narrative has a point, or a moral lesson (the answer to the "so what" that one might ask after it ends). How it is put together—the images and explanations woven into it, and the position of the narrator in relation to the events and audience—all convey something important about a narrative's meanings. In addition, a narrative is produced collaboratively; the particular context in which a narrative is produced shapes its production and interpretation. When a person's life is interrupted by an illness, narrative offers "an opportunity to knit together the split ends of time, to construct a new context," and to fit the disruption caused by illness "into a temporal framework" (Hydén 1997, 53). Narrative analysis takes the story itself as its "object of investigation" (Riessman 2008).

In its reflexivity, the narrative turn is one response to disenchantment with the "dominant 'Cartesian' paradigm of rationality" at the core of modern social science (Hinchman and Hinchman 1997, xiv). Narrative approaches counter traditional social science models of knowledge by stressing that there are multiple truths, constructed by knowers who are socially and historically located, about a world that is neither fixed nor independent of knowers. At any point in time, there is a plurality of truthful narratives that differently positioned members of a culture can reasonably claim. Because narratives are constructed at particular moments in time and directed to particular audiences, they are about pasts of the moments in which they are told; a truthful narrative might be substantially different if told in other moments or to other audiences (Williams 1984, 198).

After turning to narrative, my perspective widened and expanded and over the years has incorporated and contributed to the development of narrative studies (e.g. Bell 2002, 2004, 2006). The body of work in narrative now reaches across many fields of research, such as the study of images (Harper 2000; Rich and Patashnick 2002), politics (Polletta 2006), letters (Jolly and Stanley 2005), medicine (Charon 2006), law (Ewick and Sibley 2003), and public discourse (Cameron 2006; Baxter 2006). The core evidence in *DES Daughters* is personal narratives from in-depth interviews. The stories—personal narratives—that emerged during these interviews include rich and complex clues about the ways individual DES daughters have understood and engaged with medicine since the 1960s. But by tracing details of narratives in different contexts and genres, I am able to make sense of DES daughters' accumulated knowledge and experiences of their bodies and reveal their participation in old and new regimes of DES. The book analyzes narrative discourse in the autobiographical documentary film by DES daughter Judith Helfand, *A Healthy Baby Girl* (1996), letters to the editor of the *DES Action Voice*, panel presentations and discussion at the National Institutes of Health–sponsored 1992 DES Workshop, and the program of the thirtieth anniversary celebration of DES Action in 2008.

The multifaceted nature of embodied health movements like the DES daughters' movement opens them up to be studied in a nonlinear way. In fact, their fluidity lends itself to a narrative understanding of them. Narrative analysis emphasizes multiplicity, fluidity, and reflexivity in its approaches to understanding social life. The construction of DES daughters' stories in interviews, published accounts, workshops, and films—just like the events that the stories portrayed—took place in specific historical contexts and shifting relations of power.

Disrupting Scholarship: Feminist Transformations

In a memo dated May 3, 1987, I wrote:

> Stella had received my letter 5 years ago, recruiting subjects for my study.[3] She had saved (and not returned) the postcard. She was calling me now to find out whether I had results, because she's just beginning to think about filing a law suit. . . .
>
> It would be safe to think of subjects as cases, as individuals I interviewed at one point in time to produce data that is no longer connected to a person. It would be safe to distance myself from them during the interview, to present the same self to each of them, to remain unconnected to the particular words, emotions, and conditions of each interview. Allowing myself to empathize, to be drawn into their lives, to let their words (and world) pour over me, is much riskier. I feel responsible to them; I feel that the core of the narratives, the points, are crucial not only because I'm trying to seek a "truth" about living with risk, but because I'm trying to preserve the integrity of the truths each woman—each individual person I interview—tells. My goal then, is to speak not only to the discipline to the scholarly world, but to these women, to my subjects. In a

sense, I become, in Tracy Paget's words, a "vehicle" for them to tell their stories; I recast them in the language of science to make them acceptable, to give them scientific respectability, to explain their universality, or at least their relevance, to others. At the same time, I must inevitably distort in order to draw out. This is a problem all scholars face—the necessity of cutting and slicing and splicing—but when I remember whose life I must cut and slice and splice it make the task not only difficult but painful.

The theoretical framework of my research, and the introduction of narrative analysis, changed before I finished recruiting subjects and conducting interviews. Until the early 1990s, I employed a conventional model of qualitative interviews (Lofland 1971). I designed the study to include a purposive sample of thirty adult women—ten DES daughters who had had DES cancer, ten who had not had DES cancer, and ten women not exposed to DES—and to conduct two semi-structured, in-depth face-to-face tape-recorded interviews with each of them.[4] To identify DES daughters with a wide range of experience, I used intermediaries: clinics treating DES daughters, physicians specializing in the treatment of DES cancer, the attorneys for a class-action lawsuit, and DES Action. Each of these sources sent a letter to a random sample of potential subjects on my behalf, describing the study and asking them to contact me (by returning a postcard or telephoning me) if they were interested in learning more about my work or participating in the study. I excluded women from the study if I already knew them from my participation in women's health or DES networks. Using this strategy of recruitment, I was able to identify and interview seventeen DES daughters between 1982 and 1986. During interviews with these women, my approach was consistent with conventional understandings of qualitative interviewing. I did my best to avoid influencing the interviews and introducing bias into the collection of data (see Mishler 1986). This entailed assembling a sample of respondents and eliciting answers from them in an objective, value-free, and (ironically) disembodied way. I tried to conceive of the DES daughters as cases for producing data and of my proper role as a distanced interviewer. I tried to present the same self to each of them and to remain unconnected to the particular words, emotions, and conditions of each woman as I interviewed her.

My approach to the interviews changed over the course of the study, as my conceptions of my position as an interviewer and knower changed and

as I became more enmeshed in the world of DES daughters. My changing understanding of interviewing, recruiting subjects, and the design of
the project reflected feminist studies of sociological practice (Roberts 1981;
Stacey 1988; Personal Narratives Group 1989; Reinharz 1992). I allowed
myself to empathize with the women I interviewed, to be connected with
them, to feel responsible for them as individuals, and to contribute to the
embodied health politics of DES. I wanted to acknowledge and represent
multiple truths and to speak not only to the discipline and to the scholarly
world, but to my subjects.

Both in recruiting DES daughters and in the interviews, I became less
concerned about maintaining distance and neutrality. As I became accustomed to talking with DES daughters about my ongoing work, I felt more
comfortable about being candid about my study when I met them and
becoming more flexible and open with them during the interviews. I met
informally with DES daughters at conferences and workshops and talked
about my study with them. Often, DES daughters would volunteer for
interviews. In 1992, to complete the sample of DES daughters, I followed up
on offers by three of the DES cancer daughters and invited them to participate in the study. When one of them asked to see what I had written about
DES before the interview, I sent her a copy of one of my published articles. She began the interview by responding to the article and I incorporated
her response into my analysis of her interview (Bell 1999a, 369–370; 2009,
55–56). My shift in strategy was both a pragmatic response to the difficulty
of locating DES daughters who had developed this very rare cancer and a
reflection of transformations in the study of lives by feminist scholars (Behar
1991, 1993, 1996; Behar and Gordon 1995).

At two of the conferences I gave formal talks based on my study. In 1992,
I presented an early draft of "Looking at Bodies" with my coauthor Roberta
Apfel (Bell and Apfel 1995). The article focuses on the symbolic and material
meanings about gender and sexuality surrounding women's bodies by interpreting three accounts about the surgical removal of a woman's vagina and
its reconstruction after DES-related cancer: a presentation given by a feminist health activist at a DES Action conference, a presentation given by a
gynecologic oncologist at the 1992 NIH-sponsored DES Workshop, and
an interview from my study. Several DES daughters spoke to me after the
talk and told me they were ambivalent about making their vaginas "public."
In the conclusion to the article, Apfel and I obliquely responded to this

concern: "The three vignettes represent the sense in which our focus on vaginas risks and resists the reduction of women to an organ-specific care and an essentialist theory of gender. . . . [DES cancer daughters'] intentional reaffirmation of gender norms and sexual boundaries, combined with the uncertainty they feel after reconstruction, suggests both the importance of having a vagina and the limitations of using the vagina to define women's identities" (Bell and Apfel 1995, 16, 19).

By 1987, when I heard from Stella, I had already begun to incorporate feminist, postmodern, and narrative scholarship into my research. The memo I wrote after we talked on the phone is rich with clues about how these changing epistemologies were influencing the research process, how I was working to resolve tensions between scholarship and activism, and the risks I felt about doing the work differently. Although I did not know it then, I was still in the initial stages of the project. I had not yet even completed the interviews. Three months after writing the memo, I adopted my son, and two months later I became pregnant with my daughter.

Disrupting Scholarship: Life's Vicissitudes

E-mail to Rosanna Hertz, September 1994:

> When I realized that I was pregnant (7 years ago now!) I realized that it would mean a real slowing down of my scholarly work, but that it was worth the price. Seven years later I can think back to my rather cavalier attitude (I was SURE it would be a few years, never seven!) to changing my work rhythms along with my life course. But I must say, it remains more important to me to be the mother of two children than it would have been to be the author of a book and god knows how many refereed articles. . . . But seriously, I look around me to colleagues whose children are now in high school, see them working just as systematically and wholeheartedly as I did before having children; think about how comparatively young I am and that I too have a number of years ahead of me without young children (and with tenure); and figure that it's basically ok that I haven't done as much by now professionally because I will do it over the next 5 or 10 years instead. When I can think this way, I don't feel so crazy as I do when I think about all the projects I haven't completed at the same time my friends have completed [so] many.

E-mail to Matilda White Riley, September 1995:

> As I mentioned when you were here, I'd really appreciate an opportunity
> to talk with you sometime in the next few months. I'd like your advice
> about how to manage to fulfill my obligations at Bowdoin without
> being completely overextended here. I've found in the last year or two,
> but especially since becoming chair, that the requests from Bowdoin for
> administrative positions have increased. Simultaneously with the growth
> in the department and the multiple changes in it, the demands within
> the department have increased too. . . .
>
> I haven't been able to carve out extended periods of time for
> writing. Instead, I've had to figure out ways to write that can be
> done in brief snatches. I've never been very good at this, but at this
> stage of my research, I'm eager to produce a book manuscript, and
> this demands ongoing and extended attention. . . .
>
> What all of this means is that I'd like some advice from you
> about how to be a good citizen at Bowdoin, especially to work to
> strengthen the department, and yet to remain fully engaged in a pro-
> fessional life beyond Bowdoin.

E-mail from Matilda White Riley, September 1995:

> This is a hasty but highly sympathetic reply to your e-mail about
> the characteristic "woman's dilemma." . . . My main advice concerns
> "phases" of life. Right now you are chair—surely this assignment will be
> handed around? AND, more importantly, you have little children—they
> do not stay little for long. And after that the strains can be lessened.
> So I fear you must think of long-range scheduling of: (1) research and
> writing and (2) outside professional activities. In general, why not
> postpone (2)—you can always catch up there? And consider how to
> FOCUS writing on your most readily publishable material? Publications
> do count (outside as well as inside), but new research may be too time-
> consuming to be an immediate possibility.
>
> As women, we have extraordinarily high self-expectations. BUT,
> as I have learned, we also have predictably long lives and there
> should be time in the future for activities not feasible today.[5]

The everyday world of becoming a mother and having a family punctuated the work life I spelled out in the previous sections of this chapter: studying the literature on narrative and feminist social science; changing my approach to recruiting, conducting, transcribing, and interpreting interviews; becoming close to rather than remaining distanced from DES daughters; writing "Birth Control"; finding ways to combine my activist and scholarly identities; and so on. Rosanna Hertz and I exchanged e-mails regularly for five years when she was editor and I was on the editorial board of *Qualitative Sociology*. Our e-mails were about journal business, life at liberal arts colleges, scholarship, and taking care of our children. We gave each other advice about child care and making lists, carving out time during the week for writing, chairing departments, and balancing our commitments. For both of us, this dialogue, and the life worlds it represented, was constant.

Matilda White Riley was a mentor to me at Bowdoin. She had been president of the Eastern Sociological Society (1976) and the American Sociological Association (1985–1986), and a molder and shaper of the sociology of aging and of the interdisciplinary study of age. Her contributions to scholarship, even into her nineties, were inspirations for a vision of positive aging. She also was the first woman hired by Bowdoin as a full professor. With her women students, she shared (as she put it) a brash intellectual self-confidence and awareness of the power of co-education to infuse liberal education with excitement and challenge.

My personal ability to balance my family life with my work was uneven. While I recognized, was open to, and participated in disruptions brought about by my commitment to activism and to feminist and narrative scholarship, I often hesitated to be open about my struggle to balance my work rhythms with my life course. In my e-mail to Matilda, I left out my children, formulating the struggle as one between different obligations in my job. Matilda brought them back in and included my obligations as a mother alongside of those to my work. Rereading Matilda's response to me in preparing this chapter reminded me of my pleasure in mothering—of my deeply held belief, as I had written so emphatically to Rosanna, that it was "more important to me to be the mother of two children than it would have been to be the author of a book and god knows how many refereed articles."

The excerpt from my e-mail to Rosanna and the exchange between Matilda and me capture my ongoing struggle at a particular moment in my professional and personal life. My children had just entered elementary school and

I had just been promoted to full professor. I had begun volunteering at the school when my son entered kindergarten, and continued to do so until both children went to middle school (and parents were no longer welcome in the classroom). I wanted to be engaged in the everyday school life of my children and their classmates, and my flexible work schedule enabled me to do this. A few years later, I turned a "crisis" about my son's entry into fourth grade at the start of the school year into an article about the reproduction of social class and explored how parents and teachers and home and school are linked together through parents' unpaid labor (Bell 1999b; Smith 1987).

Strains of "this phase of life"—as Matilda put it—lasted through the time my children entered college, and not because there were any major crises. There was just the dailyness of it, and the peculiarities of my particular circumstances and choices, and the simultaneous pleasure and impossibility of balancing all of these commitments without long-term social structural and cultural changes.

Scholarship Disrupted and Transformed

One of the themes of this collection is openness. To this point, I have demonstrated my openness to learning about changing epistemologies and incorporating them into my ways of thinking, doing research, and writing. But what made me open to these changes and to slowing down my work? I do not have one simple answer. A partial answer is that I felt responsible to DES daughters and I wanted to find ways to preserve the integrity of their words and worlds. I kept trying out frameworks for understanding and following my sense of what I needed to know about DES in order to understand DES daughters' experiences and to write a book that connected individual life experiences with social structure and social change. In my quest, I kept following the DES daughters' leads. They wanted me to look at pictures. I was not initially interested, but much later on I took another look at their pictures and other visual work. They organized and advocated for DES science and I went to conferences with them. These and other times I followed DES daughters' leads just felt right to me.

Given what I believe about identity and experience and feelings and what I have written in this chapter, "feeling right" is a completely inadequate response, one that needs unpacking. Another partial answer to the question is historical time and starts with a reference to Mills's (1959, 5) concept of "sociological imagination," which "enables its possessor to understand the larger historical scene in terms of its meaning for the inner life and the external career of a variety of individuals." I came of age in the late 1960s and I went to graduate school in the mid- to late 1970s, at a time when there was much ferment in the academy: feminist and postmodern scholarship had begun to take off, and a lot of it was in Boston. Like so many in my generation, I was particularly drawn to a model of collaboration, community, and open exchange that emerged during that historical period—a model that fostered continual dialogue and exploration more than closure.

Although this might explain broadly why I was particularly open to the changing epistemologies and to slowing down, the details of my life over the thirty years of writing the book are also important; that is, the connections to and networks of scholars and activists—some of them overlapping—that I continued and expanded throughout the period. These connections flowed from, tapped into, and continually renewed my openness. For example, I met regularly with a narrative studies group in Cambridge beginning in the late 1980s and continuing to the present. The group fostered the development of individuals' narrative imaginations by responding to works in progress and in its early years organizing a series of interdisciplinary conferences. Individuals in the group contributed to the development of the field by founding a journal and publishing key texts. I was also part of a network of feminist scholarship. This consisted of ongoing exchanges of e-mails, papers in progress, face-to-face conversations, and phone calls with other feminists. They, too, were (and are) asking questions about how empathizing, being drawn into the lives of our "subjects," and attending to emotions could become acceptable social science. In addition to the network of DES activists I have described already, the "Birth Control" project also enmeshed me recurrently in close connections with women's health activists and a broader network of people committed to peace and justice. They were resources for information, critique, and reviews of birth control chapter drafts as well as sounding boards for valuing and writing about different forms of knowledge.

I could not have written a book conclusion almost thirty years ago with sentences like these:

> To study events in embodied health movements requires attention to detail, tracing multifaceted threads over time, across space, and in the talk that unfolds—such as in interviews and letters, autobiographical film and performances, and interdisciplinary scientific workshops. These social movements cannot be studied narrowly. . . . In the DES

embodied health movement, the talk that unfolds includes encounters between patients, doctors, nurses, scientists, legislators, mothers, daughters, and families. Their encounters take place in different times and locations, before and after surgery for reproductive tract cancer, surrounding infertility treatment, and in doing and undoing science as usual. . . . "They" comprise a changing constellation of people, along with individuals' perceived interests, health needs, and situations. The complexity of embodied health movements requires following the tape-recorded and transcribed talk surrounding slides and computer-generated images of internal organs and tumors in teaching hospitals and conference panels and discussions, as well as still and moving images beyond text in film and theater. The narrative analysis [in this book] integrates this wide array of practices and exemplifies their transformative possibilities. (Bell 2009, 174–75).

There were not ways of knowing in scholarship that could make these practices known. Even as ways of knowing emerged, they demanded attention to detail, patience, and a willingness to slow down. And I did. I raised two children and embraced intellectual and political challenges that I took up and integrated into my book. The projects I am currently working on build on and work within the frameworks I participated in making over the course of almost thirty years. They assume complexity, reflecting the tenets of activist, narrative, and feminist practices. I would not have chosen to slow down quite as much as I did—and I do not plan to repeat it—but in the end, I am happy I did not write the book I set out to produce almost thirty years ago.

Notes

I would like to thank Vicky Steinitz for her astute reflections about this chapter.

1. Thanks to their successful exercise of power, in 1996 Linda Gordon and Barrie Thorne persuaded the then editor of *Contemporary Sociology* to include *Our Bodies, Ourselves* in a list of the ten books since 1971 that had had the most "influence on both academic disciplines and the world" (Gordon and Thorne 1996). In her reflections on the "missing revolution in sociology" a decade later, Thorne (2006, 475) wrote that *Our Bodies, Ourselves*, "and the women's health movement of which it was a part, challenged dominant definitions of what counts as theory and as science, and highlighted the political construction of bodies and sexuality, an angle of vision only later sketched out by Foucault.

Our Bodies Ourselves . . . reflects the broad and questioning outlook, oriented to the lives and welfare of women rather than to professionalized knowledge, that continues to animate the best of feminist scholarship."

2. For recent reviews of the field, see Thoits (2010) and Avison et al. (2010).
3. "Stella" is a pseudonym.
4. Changes in the project's epistemology called into question the logic of a "control" or "comparison" group. Although I began the study by recruiting and interviewing women not exposed to DES, I decided to limit the study to twenty DES daughters, half who had had cancer and half who had not.
5. Quoted with the permission of Lucy Sallick (Riley's daughter).

References

Andrews, M., C. Squire, and M. Tamboukou. 2008. *Doing Narrative Research*. London: Sage.

Avison, W. R., C. S. Aneshensel, S. Schieman, and B. Wheaton. 2010. *Advances in the Conceptualization of the Stress Process: Essays in Honor of Leonard I. Pearlin*. New York: Springer-Verlag.

Baxter, J. 2006. *Speaking Out: The Female Voice in Public Contexts*. London: Palgrave Macmillan.

Behar, R. 1991. "The Body in the Woman, the Story in the Woman: A Book Review and Personal Essay." In *The Female Body*, edited by L. Goldstein, 267–311. Ann Arbor: University of Michigan Press.

———. 1993. *Translated Woman: Crossing the Border with Esperanza's Story*. Boston: Beacon.

———. 1996. *The Vulnerable Observer: Anthropology That Breaks Your Heart*. Boston: Beacon.

Behar, R., and D. Gordon. 1995. *Women Writing Culture*. Berkeley: University of California Press.

Bell, S. E. 1984. "Birth Control." In *The New Our Bodies, Ourselves*, edited by Boston Women's Health Book Collective, 220–62. New York: Simon and Schuster.

———. 1987. "Changing Ideas: The Medicalization of Menopause." *Social Science and Medicine* 24: 535–542.

———. 1988. "Becoming a Political Woman: The Reconstruction and Interpretation of Experience through Stories." In *Gender and Discourse: The Power of Talk*, edited by A. D. Todd and S. Fisher, 97–123. Norwood, NJ: Ablex.

———. 1992. "Birth Control." In *The New Our Bodies, Ourselves*, edited by Boston Women's Health Book Collective, 259–307. New York: Simon and Schuster.

———. 1994. "Translating Science to the People: Updating *The New Our Bodies, Ourselves*." *Women's Studies International Forum* 17: 9–18.

————. 1995. "Gendered Medical Science: Producing a Drug for Women." *Feminist Studies* 21: 469–500.

————. 1999a. "Narratives and Lives: Women's Health Politics and the Diagnosis of Cancer for DES Daughters." *Narrative Inquiry* 9: 347–89.

————. 1999b. "On the (Re)production of Social Class: Living in, with, and beyond Elementary School." In *Qualitative Sociology as Everyday Life*, edited by B. Glassner and R. Hertz, 69–77. Beverly Hills, CA: Sage.

————. 2000. "Accéder au pouvoir par les technologies: Femmes et science dans la recherche sur les microbicides." *Sciences Sociales et Santé* 18: 121–42.

————. 2002. "Photo Images: Jo Spence's Narratives of Living with Illness." *Health* 6: 5–30.

————. 2003. "Sexual Synthetics: Women, Science, and Microbicides." In *Synthetic Planet: Chemical Politics and the Hazards of Modern Life*, edited by M. J. Casper, 197–211. New York: Routledge.

————. 2004. "Intensive Performances of Mothering: A Sociological Perspective." *Qualitative Research* 4: 45–75.

————. 2006. "Living with Breast Cancer in Text and Image: Making Art to Make Sense." *Qualitative Research in Psychology* 3: 31–44.

————. 2009. *DES Daughters: Embodied Knowledge and the Transformation of Women's Health Politics*. Philadelphia: Temple University Press.

Bell, S. E., and R. J. Apfel. 1995. "Looking at Bodies: Insights and Inquiries about DES-related Cancer." *Qualitative Sociology* 18: 3–19.

Bell, S. E., and L. Wise. 1998. "Birth Control." In *Our Bodies, Ourselves for the New Century*, edited by Boston Women's Health Book Collective, 288–340. New York: Simon and Schuster.

Brown, P., S. Zavestoski, S. McCormick, B. Mayer, R. Morello-Frosh, and R. G. Altman. 2004. "Embodied Health Movements: New Approaches to Social Movements in Health." *Sociology of Health & Illness* 26: 50–80.

Cameron, D. 2006. "Theorising the Female Voice in Public Contexts." In *Speaking Out: The Female Voice in Public Contexts*, edited by J. Baxter, 3–20. London: Palgrave Macmillan.

Charon, R. 2006. *Narrative Medicine: Honoring the Stories of Illness*. New York: Oxford University Press.

Coelho, G. V., D. A. Hamburg, and J. E. Adams. 1974. *Coping and Adaptation*. New York: Basic Books.

Epstein, S. 2000. "Democracy, Expertise, and AIDS Treatment Activism." In *Science, Technology, and Democracy*, edited by D. L. Kleinman, 15–32. Albany: State University of New York Press.

Ewick, P., and S. Sibley. 2003. "Narrating Social Structure: Stories of Resistance to Legal Authority." *American Journal of Sociology* 208: 1328–72.

Foucault, M. 1978. *The History of Sexuality*, vol. 1. New York: Pantheon Books.

Frank, A. W. 2010. "Book Review of DES Daughters." *Sociology of Health & Illness* 32: 817–18.

Gordon, L., and B. Thorne. 1996. "Women's Bodies and Feminist Subversions." *Contemporary Sociology* 25: 322–25.

Haraway, D. J. 1988. "Situated Knowledges: The Science Question in Feminism and the Privilege of Partial Perspective." *Feminist Studies* 14: 575–99.

———. 1991. "A Cyborg Manifesto: Science, Technology, and Socialist-Feminism in the Late Twentieth Century." In *Simians, Cyborgs, and Women: The Reinvention of Nature*, edited by D. J. Haraway, 149–181. New York: Routledge.

Harper, D. 2000. "Reimagining Visual Methods." In *Handbook of Qualitative Research*, edited by N. K. Denzin and Y. S. Lincoln, 717–32. London: Sage.

Helfand, J. 1996. *A Healthy Baby Girl* (film). New York: Women Make Movies.

Herbst, A. L., H. Ulfelder, and D. C. Poskanzer. 1971. "Adenocarcinoma of the Vagina: Association of Maternal Stilbestrol Therapy with Tumor Appearance in Young Women." *New England Journal of Medicine* 284: 878–81.

Hinchman, L. P., and S. K. Hinchman. 1997. *Memory, Identity, Community: The Idea of Narrative in the Human Sciences*. Albany: State University of New York Press.

Hydén, L.-C. 1997. "Illness and Narrative." *Sociology of Health & Illness* 19: 48–69.

Jolly, M., and L. Stanley. 2005. "Letters as/not a Genre." *Life Writing* 2: 75–101.

Klawiter, M. 2008. *The Biopolitics of Breast Cancer: Changing Cultures of Disease and Activism*. Minneapolis: University of Minnesota Press.

Kleinman, A. 1988. *The Illness Narratives: Suffering, Healing, and the Human Condition*. New York: Basic Books.

Labov, W. 1972. *Language in the Inner City: Studies in the Black English Vernacular*. Philadelphia: University of Pennsylvania Press.

Labov, W., and J. Waletzky. 1967. "Narrative Analysis: Oral Versions of Personal Experience." In *Essays on the Verbal and Visual Arts*, edited by J. Helms, 12–44. Seattle: University of Washington Press.

Layne, L. L. 2003. *Motherhood Lost: A Feminist Account of Pregnancy Loss in America*. New York: Routledge.

Lofland, J. 1971. *Analyzing Social Settings: A Guide to Qualitative Observation and Analysis*. Belmont, CA: Wadsworth.

Martin, E. 1987. *The Woman in the Body: A Cultural Analysis of Reproduction*. Boston: Beacon.

Mills, C. W. 1959. *The Sociological Imagination*. New York: Oxford University Press.

Mishler, E. G. 1986. *Research Interviewing: Context and Narrative*. Cambridge, MA: Harvard University Press.

Mitchell, W. J. T. 1981. *On Narrative*. Chicago: University of Chicago Press.

Paget, M. A. 1982. "Your Son Is Cured Now; You May Take Him Home." *Culture, Medicine and Psychiatry* 6: 237–59.

———. 1983. "Experience and Knowledge." *Human Studies* 6: 67–90.

Pearlin, L. I., and C. Schooler. 1978. "The Structure of Coping." *Journal of Health and Social Behavior* 19: 2–21.

Personal Narratives Group. 1989. *Interpreting Women's Lives: Feminist Theory and Personal Narratives*. Bloomington: Indiana University Press.

Polletta, F. 2006. *It Was Like a Fever: Storytelling in Protest and Politics*. Chicago: University of Chicago Press.

Polletta, F, P. C. B. Chen, B. G. Gardner, and A. Motes. 2011. "The Sociology of Storytelling." *Annual Review of Sociology* 37: 109–30.

Reinharz, S. 1992. *Feminist Methods in Social Research*. With Lynn Davidman. New York: Oxford University Press.

Rich, M., and J. Patashnick. 2002. "Narrative Research with Audiovisual Data: Video-Intervention/Prevention Assessment (VIA) and NVivo." *International Journal of Social Research Methodology* 5: 245–61.

Riessman, C. K. 2008. *Narrative Methods for the Human Sciences*. Thousand Oaks, CA: Sage.

Roberts, H. 1981. *Doing Feminist Research*. London: Routledge and Kegan Paul.

Scott, J. 1991. "Experience." *Critical Inquiry* 17: 773–97.

Smith, D. 1987. *The Everyday World as Problematic*. Boston: Northeastern University Press.

Stacey, J. 1988. "Can There Be a Feminist Ethnography?" *Women's Studies International Forum* 11: 21–27.

Thoits, P. A. 1982. "Conceptual, Methodological, and Theoretical Problems in Studying Social Support as a Buffer against Stress." *Journal of Health and Social Behavior* 23: 145–59.

———. 2010. "Stress and Health: Major Findings and Policy Implications." *Journal of Health and Social Behavior* 51: S41–S53.

Thorne, B. 2006. "How Can Feminist Sociology Sustain Its Critical Edge?" *Social Problems* 53: 473–78.

Williams, G. 1984. "The Genesis of Chronic Illness: Narrative Re-construction." *Sociology of Health & Illness* 6: 175–200.

7

A Sociology of Inclusion and Exclusion through the Lens of the Maid's Daughter

Mary Romero

I n my life history of Olivia, I interviewed one Chicana over a twenty-year span; she was the daughter of a live-in domestic worker in a gated Los Angeles community.[1] Olivia's mother, Carmen, was an immigrant from Mexico who had started working as a live-in maid in the Country Club area in El Paso, Texas. In her mid- to late twenties, Carmen accompanied friends in search of employment to Los Angeles. Finding the work in the garment district difficult and unappealing, she turned again to domestic work and began working in a gated community. After the birth of her daughter, Carmen returned to the border area, leaving her mother and sister to raise Olivia as she worked as a live-in maid in El Paso. When Olivia was three, Carmen made arrangements to live-in with her daughter in Los Angeles. There, Olivia and Carmen negotiated a mother-daughter relationship within the confines of the employers' household, trapped in the contradictory boundaries of "being like one of the family." Returning every summer to Mexico, Olivia spent time with her grandmother, aunts, and cousins, never losing sight of her family or culture.

Olivia's experiences offered the ingredients for examining the reproduction of privilege in opposition to the national narrative that claims meritocracy, equality, and assimilation as the means to material success in the United States. Moving from experiences in the gated community and

Country Club to meals with Mexican immigrants in Los Angeles and her family in Mexico, Olivia compared and contrasted personal choices and was aware of the different consequences and the vastly unique opportunities gained by being a member of the upper class. These contrasting social settings and relations constantly challenged Olivia's perceptions of her mother. Among her employers, Carmen was the ideal maid, but among her fellow immigrant workers, she was a valued friend who helped find others employment and to negotiate above-average working conditions. Among her family members in Mexico, Carmen was the major wage earner and had their respect and admiration. Rather than following instructions as she did in the homes of her employers, Carmen made the major financial decisions in her family. When Olivia's experiences outside the gated community are not included in the picture, Carmen appears as a low-wage worker in a dead-end job instead of an entrepreneur engaged in numerous asset-building activities. Carmen may have been merely a trusted maid in her employers' world, but in the immigrant community and within her family, she was a trusted adviser and a financial success. If I had not allowed life to take its course, I would have ended up with one stop-action photograph rather than the many photos of a journey that provided meaning to past experiences.

The following chapter is a reflection on the methodology I used to study the children of domestic workers and more specifically on the life story of one daughter of a live-in maid. Rather than beginning with a precise research question and limiting my data collection to a specific time period, I developed research foci as I collected and analyzed the data, wrote extensive research notes, and further developed the literature review. Like other researchers, I was faced with the decision of when to stop collecting data (Lareau 1989). However, I based my decision not on whether I had reached a saturation point in the narrative, but on what I would capture of Olivia's stages of life and her construction of identity and meaning. Approaching the study of domestic service from the perspective of the maid's daughter who lived in her mother's workplace offered both research challenges and opportunities. I began the study by examining the access children had to their mothers' work as domestics. I used this data to inform many of the questions I asked in conducting a life story with Olivia. Learning to interview the same person over twenty years took on its own process and routine, which shaped the researcher-subject relationship. I conclude this chapter with a reflection on constructing a life story.

Who Takes Care of the Maid's Children?

Olivia first approached me at a conference in El Paso, Texas, after I had presented a paper on the experiences of Chicana domestic workers. However, it was not until a year later, at the next annual conference, when she confided that she had grown up in the same house that her mother worked in as a live-in maid. This meeting was very emotional for Olivia: she had concealed her background because she wanted to be identified not with the social world of her mother's employers but rather with the Mexican immigrant workers who cleaned their houses, cared for their children, cooked their meals, washed and ironed their clothes, cut the grass, and pruned their gardens. A recent college graduate working for a civil rights organization, Olivia had become increasingly uncomfortable with the disconnect between the cultural capital she had acquired from being raised in an upper-middle-class household and community and the working-class ethnic identity she claimed as the daughter of a Mexican immigrant woman employed as a domestic. Our paths crossed at an opportune time in Olivia's life. She was at a point in her life where she wanted to talk about her experiences with members of the Smith family, her mother's employers. For her, "being one of the family" held both truths and contradictions. The fact that she was no longer living near her mother, but residing in another state, increased the urgency of her need to understand the mother-daughter tensions that remained after years of negotiating their relationship within the dynamic of her mother's employment. Olivia was ready to tell her story from the standpoint of the maid's daughter.

As I began analyzing Olivia's narrative, I realized that my first book, *Maid in the USA* ([1992] 2002), had focused entirely on the employer's home; I had not included a comparable examination of employees' families. While I did compare and contrast the differences found among employer and employee spouses, I did not examine the different division of household labor among the children. As Olivia recalled her mother's work as a domestic, she pointed to the ways she had learned to be responsible for cleaning, cooking, and doing laundry, as well as how she had heard about and sometimes seen the vastly different houses and family life in relation to her family in Mexico or immigrant families in Los Angeles. Rarely has the dilemma of women's work been examined from the child's viewpoint. What does it mean when working mothers are too tired to spend quality time with their children at the end of the day? How does the child interpret work obligations that extend into family time?

How does their mother's occupation shape the way that children are treated by their employers and the larger community? These are all questions concerning mothers who care for their employers' children and clean their houses—raised from the perspective of employees' children. Low wages and lack of benefits in domestic service point to the ways that carework is unequally distributed among families, communities, and nations. This research inquiry pointed to the reproduction of privilege.

Interviewing over Life Stages

My first interview with Olivia was unlike any interviewing I had ever done and may hold a clue to why the interview process extended over two decades. In previous interviews, I had always been able to mark a beginning and an end. As a graduate student, I learned that many times the interview actually begins when the recorder is turned off. I soon learned to keep the recorder running as I finished up—just in case my interviewee began to elaborate on points made during the "formal" interview. I had never interviewed anyone as assertive as Olivia. Any concerns about getting her to talk or to discuss questions that might cause discomfort were immediately erased. As we sat down to begin the interview, I turned on the tape recorder and before I had even voice-recorded the date and setting, Olivia began her story as the maid's daughter: "My mom was born in a place called Piedras Negras—not the border Piedras Negras but a small town in Aguascalientes, Mexico. Her father was from the state of Chihuahua. She grew up with my paternal grandfather's relatives and spent a lot of time with her aunts and grew up with them." As each audio tape ended, she waited as I turned it over or started a new tape. Olivia continued for six hours without any other type of interruption, and then announced that we had done enough for the day and turned the recorder off. Without further discussion, we turned our attention to dinner and talked about university life and politics.

Olivia is the only person I have ever interviewed who started the interview without any preliminaries and had a beginning to her story. However, any idea of her telling her story with a beginning and end was quickly dispelled in the following interviews. Future interviews took on an "Olivia is in charge" format but did not follow the same chronological order as her first interview. Many of the interviews were scheduled in response to Olivia's interactions with her mom or a member of the employers' family.

For example, trips to Los Angeles resulted in revisiting old arguments or sentiments, or reporting new turns in her mother's relationships with the employers. She began such interviews with a detailed description of the incident or story and then wove in other memories or information that offered possible explanations. Since she was so easily distracted from her stories, which reminded her of other incidents, I tried to avoid interruptions. While she talked, I kept notes of items to go back and ask her about. These questions were usually for clarification, but sometimes they were requests for her to elaborate on various points of the story or the meaning she attached to an incident or comment. Later, as I transcribed and analyzed the tapes, I kept a journal of questions and topics requiring more detail. This journal came in handy during interviews scheduled around my travels rather than in response to her contacting me to share additional stories and news.

Olivia is a very engaging storyteller and gets into character as she describes incidents. She loudly expresses her outrage and sprinkles humor throughout her narration of events that break the social norms. After the first six-hour interview, I walked away unaware of how she had been affected by telling me about her life in the gated community. The next day, as we walked along the Colorado River, she reflected on the stories and incidents she had described the previous day. Her reflections pointed to unresolved tensions in her life. For the first couple of years, Olivia continued with a period of reflection after each interview session. At first, these reflections seemed too personal to record, but sensing that Olivia did not share the same boundaries as I did, I asked her permission to keep the tape running and she agreed. Gradually, the tape recorder accompanied us everywhere, even when we were driving, cooking, or taking walks. As the years went by, these periods of reflection became fewer, occurring only when the interview included new information or after Olivia experienced a specific event. Listening to her reflections was important: in the early years of the project, they helped me identify ongoing tensions, and later they announced Olivia's acceptance of circumstances she could not change or simply presented an aspect of who she is.

I began interviewing Olivia when she was in her mid-twenties and a few years out of college. She was living away from her family and was working full time for a civil rights organization. We began the project at a time when she was recognizing that her assumption that leaving California would result in an end to the paternalistic relationship and condescending interactions with the employers had not been correct. Her mother continued to work for the Smith family, and since her mother continued to work on a live-in basis, Olivia was expected to stay at the employers' home when she visited her mother. Given her mother's age and health problems, Olivia needed to maintain ongoing communication with the employers who shared information that her mother tried to conceal from her. At the same time, Olivia's involvement in civil rights politics became acknowledged by the employers as a lifetime commitment rather than an adolescent fad, which resulted in increased racial and class tensions between them. Furthermore, Olivia was recognizing that even though she no longer lived with her mother's employers, they continued to shape who she is. Submerging herself among immigrant, working-class, and first-generation college students of color, she became painfully aware of the cultural capital that she took for granted and the questions of ethnic and class authenticity that arose from uncomfortable interactions. Committed to using her cultural capital to increase her effectiveness as a civil rights advocate, she also was aware of her mannerisms, which intimidated others and marked her as an outsider.

Olivia in her thirties was occupied with beginning a family, negotiating her mother's retirement, and building her career. Carmen had lived most of her adult life as a live-in maid and Olivia had heard her mother and the employers always tell each other they would grow old together. But, Olivia also knew that her mother owned property in Mexico and had told her family she would retire near them in Juarez. However, when Olivia asked her about this, Carmen dismissed the Juarez plan, rejecting life there as incompatible with her attachment to Los Angeles. Carmen eventually retired by moving in with Olivia over a period of several years, caring for Olivia's children and keeping the house while taking regular trips to Mexico to visit her sisters; she also flew back to Los Angeles to help with weddings and births. Gradually, the visits to Los Angeles were replaced with phone calls, which became her only contact with the employers. In my interviews with Olivia during this period, she moved away from the painful recollections of having to spend time with Mr. and Mrs. Smith at home; of longing for her mother, who was always working; and of yearning for more cultural diversity. Now, Olivia told stories of reconciling her relationship with Mr. and Mrs. Smith by seeking business advice related to her new job and when negotiating another position. Her relationship with her mother began to change as they spent more time together and Olivia came to recognize how resourceful and smart Carmen was.

As Carmen retired and started to live full time with Olivia, both women had to negotiate their relationship outside the employers' residence. As the primary wage earner of the family, Olivia makes most of its decisions but recognizes that Carmen is managing the family in the same way she managed many of her former employers' families. At first, Carmen's behavior in Olivia's home was not much different than it had been when she was a live-in maid. This alarmed Olivia, but nothing she said or did changed her mother's work habits. As the grandchildren got older, however, Carmen participated in their sports events and school activities in ways that she had missed out on when Olivia was growing up. In the interviews during this stage of her life, Olivia was much less emotional about and far more accepting of the fact that she was not going to change her mother, but remained steadfast about what she wanted for her own children. By starting her own business and working more independently, she has embraced the skills developed from her past experiences and is focusing on the projects she wants to contract for. The work arrangement allows her to spend more time with her children.

If I had approached Olivia's life story project as a rigid research question and limited the research period to a few months or years, I would have failed to fully understand the nuances of her experiences as "one of the family" and its long-term impact on the mother-daughter relationship. Any predetermined research period would not have acknowledged Olivia's own life processes in making sense of her experiences. Olivia was an adult woman with her own children when she was exposed to the ways that she and her mother had affected the Smith family. She learned that the Smith children had appropriated Mexican culture and claimed to have a Mexican mother. More surprising was the recognition that Mr. Smith had been proud of her: over the years, even in her absence, he had continued to watch her career and talk to his friends about her. As an adolescent, she had thought of Mr. and Mrs. Smith's interest in her only as a sociology project, in which they experimented with her life to see how assimilation might lead to financial success. She had subsequently rejected assimilation and committed herself to a bicultural path to success, not recognizing at the time that they would come around to accepting her choices, even though they did not agree with all of them, and that they were proud of her. My narrative attempts to convey the ways that children learn their own status within various social settings and recognize the changes as they move from one social group to another. However, the narrative I constructed would not have been possible until Olivia had reached a stage in her life where she felt a sense of belonging.

The two-decade research period also captured the change in our nation and the growing influence Mexican culture has had on popular culture, as well as how it is changing the demographics of the country. Just as Olivia struggled to maintain her bilingual skills, Spanish-language radio, TV, and newspapers gained a larger market in the United States. The culture she yearned for as an adolescent is now visible in concert halls, soccer fields, chain restaurants, museums, and even local gyms (in their offering of Zumba classes). Olivia's story captures the changing cultural and racial terrain, with maids' daughters like herself moving from living outside to inside the American Dream. Had I written the book a few years after meeting Olivia, my study on domestic workers would not have understood the role of globalized carework in the production of inequality between families, communities, and nations. The U.S. population is growing older and few women remain outside the labor force, removing them as a potential pool of caregivers. Elderly care is taking its place alongside child care as a major source of employment for women immigrant workers. In providing carework, Latina immigrant mothers "mother at a distance" by leaving their children with family members in their homeland or adapting a wide range of strategies for care of their children in the United States. Low wages and the absence of benefits—maintained through the lack of state or federal legislation—contribute to reproducing the working poor.

Composing a Life

A life story told over years captures the changing positions in a person's social position, along with that person's ways of adjusting priorities, defining tensions, and dealing with contradictions. As I quickly learned, over time our storytelling of significant events in our lives frequently incorporates new details, and sometimes different meanings, that might come to represent important turns in a life. Narrating a life over decades adds new adventures and incidents that might disrupt social relationships or begin to redefine them. Unfortunately, writing a life story takes a lot of editing, which means making choices that shape the telling of the story. The choices I made were largely made as a sociologist analyzing privilege, power relations, identity, and resistance.

As I worked on my book about Olivia, I was overwhelmed by the thought of organizing over five hundred pages of transcripts into sociology. As I transcribed the tapes, I began to organize the stories chronologically but realized the reflections did not neatly fit into different time periods of her life. I was also confronted with the repetition of stories and the unique features of each telling. Each telling of a story took it in a slightly different direction. After several attempts at writing the book, I began to doubt my ability to finish the book. Every attempt ended in a complete tangle of disjointed events and time periods. I turned to published life stories in desperation, hoping to find a method to write the book. I finally began mapping out themes. This turned out to be quite easy, since I had written shorter pieces over the years that had already identified the most salient themes in the narrative. Next, I began grouping together the major events in her life that had taken on special meaning. Some of these had been turning points or events that changed her social circumstances, but most of them represented the sum of rituals to define privilege, power relations, and social relationships. These events revealed tensions and contradictions resulting from Olivia's status as "one of the family," the employers' choices to include or exclude her, and the changing expectations she experienced as the maid's daughter.

Olivia began her first interview with me by telling her family story, recounting not lived experience but stories passed down as family lore. She gradually gave witness to her own stories of family life, many of them set in the employers' home, where she learned the social cues of when to act like a member of the employers' family and when to resume her social position as the maid's daughter. Olivia's stories of the Smith family were not about lineage or ancestral bloodlines, but rather her obligation to her mother's employers and the pseudo-family relations placed on her as the child of the live-in maid. She had to assume a position alongside the employers when they wanted her to act "like one of the family" and in other settings she was expected to fulfill the role and status of the maid's daughter. Olivia's family stories included her construction of sharing time (including holidays) with immigrant workers living in Pico Union and attending maid gatherings in the gated community, which represented family time to her as she was growing up because they were activities she participated in with her mother. Analyzing these family stories captured the themes of Olivia's search for identity and belonging, which are structured around the power relations between employer and employee, upper class and working class, English-speaking and Spanish-speaking, and citizen and immigrant. For Olivia, "being one of the family" has been significant in locating herself in the world of employers and the nation that defines her mother as a noncitizen. The family became a useful metaphor in examining home-work boundaries and the class-, race-, and gender-based social order of globalized carework in the United States.

During the course of the project, Olivia had always generously answered my questions and offered to share stories that she thought might be relevant to the project. I never ceased to be a participant observer while in her company. We had developed a strong sense of trust over the years. While we enjoyed each other's company, our interaction had developed a pattern of me listening and Olivia talking, which at times became exhausting. The conversation, rightly so, always turned back to her experiences and social interaction. As Olivia lived her life, she never experienced the "end" to being the maid's daughter, but I faced the reality of needing to finish the project.

Finding an ending to Olivia's story for the reader was easier than I had thought. The answer was one more interview session toward the end of my writing the book. Entering the social world that Olivia had created for herself gave me the confidence that I would end the book with a conclusion that did justice to her story as the maid's daughter. As I entered her home and hugged Carmen, I was immediately struck by the way Olivia had blended aspects of Mrs. Smith's and Carmen's parenting practices, and by the presence of Spanish and English on the TV and the radio. Later, as we drove off to the gym for a Zumba class, I witnessed how she had chosen social activities that were both multiracial and multicultural. The tensions of being pulled by different social worlds were completely gone. Olivia had succeeded in being successful by maintaining her ethnic roots and continuing to fight for civil rights.

Now the book is complete (Romero 2011), and I am delighted that Olivia has embraced it. I was a bit concerned when she did not read the draft I sent her. Later, I discovered that she gave the manuscript to a friend to read first. After the friend assured her that it was fine, she read the draft. I was surprised at her hesitation, because she had never commented on the papers and articles I had sent her before, or the earlier versions of the book (long since discarded) I had shown to her. However, I came to realize that the close-up sociological analysis of her entire life was a bit intimidating. After the book was released, she did express some concern about how some of her acquaintances had made her aware of the ways they were able to identify her. I thought I had taken adequate precautions, but I had not anticipated her mentioning her presence in my book to a chosen few who were not depicted in a particularly good light in her stories. These encounters were not positive experiences for her and she has become more careful about revealing her identity. Fortunately, she has no regrets about being the subject of my project.

Olivia continues to be "the maid's daughter" in the stories she shares with me when I drop into town and we meet for dinner. For some time now, I have been aware of the way that the interview process has left its mark on our personal interactions. I have taken a passive role as listener and limit my own stories to responding to her questions. As a friend, I am interested in knowing about her adventures but am no longer interested in the sociology of her life. I enjoy seeing photos of her daughter playing baseball and I always inquire about her mother. I continue to be impressed with her ability to blend her wide range of multicultural and bilingual skills into her work. Her life in corporate America and mine in the academy do not offer many mutual points for conversation, but our interest in national politics—particularly the role Latinos play—continues to be a major point of discussion. I am glad the project is over and I do believe that we will have an ongoing friendship based on our twenty-year journey into the life of the maid's daughter.

Note

1. "Olivia," "Carmen," and "the Smith family" are pseudonyms.

References

Lareau, A. 1989. "Appendix: Common Problems in Field Work: A Personal Essay." In *Home Advantage: Social Class, and Parental Intervention in Elementary Education*, 197–233. London: Falmer Press.

Romero, M. (1992) 2002. *Maid in the USA*. 10th anniv. ed. New York: Routledge.

———. 2011. *The Maid's Daughter: Living Inside and Outside the American Dream*. New York: New York University Press.

8

Getting to the Dark Side of the Moon

Researching the Lives of Women in Cartography

Will C. van den Hoonaard

L ittle did I suspect that a research project conceived by my enthusiasm for maps would lead me to embark on a convoluted but very instructive journey through the occupations inhabited by women cartographers. Unlike many other travels, however, its precise start eludes me. I also find myself not knowing when the journey will actually come to a close. Can it already be twenty-one years long? What explains its long duration? There is an intermingling of my own interests and talents, of the nature of the research itself, and of the new, contemporary demands of interdisciplinary scholarship. All three elements have contributed to the protracted length—and ultimately to the complexity—of my research.

This chapter locates the original impetus for my project and explores the long period of gestation in a field that required me, as a former cartographic editor, to abandon previously held concepts of cartography in order to view the field in a new way. Because I was totally unfamiliar with contemporary aspects of cartography, I began my sociological work from the margins of the "map worlds" and gradually worked toward the center of that universe. This working from the margins allowed me to take in a broader, more relaxed picture of the structure of cartography and the social dynamics of its incumbents. It also gave the international community of cartographers an opportunity to become familiar with me and my particular research interests. All this, however, took time. The final outcome of that research—*Map Worlds: A History of Women in Cartography* (2013)—describes the world of women map makers, beginning in the Golden Age of Cartography in the sixteenth-century Low Countries and ending with tactile maps in contemporary Brazil.[1] As developers of resources that allowed early map ateliers to flourish through marital liaisons, women had an unmistakable role. Other women cartographers, working from the margins, produced maps to record painful tribal memories or sought to remedy social injustices in the nineteenth century. In contemporary times, one woman produced a revolution in the way we think about continents, likened to the Copernican revolution. Several others created order out of the disorder of the lunar landscape after a three-hundred-year accretion of confusing naming practices, while still others turned the art and science of making maps inside out, exposing the hidden, unconscious, and subliminal "text" of maps. What all these outstanding women map makers share is their interest in social justice and making maps work for the betterment of humanity. *Map Worlds* set itself the task of recovering these women from obscurity. It also recounts the experiences of women within contemporary cartography. Oftentimes, the world of women cartographers seems to be hidden, much like the so-called dark side of the moon, but as every thinking person knows, the invisible side of the moon bathes as equally in the sunlight as the one that faces us.

Opening Scene: The Start of the Journey

I clearly recall a warm and pleasant evening in May 1994, rifling through the glove compartment of my car, looking for city maps. A few hours earlier, I had been steeped in a conversation with participants at the "Canadian Qualitatives" conference at the University of Waterloo about wayfaring through cities. Someone's comment had prompted me to wonder about graphic representations in city maps. By a stroke of serendipity, my eyes fell on how colors were patterned on maps. I noticed that buildings associated with "masculine" identities (justice, police, and city hall) were overwhelmingly portrayed in black while buildings linked to "feminine" identities (hospitals, clinics, schools, and day care centers) were in pinks or reds. I also noticed how buildings for generic uses were recast in masculine nomenclatures: skating rinks were "hockey" rinks (long before women started to play hockey). A few days later, as I was driving to my university in Fredericton, I realized that most of the people waiting at bus stops were children, women, or young university students. This observation triggered an insight that would open a long stretch of research: map makers were men and had no interest in marking city maps with actual bus *stops*—that is, they indicated only the bus *lines*. Men, it seemed to me, drove cars to work, and were oblivious to the needs of those who had to take the bus. Then a whole range of missing items became apparent: city maps did not indicate public toilets, paths that could be used as short cuts, or distinctive attributes of playgrounds (such as the presence of a sandbox or swings). I immediately conveyed these impressions in an article for our local newspaper (van den Hoonaard 1994).

A year later, by chance, I met Dr. Eva Siekierska, who happened to be a cartographer. When she mentioned the establishment of the Gender Commission of the International Cartographic Association, I realized that I had already become intrigued by the status and role of women in cartography. By April 1997, I received a grant from the Social Sciences and Humanities Research Council of Canada to conduct a study titled "A Historical and Contemporary Study of Women in Mapmaking." My initial enthusiasm, along with that support, would take me through another fifteen years of scholarship in "map worlds." I completed the first draft of a manuscript in 2003 (some nine years after having informally started exploring this topic, or five years after having obtained the research grant); I completed the second draft nine years later.

Map Worlds

The term "map worlds" is derived from Howard S. Becker's (1982) study on the creation, production, and distribution of art. He adapts the term used by artists to refer to the whole borderless community that makes art possible—namely, "art worlds." The social organization of art worlds requires a division of labor, cooperative links, conventions, the mobilization of resources of all kinds, patronage, sales by dealers, agents, culture industries, education or training, and accreditation. It is a universe where the initiative and work of an artist is linked in many tangible and intangible ways to a wide variety of things that make his or her art possible, from someone making a particular color of chalk to the organization of an art gallery. We can extend the idea of "worlds" to other areas of human endeavor, be they music, schooling, plumbing, nursing, or the making of maps.

The concept of map worlds embraces the totality of relationships, norms, practices, and technologies that shape and constitute the world of map makers. While "map trades" are about the retail products associated with maps per se, map worlds are about the wider context of cartography (in which "map trades" are located), suggesting that many more elements contribute to the field than what one normally thinks of as map making. Map worlds are an explicit recognition that cartography is multifaceted; there are no margins in this conception of map worlds, where boundaries are contiguous. All kinds of relations, practices, and ideas occur on the borderline of map worlds, involving powerful forms of knowledge, struggles, and tensions, and invoking change and interchange.

When I began my research on gender and cartography, I assumed I had some of the necessary skills to study that aspect of map worlds since I had been an assistant map editor in one of Europe's largest city-map firms in the mid-1960s. I soon learned otherwise. In the thirty-four years since my early involvement with cartography, the field had changed utterly. I was experiencing *frozen time*, much like the Japanese soldier who had been holed up in a cave in Malaysia, believing that the war was still on. He emerged from the cave to discover the war was long over: he lost his bearings and was confounded by his new experience. My experience, though less dramatic and earth-shattering, was not unlike that soldier's. I was returning to a field where digital imaging had long ago replaced hand-held tools such as the awl or Letraset sheets. Indeed, I had stepped into an entirely new world and in a new position. No longer was I a cartographer; now I was studying "them," from the perspective of an outsider to the discipline and from the perspective of a man trying to understand issues confronting women.[2]

I was now interested in studying the everyday life of *women* cartographers (i.e., social behavior and interaction), *their* community (i.e., values and norms), and *their* social organization ("map worlds"). But without proper training in geodesy and geomatics, which have become the home of cartography, I felt quite unequipped to deal with the new realities of cartography. My interviews with the women cartographers who were the focus of my study only underscored that weakness. In an effort to "catch up," I began at the margins. At a 1999 conference of the International Cartographic Association in Ottawa, I explored the commercial exhibits (van den Hoonaard 1999) and noticed that although the established cartographic agencies, staffed by well-dressed men, were located at the center of the exhibition hall, the circle of exhibitors spun from the center. And it was at the margins that I found the new companies, often staffed by young women. Moreover, I observed that although most of the exhibitors were competing for clients, the competition was subdued by a sense of community among these young women: when one exhibitor had to take a lunch break or go to the washroom, a neighbor did not hesitate to step in and watch over the booth.

Working with women cartographers on the Commission on Children and Cartography became another occasion to observe activities "at the margin" that could help me better understand map worlds (and the place of women in those worlds) and in that way understand issues of gender. Just as I observed that the maps and exhibits were gendered in particular ways, so I began to understand that issues crucial to women were often perceived as being marginal to the field and often entirely invisible to the men at the center. Later, when I wrote about the children of women cartographers, reviewers of my manuscript perversely assumed that I was trivializing the women's lives. This might have been particularly the case because the manuscript was doing something different from other biographies about cartographers. Interestingly, however, it was the women who had included that information about their families in their explanations about what had been important to them and their careers. As Cecilia Ridgeway (2011) notes, when people face unknown situations and risk uncertainty, they fall back on familiar gender stereotypes. I called such preconceptions the "gender stone" because I stumbled on it and almost lost my way.

International Organizations, Ambiguous Boundaries, and Interdisciplinarity

While my general initial unfamiliarity with both the new cartography and the specific issues of gender led me to adopt a strategy of starting at the margins, there were three other reasons for slow progress. First, map worlds are an international community and its incumbents engage in extensive travels to virtually every corner of the globe. If I wanted to study that universe, I too had to undertake time-consuming and expensive international travel. Second, and very much related, cartographers inhabit many settings—government agencies, contracting firms, mapping companies, and universities—and are involved in many tasks, as GIS specialists, academic conceptualists, tactile-map creators, geodesists, elementary-school instructors, software engineers, geography teachers, map librarians, and map archivists. Some settings are more closely aligned to cartography than others, but all touch on maps, whether directly or indirectly. Quite simply, there is no widely accepted idea about who is or is not a cartographer.

Over what seemed to be an endless period of time, I attended a range of gatherings in a wide variety of places. In Canada, I turned to the activities of the Canadian Cartographic Association; internationally, I focused on the International Cartographic Association (ICA). I also tried to tap into other national and international events, such as the Summer School on Cartography organized by the Norwegian Association of Cartographers, and the activities of two key ICA commissions (Gender and Children). These commissions also held in-house meetings that were sometimes separate from the international gatherings. Some meetings only took place once every two years; if I missed one, I then experienced a four-year gap in establishing some contacts and making links to others. In addition to attending meetings as much as opportunity allowed, I paid visits to map-making firms in Sweden, Hungary, and Slovenia. These visits were made possible by paid lectures—unrelated to cartography—I delivered in those three countries. I also visited a renowned cartographic institute in the Netherlands.

The third factor that slowed down the research was that of interdisciplinarity. I finished the first full draft of *Map Worlds* in 2003. The reviewers of the initial draft were cartographers who examined the book exclusively through their own disciplinary lens. Their critiques were so profound (and true) that I could not bear to look at them again for at least five years. I then began to reconstruct the book. Although I thought that my own lack of intimate knowledge of the history of cartography and of its current practices was fair game for the reviewers and I tried to address that issue, what unhinged me more was their lack of understanding—let alone appreciation—of sociological concepts, language, and perspectives. Their sharpest criticism addressed the qualitative nature of the data I had obtained through my interviews with women cartographers. The reviewers insisted that the sample was not representative (besides being too small), that the quotations were too long, and that the information was not about cartography (but about the experiences of women in map worlds). They also wanted to know why I had not interviewed men. In short, they did not understand either what I was doing or why I was doing it.

Of course, I am not alone in the experience of crossing disciplinary boundaries and facing challenges by those outside my own field. In fact, universities and research councils today promote interdisciplinary work, and the costs of "going solo" are high. In my case, if I wanted the book to be successful, I would have to pay close attention not only to what the early reviewers had spotted as my weak knowledge of cartography and their disinterest in women's lives, but also to try to frame the qualitative data in a way that would make it acceptable to someone operating from an entirely different research paradigm. Ultimately, what I chose to do was to relocate my qualitative interview data in a different section of the book by incorporating new sections that dealt with the biographies of women pioneers in cartography. These new sections would fall between the much-revised sections of historical cartography (going back seven hundred years) and the data from the interviews. The new sections would be perceived as "factual" by reviewers of the revised book manuscript and heighten the sense that the book is about cartography after all.

This new vision of the manuscript entailed a one-and-a-half-year process of soliciting the names of women pioneers from those who know the field—namely, cartographers. This process generated twenty-eight names, from the eighteenth century up to the present. I touched base with each of the dozen pioneers still alive and submitted my initial narrative about each of their lives to them, asking them to approve what I had written or to let me know of changes they wanted me to make. Interestingly, a number of women pioneers thought that their contributions were not worthy of any mention despite the advocacy of them by others. Others refused to be singled out as the representative of a given country and insisted that colleagues be included in my narrative. In short, this process of building the pioneers' vignettes turned out to be far more elaborate than I had expected. By 2012, I had finally completed an eleventh draft of *Map Worlds* and turned it in to Wilfrid Laurier University Press for publication in 2013.

Concluding Thoughts

Among the reasons for "slow sociology" in this project—out-of-date knowledge, time-consuming and expensive international travel, the ambiguous boundaries of map worlds, the "gender stone"—the issue of interdisciplinarity was perhaps the most vexing because it created a clash of perspectives, understandings, and approaches. My strategy was to try to accommodate that friction without surrendering my own discipline of sociology. There is no easy, take-home message here—no how to "do it yourself" set of instructions. Each scholar who leaves the comfort of his or her own back-yard will have to make adjustments to "fit" into a new environment. The distinctive nature of those adjustments will depend on the particularities of that new environment. What will be common in *all* such situations is that a scholar will emerge from the process with a richer understanding of his or her *own* discipline as he or she seeks to make it accessible to those to whom it initially makes little, or limited, sense. In my case, I came away with a far fuller interpretation of map worlds and of the place of gender both at the margins and in the center of that universe.

Notes

1. The cartographic work of Dr. Kira Shingareva of Russia inspired me when I set the title of this chapter. Dr. Shingareva was part of the first group to map the reverse side of the moon, in 1965. She died in September 2013, two weeks after my book *Map Worlds* was published.

2. In 2000, I expressed this excitement (and, I confess, some worries) in a paper at the joint conference of the Association of Canadian Map Libraries and Archives, the Cartographic Association of Canada, and the Western Association of Map Libraries (van den Hoonaard 2000a) entitled "'What's a Nice Sociologist like You Doing in a Place like This?' A Sociological Exploration of the World of Cartographers."

References

Becker, H. S. 1982. *Art Worlds*. Berkeley: University of California Press.

Macionis, J. J., and L. M. Gerber. 1999. *Sociology*. 3rd ed. Toronto: Prentice Hall Allyn and Bacon.

Ridgeway, C. L. 2011. *Framed by Gender: How Gender Inequality Persists in the Modern World*. New York: Oxford University Press.

van den Hoonaard, W. C. 1994 "Do City Maps Show Gender Bias?" *Fredericton (NB) Daily Gleaner*, June 23: 7.

———. 1999. "Map Worlds: A Conceptual Framework for the Study of Gender and Cartography." In *Touch the Past, Visualize the Future: Proceedings, ICA 1999* [19th International Cartographic Conference and 11th General Assembly of the International Cartographic Association], edited by C. Peter Keller, 387–400. Ottawa: Organizing Committee for Ottawa ICA 1999.

———. 2000a. "'What's a Nice Sociologist like You Doing in a Place like This?' A Sociological Exploration of the World of Cartographers." Paper presented at a joint conference of the Association of Canadian Map Libraries and Archives, the Canadian Cartographic Association, and the Western Association of Map Libraries, Edmonton, May 31–June 4.

———. 2000b. "Getting There without Aiming at It: Women's Experiences in Becoming Cartographers." *Cartographic* 37 (3): 47–60.

———. 2000c. "Mapping a Conference: A Participant-Observation Analysis of a Cartographers' World." *Association of Canadian Map Libraries and Archives Bulletin* 107: 23–28.

———. 2008. "And Speaking of Map Worlds: A University Course on Maps by a Non-Cartographer for Non-Cartography Students." *Association of Canadian Map Libraries and Archives Bulletin* 132 (Spring/Summer): 10–15.

———. 2013. *Map Worlds: A History of Women in Cartography*. Waterloo, ON: Wilfrid Laurier University Press.

Whyte, W. F. 1955. *Street Corner Society: The Social Structure of an Italian Slum*. Chicago: University of Chicago Press.

9

Getting It Right

Pamela Stone

I first got the idea for the study that became *Opting Out?* (Stone 2007) when I dropped off my younger son, Nick, for a playdate. He was in kindergarten, eagerly learning the ropes of school and making new friends. So, come to think of it, was I. His newfound friend's mother (whom I'll call Karen) became my newfound friend. And at this particular playdate, I wasn't only dropping off my son, I was dropping off a present to Karen, a "stay-at-home" mom who'd just given birth to her third child. As I was leaving, she told me with obvious excitement that she had an announcement to make: she was going back to work. When I asked if she was returning to her former company, a prestigious investment banking firm, she looked at me as if I were, frankly, nuts. Waving that off as an impossibility, she told me she'd taken a position as a receptionist in a residential real estate office in our small suburban town, just to get out of the house and do something and because, with three children now, she'd lined up a live-in au pair anyway. I found elements of Karen's story striking: the sudden timing of her going to work immediately after the birth of her third child, considering she had been out of the workforce for years; her complete dismissal of the idea of returning to her former job and instead taking a job for which she was wildly over-qualified; her enthusiasm about the prospect of returning to work; and the absence of any obvious economic reason for her to do so, given what I knew about her family's circumstances. Parts of Karen's story resonated with what I knew from my own scholarly expertise in women and work, but parts were novel, and confounding.

I can still recall the feeling of epiphany I had as I walked to my car after that conversation—that "click" moment of sociological imagination when

I realized I had found a subject that joined the personal and the sociological. The experience planted the seeds of my interest in other high-achieving women whose lives had taken turns that were to me, and perhaps to them, surprising and seemingly unpredicted. Nick was in kindergarten when I dropped him off for that playdate, and in college when *Opting Out?* was published—a long gestation period. Let me hasten to clarify (without seeming overly defensive, which I no doubt will anyway) that much of that period was devoted to other things. Professionally, being a department chair took up a lot of my time. On the home front, raising our two boys with my husband kept things busy. Along the way, a broken leg and herniated disc made for some unexpected downtime. Yet with all this on the work, family, and medical fronts, in hindsight, probably contributing equally to the number of years it took me to design, carry out, write up, and publish this study was the nature of the topic itself and its evolution from obscurity to highly charged visibility. Writing this leads me to reflect not only on why it took so long, but on what I was doing all that time. Looking back, I realize that many of the periods I regarded as frustrating and fallow—as wheel-spinning or unproductive—were, quite simply, not.

It is easier to say this now, when the story has a happy ending (a published book and promotion to full professor), than it was to live through, but it wasn't only life that got in the way of research and slowed it: it *was* the subject itself. When I was talking with Karen, my immediate inspiration, it was the mid-1990s; it was not until the late 1990s that I began working on the subject in earnest. This was before the *New York Times Magazine* cover story by Lisa Belkin (2003) defined what I was studying as the "opt-out revolution." That story, the most-commented on in the history of the magazine, unleashed a veritable torrent of discussion. It was the elephant in the room that I, even in the quieter confines of academia, could not ignore. While one might imagine that a desire to be responsive to the media controversy generated by this story would have speeded up my timetable, it had in fact the opposite effect, as I'll describe. "Getting it right" (sidestepping ontological and epistemological debates, I believe empirical research yields some approximation of, and insights into, reality) was already a concern, but became even more important to me after the *Times* story. My desire to "get it right" was part of why *Opting Out?* had such a long gestation period, but there were other reasons as well, rooted in where I was in my career, decisions I made about the kind of work I wanted to do, and the kind of research I felt I had to do once I figured out what I really wanted to know.

Career Context

By the time of that playdate, I'd been department chair long enough to realize that the demands of chairing had taken their toll on my research. Most of what I was doing with regard to research at that point could be characterized, I suppose, as plotting my comeback, which took the form of wrestling with wrenching self-doubt about my ability to revive my research agenda, whether with old or with new projects. Despite knowing better, I'd agreed to serve as chair while an associate professor, and was still at that rank. When I finally decided to begin working on the project that became *Opting Out?* I had tenure, but was keenly aware of the need to make up for lost time. I wanted to be promoted—not just for a sense of personal accomplishment but as a demonstration that, as a woman, I was holding up the side. I also knew that I was facing an academic Catch-22: my publication slowdown and time-in-rank were going to make it hard for me to acquire the resources (i.e., grants) that I needed to support the research and publication necessary to move forward in my career.

I had to balance a sense of urgency about what I wanted to do with pragmatism about what I could do. Objectively, the situation was pretty bleak. Trained in quantitative research, primarily secondary data analysis, my first instinct was to build on my prior track record. I applied for a grant from a special National Science Foundation (NSF) program designed to support women scientists whose careers had been interrupted—perfect, I thought. Intrigued by Karen, I'd been accumulating examples of women like her whom I'd come to know. With an eye to what their decisions portended for the larger issue of gender inequality, I proposed a project in which I would analyze career interruption (versus persistence) and career outcomes among college-educated women using National Longitudinal Surveys (NLS) data. My application was turned down.

This could have been pretty devastating, I suppose, but years of thinking about and sporadically working on this subject had yielded a few insights that kept me motivated and kept me going. First, my efforts at literature review had revealed that there was no research on this phenomenon of women of the feminist revolution and beyond who had pursued professional careers in formerly male-dominated fields and left them. Second, the continuing absence of women at the top of these fields begged to be explained, and there were beginning to be signs that some part of the explanation might lie with the fact that a not insignificant fraction of women were leaving the labor force in fields in which "being in it to win it" was a necessary if not sufficient condition for success. Third, while there was little to no academic research on the topic, it had attracted some attention in the media, which seemed to me (and to feminist analysts such as Faludi [1991]) to be framing it in terms of "choice feminism" in ways that demanded further interrogation. A content analysis I did of these stories about what came to be called "opting out" (later updated in Kuperberg and Stone 2008) confirmed that the dominant narrative in the media reflected the reductionist rational choice model that I (and many other sociologists of gender inequality) had spent my career challenging. Women were "choosing" to go home, their decisions framed as proof of the rise of a neo-traditionalist gender ideology that reflected separate spheres and favored motherhood and domesticity over career. Fourth, and probably not least, I was putting faces to phenomena, perhaps for the first time in my career. Women like Karen and others I'd gotten to know through the "mom work" I was doing alongside my work as chair and professor personified issues I'd engaged with throughout my career. And they did so in ways that were complex, confusing, and counterintuitive.

During this period, when my CV would make it appear that I was not doing a whole lot of research, I came to discover that Karen was not an isolated exception. One example that sticks in my mind occurred while I was brainstorming with the PTA executive committee of which I was a member about the slate of officers for an upcoming election. Candidate after candidate was an at-home mother described in terms of her former profession—the ex-corporate CFO (chief financial officer), for example, who would make an ideal PTA treasurer. While not formally "in the field," this experience and others like it gave me insights into the lives of former professionals turned at-home mothers that no doubt informed my future study of them. More importantly at this point, however, these women fascinated me and piqued my interest. I wanted to find out more about them. And I was propelled to do so more by sheer curiosity about the intellectual puzzle they represented than by anything else, since what I wanted to study was still a problem that had no name and, based on my NSF experience, not one other scholars found particularly important or compelling or researchable. In fact, one of the reviewers of my failed NSF proposal assumed that "opting out" was so rare a phenomenon among college-educated women that there wouldn't be enough women ("a big enough N") to study. While it's true that "opting out" *is* a minority phenomenon, it is not so rare that small Ns posed a fatal problem.

Having lost time on the unsuccessful grant application, I had better luck when I applied for a fellowship at Radcliffe the year after I stepped down as chair and was on sabbatical. Radcliffe, formerly the women's college of Harvard, was at this point a research institute within the university. It had a special interest in the subject, an earlier study having shown that women graduates of Harvard's professional schools had an unanticipated high rate of being out of the labor force ten years past graduation (Swiss and Walker 1993). My time there gave me the unencumbered ability to pursue my research and the intellectual companionship of an outstanding group of scholars. But now I had to face some stark realities about the contested nature of what I was studying and I was at a crossroads about how to go about studying it.

Forbidden Subjects

I knew when I first became interested in the subject of professional women at home that it was potentially controversial. It was probably no accident that there was so little research on the subject, because academic researchers, especially then, which was just before the explosion of interest in unpaid or caregiving work, tended to focus on women's paid work experiences. As I wrote in my study of women with superb professional pedigrees who are at-home mothers, even "acknowledging their existence *does* seem a dirty little secret" (Stone 2007, 8). There was about these women, as Ann Crittenden (2001) pointed out earlier in *The Price of Motherhood*, a hint of taboo. To study them, I had to wade into the battlefield of the mommy wars, which pitted stay-at-home moms against working moms. I had to shed light on a group of women who were often viewed as naive (at best) or as hapless victims of false consciousness or even as traitors to the feminist cause—a group that many observers would rather just ignore, hoping the women would learn the error of their ways. These sentiments were already evident in the popular literature of the 1990s, but would reemerge even more pointedly and vehemently after "opting out" became a high-profile phenomenon, as exemplified by books such as Hirshman's *Get to Work* (2006) and Bennetts's (2007) *The Feminine Mistake*.

As I talked more about my then very nascent work in progress, I sensed interest—tempered with wariness—among my colleagues, many of whom reported, sometimes *sotto voce*, knowing women similar to those I had encountered. This was a wariness I shared. I had to be open to the possibility that prevailing media explanations might be correct—that women *were* changing their preferences about work and family, that so-called neo-traditionalism was real. At that moment, in the late 1990s, for example, we were beginning to see evidence of a now well-documented stall in the gender revolution (Cotter, Hermsen, and Vanneman 2007). Going where the data led me also meant that I had to be attuned to the implications of my findings. This idea of "getting it right," which hovers over most researchers, was hovering that much closer in light of what my research might have to say about high-achieving women, about the gender wars, and about our understanding of gender inequality and reasons for the stall in closing the gender gap—about issues that had shaped my own coming of age and my life's work. Was I opening a Pandora's box?

To address these concerns, I felt I needed to get a better sense of national trends in the behavior I was observing firsthand in my relatively affluent suburban community. My quantitative training compels me to ask questions like how much, how many, and how representative? At this point, which was still years before the "opt-out revolution" article, there was relatively little attention being paid to the now well-documented leveling off of women's (especially mothers') labor force participation in the 1990s. From my review of popular literature, I had identified college-educated married moms as being the target demographic for further study; I knew both from existing research and my own observations that they were in a position to exercise the option to quit working. When I analyzed Current Population Survey data for this particular group, I found that there was indeed evidence of a decline (this analysis covered the years 1977 to 1998) in this group's labor force participation and that a relatively sizable share (on the order of one in five) were at home taking care of family. This analysis, which I subsequently updated (Reimers and Stone 2008), gave me a basis for going forward—it appeared that something was happening and it wasn't only in my backyard.

Having satisfied myself that the subject was worth studying based on recent trends, I then had to confront the question of how to study it. The fellowship gave me a year during which I ultimately decided to jettison a quantitative approach in favor of a qualitative one. This was, admittedly, a risky decision for a variety of reasons, the foremost being that I had no training whatsoever in qualitative methods (and respected the methods enough to know there was a lot I needed to learn). Furthermore, feeling out of sync with my career already, I knew that qualitative work was typically slower going than quantitative (though I think the amount of time needed to do good secondary analysis is often underestimated too). Finally, my area of inquiry, gender, attracts some of the best qualitative researchers in sociology, so I was entering a new arena that was competitive and exacting.

Offsetting these considerations, and finally winning the day, were others, some tied to question and method, some tied to personal predilection. One of the frustrations of working on gender inequality using a quantitative orientation is that one has to wrestle with the hegemony of economists' rational choice models (which offer essentially the same explanation for women's behavior and gendered outcomes as voiced by the media). In these models, outcomes are revealed preferences. Thus, attitudes, tastes, and preferences that underlie women's choices don't need to be measured, and usually aren't, typically consigned to the so-called black box. The direct effects of tastes and preferences, along with other effects (like that of discrimination), are captured empirically in residuals or unexplained variation. For me, as for most sociologists, tastes and preferences are important and distinct from actual behavior. Behavior is seen as reflecting both individual-level influences—human capital endowments and attitudes, for instance—and supra-individual opportunities and constraints, typically framed as structure. Given the centrality of "choice" in the media narratives and in the prevailing academic paradigm, it seemed critical to interrogate choice—to attend to aspects of both individual decision-making and structure. Working quantitatively, this is hard to do, even if one is so inclined. The reality of secondary data analysis is that attitudinal indicators or others that tap into motivations are typically pretty sparse in large nationally representative datasets. If I wanted to unpack "choice" to understand what women really want—their preferences for work, family, or a combination thereof—and the context within which they were forming their preferences and making (and framing) their decisions, I needed to use qualitative methods.

Making the case for a qualitative approach even more compelling was the absence of research on the subject, classically a situation calling for exploratory, hypothesis-generating qualitative techniques. These women and their motives were opaque to me and there were a number of plausible competing hypotheses—the push of hostile or unfriendly workplaces, the pull of children and family, changing attitudes and preferences, and, in an era of heightening income inequality, the resurgent power of a previously declining income effect. Finally, given that I was treading in waters known to be contested ("mommy war" territory), the framing of specific questions posed special challenges. Designing my own survey was premature. Given my interests, and given my prior research (my dissertation, for example, had used a two-wave longitudinal survey to examine the persistent effect of adolescent aspirations on women's adult labor force participation), and given the existing research (Gerson's [1985] *Hard Choices* was a particular influence), the semi-structured life-history interview seemed the perfect fit.

Retooling

During my sabbatical, I was fortunate to be surrounded by colleagues who were premier scholars of gender, many of whom were also expert qualitative researchers. I did a lot of reading based on their suggestions, but as I've found is true for learning any method, talking to knowledgeable practitioners about their experiences could get me only so far: the best way to learn a method is finally just to do it. I also admit to finding the recommended reading somewhat frustrating. While I knew that qualitative approaches did not lend themselves to the more standardized process of quantitative analysis, I was nonetheless a little surprised to find how "gestaltish" it all seemed to be. Descriptions of coding, for example, left me completely baffled, and led me to work out coding schemes on my own. Subsequently, I've been heartened to learn that qualitative coding appears to be challenging for everyone, but at the time I thought it was just me. I was also somewhat amazed to find out how some of the people whose work I most respected analyzed their data (typically from interviews). A common technique appeared to consist of putting quotes on pieces of paper or index cards and arranging and rearranging them (often on the floor) to see patterns. While this clearly worked for my colleagues, this is where my quantitative side kicked in—I needed a computer. Thankfully, there were a number of text analysis software packages available and a growing interest in their use. A workshop in ATLAS.ti saved the day and gave me the security blanket of computerization.

I also was fortunate to have hired an outstanding research assistant, Meg Lovejoy (then a doctoral candidate at Brandeis, now a PhD), who was not only well trained in qualitative methodology but gifted at it. In doing my study, I arrived at a kind of hybridized qualitative-quantitative approach. Whenever I was leaning too much toward the latter, Meg would pull me back with a gentle reminder that I was being quantitative. Nonetheless, from the outset, it was important to me to try to address the inherent subjectivity of qualitative research. I did this in a number of ways. First, and most importantly, I double-coded all my interviews (with Meg as the second, independent coder). Second, I made use of ATLAS's capacity to break out and count codes by categories. While frequency per se wasn't the final yardstick, simple counts to understand the prevalence and patterning of emerging themes reassured my quantitative side and confirmed (or sometimes didn't) that I was hearing what I thought I was. Third, I compared attitudes, tastes, and preferences to behavior and circumstance, looking for points of congruence (or lack thereof).

There were two major challenges to the analysis. First was parsing out what I called "choice rhetoric"—the extent to which women framed their decisions in the language of choice and preference—and distinguishing this from the reality of their options, or structure; the second was trying to understand the relative weighting of workplace versus family influences on women's decision-making. Not only were these the central questions of my study, they were central questions in the larger media accounts of women's lives and options with regard to work and family. Being confident in my conclusions required performing numerous iterations, when I would painstakingly comb through interviews. Meg and I worked out narrative summaries for each woman in addition to coding (and in hindsight, probably overcoding) their interviews in order to try to distill the key influences on and circumstances surrounding their decisions. But to someone who was new to the methodology, and increasingly conscious of the importance of what I was discovering (about which, more below), this stage—which occurred over years, not weeks or months—was critical to feeling I could move forward to present these results.

While at Radcliffe, I made some other design decisions. My first intention had been to study professional women who were mothers, both currently working and at home. The question then was broader: Why did some continue with their careers and others not? What were the factors differentiating continuity from interruption? What was the mix of work and family influences leading to one decision or the other? I began to do some preliminary interviews, some with working mothers, some with at-home mothers. What I heard from the working mothers confirmed the research we already had on hand, pointing to the importance of (truly) supportive bosses and husbands and to the size and importance of women's relative contribution to household income. What I was hearing from the at-home mothers, however, was surprising and countered the prevailing narrative: they were telling me very little about motherhood, but a lot about unyielding workplaces. I could have continued with the kind of balanced design I'd originally envisioned—that is, to include both groups of women—but as I took stock of the time and money required to arrange, conduct, transcribe, and analyze each interview (in addition to the considerable legwork necessary to identify women for the study in the first place), I decided after these early interviews to focus only on the at-home mothers, who were underresearched and little understood.

From this point on, my course was set. For details of my methodology, see Stone 2007. Exactly as described in the texts on qualitative methodology I'd been reading, I hit the "saturation point" fairly quickly, at around fifteen interviews. Still nagged by my quantitative mindset, no doubt, I continued interviewing to boost the final N to 54. I also wanted to see if what I was finding held up across regions, age cohorts, and occupation types (it did), and was guided in my additional interviews by a rough quota sampling design.

The time at Radcliffe, then, turned out to be pivotal and critical. The work I did there solidified and encouraged my interest in the subject. It helped me frame my methodological orientation and gave me the initial opportunity to retrain myself and retool my skills, which was in some ways a never-ending process that lasted the duration of the project. It also gave me the chance to conduct some preliminary interviews that resulted in a major change to my research design (to focus only on the group who had left the labor force)—a decision informed by pragmatic resource considerations as well as by emerging findings. In the years after my sabbatical, I continued my interviews, which took me across the country, and I presented some preliminary results, but otherwise mostly engaged in the continual analysis and meaning-making that is part of the reflexive process of qualitative research.

I was to encounter yet another interruption, which occurred just about when I thought I was finishing my interviews. In the weeks—and months—after 9/11, work and family, especially the importance of family at a time of tragedy, were major themes in the national narrative of comprehending and healing. Work-family narratives were also a crucial part of what I was trying to pull apart and distinguish between. Not to trivialize the event, but from my perspective, 9/11 posed a threat to the internal validity of my study, specifically in the form of a history effect (Shadish, Cook, and Campbell 2002). I was concerned that 9/11 and its aftermath would raise the salience of family in women's retrospective accounts of their decision-making. To avoid this and the possible bias it introduced, I suspended interviewing for a year—another painful delay, but one I thought justified and necessary from the point of view of research design.

From the Problem That Had No Name to "Opting Out"

What I found as I did those initial interviews was how much I enjoyed them. I was astonished, and grateful, that women were so willing to talk with me. Having guaranteed them anonymity, I nonetheless marveled at their candor and openness. Because my research until that point consisted almost entirely of secondary data analysis, I had never actually talked with my subjects, much less interviewed them in their own living rooms. This firsthand experience further heightened my sense of wanting to get it right—to fully and accurately convey the lives these women were sharing with me—and became another reason why analysis of their stories was so time-consuming. I also knew that the women I was interviewing would likely read my book, or certainly have easy access to it. Not only did I want to get it right, I wanted to write it up in a style that was accessible to them and women like them.

By 2003, five years after my initial year at Radcliffe, I had finally reached the point, after endless analysis, of being fully confident in my results, having checked them in numerous ways and finding them robust. I was ready to go public and to begin writing the book that I had always anticipated would be the major end result. Propitiously, I was also invited to give a paper at a conference at the University of Pennsylvania. Sponsored by the Sloan Foundation, its focus was on assessing the progress of women in the professions. Jerry Jacobs, the organizer, knew of my work and asked me to talk about it. That conference, as I recall, was on a Friday; the weekend before, the *New York Times Magazine* featured a cover story titled "The Opt-Out Revolution" by its work-life reporter Lisa Belkin (2003), with the teaser "Why Don't More Women Get to the Top? They Choose Not To." When I first saw it, and understood what it was about, I couldn't read it, certain that the years of research I'd been doing had just been scooped, and sure that (as is often the case) the cover story was a prelude to a forthcoming book. When I finally read it, I realized that Belkin and I had heard different things and come to different conclusions. More significantly, perhaps, by the end of the week it was clear that the topic I'd been working on for years—the problem that hadn't been recognized as a problem and that had no name—had morphed, literally overnight, into a subject of considerable interest and controversy.

Meanwhile, I presented my paper and received excellent comments from Heidi Hartmann, a scholar whose opinion I valued. While generally laudatory, she wondered whether my sample was not skewed a little old and whether what I was picking up reflected experiences of an older cohort of women (i.e., women in their forties). While I had tried to sample from a range of ages, the fact was that the majority of my sample at that time was indeed women in their forties, which was not surprising given that these were professional women who'd deferred marriage and childbearing while pursuing advanced education and training in their twenties. Nonetheless, this critique resonated with me. When I'd thought no one would be listening—when my problem still had no name—I'd been okay with this weakness, reasoning that no study is perfect. Now that it was possible, thanks to the *Times* story, that my work might actually find an audience, and because it was clear from my results that I would be challenging a high-profile interpretation, I felt an added pressure to respond to the comment of an eminent scholar and, again, to get it right. In this instance, this translated into going back into the field to interview an additional eleven women in their thirties so that the final sample was evenly split between thirty- and forty-year olds, which added at least another year to the study.

At this point, time was of particular essence, not only because of the length of time I'd already invested, but because of the controversy the article had ignited and my desire to see my research enlighten the ensuing discussion. What I haven't mentioned yet is funding. Part of the relatively slow pace of my work was due to the need to raise money to support it. Because I hadn't been publishing regularly, I did not feel I was competitive for major external funding. Instead, I turned to relatively small (but critical) internal grants from my institution, including invaluable support from an NSF ADVANCE grant to Hunter College (Virginia Valian and Vita Rabinowitz, PIs) to promote the careers of women in science. I'd exhausted those options and needed more money faster than internal funding could provide. I applied to the Sloan Foundation and was funded by Kathleen Christensen's program in Work and Family, in part I think because I was the only person out there who had actually conducted research on "opting out," for which I will take some credit for prescience. With Sloan's support, I was able at last to complete the remaining interviews, the results of which confirmed what I had previously found. I was also able to get some release time to write. Having spent years with these results paid off in that I completed the manuscript relatively quickly, aided by Naomi Schneider, my wonderful editor at the University of California Press, who facilitated its path to publication in 2007. Remarkably, four years after the "opting out" article's publication, interest in the subject remained high, giving me the opportunity to provide the counternarrative—to tell the stories of women who were being talked about, and talked at, but rarely given voice.

Decisions about research design were not just technical decisions made to meet academic standards, but to enhance the credibility of what I was finding. Was I overly cautious? Probably, but chalk that up not only to the challenges I've described, but to the burden of being a rookie at qualitative methods and, no doubt, trying harder. The study was better for the decisions I made, even though each one incurred a delay. In the end, it was the methodology itself—the fact that I so closely engaged with the women I was studying—that really motivated me, because getting it right wasn't an intellectual exercise, it was an obligation to them. In hindsight, the fact that I probably identified with women's stories of careers interrupted, having seen my own research career interrupted, also gave me an empathy and insight into their lives that I would otherwise not have had. If so, perhaps it was worth the interruption.

References

Belkin, L. 2003. "The Opt-Out Revolution." *New York Times Magazine*, October 26, 42–47, 58, 85–86.

Bennetts, L. 2007. *The Feminine Mistake: Are We Giving Up Too Much?* New York: Hyperion.

Cotter, D A., J. M. Hermsen, and R. Vanneman. 2007. *The Stalled Gender Revolution* (project website hosted at Reeve Vanneman's University of Maryland faculty page). *www.vanneman.umd.edu/endofgr/default.html.*

Crittenden, A. 2001. *The Price of Motherhood.* New York: Metropolitan Books.

Faludi, S. 1991. *Backlash: The Undeclared War against American Women.* New York: Crown.

Gerson, K. 1985. *Hard Choices: How Women Decide about Work, Career, and Motherhood.* Berkeley: University of California Press.

Hirshman, L. 2006. *Get to Work: A Manifesto for Women of the World.* New York: Penguin.

Kuperberg, A., and P. Stone. 2008. "The Media Depiction of Women Who Opt Out." *Gender & Society* 22 (4): 497–517.

Reimers, C., and P. Stone. 2008. "Explaining Trends in Opting Out among Women: 1981–2006." Paper presented at the annual meeting of the Population Association of America, New Orleans, April 7.

Shadish, W. R., T. D. Cook, and D. T. Campbell. 2002. *Experimental and Quasi-experimental Designs for Generalized Causal Inference.* Boston: Houghton Mifflin.

Stone, P. 2007. *Opting Out? Why Women Really Quit Careers and Head Home.* Berkeley: University of California Press.

Swiss, D. J., and J. P. Walker. 1993. *Women and the Work/Family Dilemma: How Today's Professional Women Are Confronting the Maternal Wall.* New York: Wiley.

10

"Breakfast at Elmo's"

Adolescent Boys and Disruptive Politics in the Kinscripts Narrative

Linda M. Burton and Carol B. Stack

O n Thursday mornings, we find ourselves sitting across from each other in *our* corner booth at Elmo's Diner in Durham, North Carolina. We nearly disappear into the roomy, slightly tattered green leather cushions, anchored in the comfort of the history we share—that is, our long engagement as friends and coconspirators in the world of kinship, poverty, and ethnography. Despite our access to the long menus that flank the table, the server who greets us knows that we won't bother to look because we always order the Egg Deal. We find solace in the predictability of the setting, our conversations, and the Egg Deal.

Between us, we have amassed about seventy-five years of experience as ethnographers, working and communing with low-income rural and urban families across generations, time, and place. Even before Linda's orange juice and Carol's coffee are delivered to the breakfast table, we spread out our fieldnotes and memos, aligning the salt, pepper, and other condiments so that they are equidistant to our reach. We approach our ongoing disciplined discussions about our research on poverty and families in much the same way. We are eager to launch our discussion on this particular day because Margaret Nelson, Anita Garey, and Rosanna Hertz have invited us to contribute a chapter to an edited volume that will allow us to talk frankly about aspects of our work that we have rarely had the forum to provide details about—that is, how slow ethnography and disruptions rooted in the politics of science shaped the pathways we followed in constructing narratives about our observations of low-income males and their labor in families.

We joke with each other, suggesting that Margaret, Anita, and Rosanna have been stealthy, silent partners in our ongoing breakfast conversations, and that our current writing project for them is a reflection (though only in part) of their numinous presence. You see, in nearly fourteen months of breakfast tête-à-têtes, we have dutifully challenged each other to "get a handle on" how the processes of slow ethnography and disruptions owing to the politics of science have moved us along at a snail's pace in writing about something we actually know quite a bit about—boys, men, and families. We ask each other on a fairly consistent basis: why is it taking us so long to write a full-monty narrative about the boys' and men's lives that are so deeply entrenched in our ethnographies and theoretical discourse on poverty and kinscripts?

"Kinscripts," an article we wrote, now some two decades ago (Stack and Burton 1993), depicts one of the ways that we craft theory about kin processes through ethnography. For this effort, we combined our individual longitudinal ethnographic datasets on mostly African American, but also some White and Latino, low-income urban and rural families. We painstakingly culled through reams of fieldnotes and transcripts over a period of six years, recalling vivid images of the families, women, men, and children we studied at every step and harkening back to their voices and their understandings of kin roles and relations and how they work. Throughout the process, we invoked our credo of holding each other accountable for how we interpreted the data as a whole. It is because of this credo that as we wrote the present chapter, we decided to make readers privy to reflexive insights about us that likely shaped kinscripts (Naples 2003).

We invented the kinscripts framework to organize and interpret observations of: (1) the temporal and interdependent dimensions of family role transitions; (2) the creation and intergenerational transmission of family norms; and (3) the dynamics of negotiation, exchange, and conflict within families as they construct the family life course. Across our ethnographies, we could see that the dominant lens for understanding families and their outcomes was to assess their *kin-work* (the labor individuals do in families), *kin-time* (the temporal nature of individuals' engagement in labor and the expectations from others about them doing so), and *kinscription* (how individuals are ushered or recruited into doing family labor). This perspective helped us to interpret and understand the family work of women in our studies whose lives we chose to write about in greater detail first. But, our gaze both in the field and as we wrote was also fixed on the labor of boys and men trudging through childhood, adolescence, and adulthood, both inside and outside of families.

As we breakfast at Elmo's week after week, we speak feverishly about the boys and men we came to know and understand using the kinscripts lens and about what we have and haven't done in telling their full stories even though they were active participants in our ethnographies from day one. As such, in this chapter, we humbly reveal a confluence of forces that some-times drove us to park boys and men in the background of our narratives on the labor of kin. We talk about why understanding the lives of low-income males, particularly adolescents, required a slower ethnographic timetable that involved us "being there" and "lingering" in the field for very long peri-ods of time. And, we also reflect on how the kinwork of males inside low-income families has been marginalized in the scientific and public policy discourse on poverty, and consequently created disruptions for us in bring-ing boys and men to front and center in the theoretical and empirical evolu-tion of kinscripts.

Kinscripts: A Reflexive Lens

As we move forward in our breakfast deliberations from week to week, we have decided to focus our current efforts on bringing the family labor of adolescent boys to center stage before we develop detailed narratives about their fathers and the other adult men in their lives. As we make these kinds of decisions, our discussions occasionally shift to our early years as collabo-rators as well as our own life course experiences with families and adoles-cent males. Our journey as ethnographic partners and vessels of kinscripts began on February 25, 1985, when Linda called Carol out of the blue—we had never met—with a straightforward, yet naive, request. She wanted to come to Durham, North Carolina, to work with Carol. Carol agreed with-out knowing Linda from Adam. We both simply trusted our instincts. Our ethnographic collaboration on the work of kin was launched in the summer of 1985.

When Linda came to Durham to work with Carol, we had two ethno-graphic studies on family networks between us: Linda's dissertation, "Early and On-Time Grandmotherhood in Multigeneration Black Families"

(Burton 1985), and *All Our Kin* (Stack 1974), the book based on Carol's dissertation. The worldviews we showcased in those works emerged from our academic disciplines (sociology and anthropology), the times, and our own family backgrounds. Carol was born in the East Bronx in New York City. Her family migrated first to Albuquerque, New Mexico, and then on to Southern California, where her sister was born. Carol grew up in a large, extended, working-poor, immigrant Jewish family whose members gathered around one another in the San Gabriel Valley in Southern California. Carol married as a young graduate student, had one son, and divorced. She spent the early part of her academic career at Duke University before moving to the University of California at Berkeley, where she lived and taught for several decades. Upon retiring from Berkeley, she returned to Durham.

Linda grew up in a working-poor African American family that migrated from New Orleans, Louisiana, to Los Angeles, California. She had two sisters and spent most of her life in South Central Los Angeles and Compton, California, also around a sizable extended family network. Linda married directly out of high school, had four children (three girls and one boy) rather quickly, and divorced. Her academic career took her first to Penn State University, from where she initially traveled to Durham to meet with Carol. Linda remained at Penn State for over twenty years before moving to Duke University nearly seven years ago. With this move, Carol and Linda were reunited in their adopted "homeplace," Durham.

We both grew up with strong mothers and very generous fathers, and ironically, throughout our childhood and early adult years had resided at different ends of the 110 Freeway—a bypass that connected northeast and southwest Los Angeles. Life was much quieter and safer in South Pasadena for Carol than it was in Compton's "Bloods and Crips territory" for Linda. At one point, Linda lived across the street from Stanley "Tookie" Williams, the leader of the Crips.

In the early 1950s, Carol spent time on her father's bread truck near the community where Linda would later go to elementary school. Linda's father was janitor in a Mexican café in East Los Angeles. Both our fathers traversed diverse cultures and spaces on a daily basis and were quite adept at doing so. They were lifelong caregivers, attentive and generous to others and to us to a fault, even though they were always financially in dire straits. As such, it is not hard to detect the commonalities we shared as we came of age as single mothers; as we watched our own mothers struggle to make do with the meager resources our fathers provided; and as we took part in the care our fathers provided to other family members, friends, and sometimes strangers off the street. These life experiences, no doubt, shaped the ways we approached our research.

Coming Together in Front Porch Dialogues

Linda recalls the day she met Carol in person:

> Our first serious conversation was on Carol's front porch in North Carolina (where she was teaching at Duke). It was so candid and unexpected, much like ethnography. We had no history together. We had just met. But an immediate path was forged for us on that day—a path characterized by mutual trust, honesty, and an unwavering sense of responsibility to represent and interpret the lives we became a part of in our work. We both wanted our research to mirror our respondents' realities. I knew then that this path would be a long engagement requiring more conceptual, emotional, and physical labor than any graduate class that I had ever taken or job I had ever worked.

Carol's thoughts:

> At the time I was the single mom of a teenage son, and I was also in the middle of doing an ethnography on African American return migration to the rural South. Summertime was for research, and I fully intended to spend my summer in northeast North Carolina. I listened closely to what Linda had in mind, and thank goodness I said yes. Whatever our initial intentions were, we soon began talking about our basic frustration with language and terminology in our respective fields that made it so hard to portray what we were observing. The formal kinship terminology in anthropology left me without a satisfactory way to describe the intricacies and dynamics of caregiving and care-receiving among the extended families in my study.

On Carol's front porch we relived our data, and we talked, and talked, and talked. We shared the everyday practices we saw in low-income families in a midwestern city and in South Central Los Angeles. We also began to talk about our ethnographic practices, and seriously engaged the topic of nuanced, understated, and often-misunderstood aspects of families and poverty. Through our conversation, we found our own blind spots and missing pieces of the jigsaw puzzles in our ethnographies. Carol's ethnographic gaze was wide. As she crafted her dissertation, she and her young son had moved in and among a stretch of kin networks, living in harsh conditions that were labeled in political circles as a culture of poverty. She began with an interest in the strategies that large extended families used to survive urban poverty, the networks they formed, and their individual and cultural sense of what they owed to themselves and what they owed to others. Linda's research eyes were directed toward time, place, generational depth, and recurring family roles and patterns across the life course. This work tethered her initially to the field of aging and the role of young grandmothers caring for children in the throes of urban poverty and neighborhood violence. Carol wrote about social and cultural patterns within families. Linda wrote about family structures, roles, and communities that created an accelerated life course for poor African Americans. But neither of us had found fitting language to describe the paradoxes and complexities of poverty and family labor that we had come to know through our work. Carol's memory of these discussions is that "we stripped away any pretense of claiming that we had done justice to or succeeded in describing the kin networks that characterized our work. I came from a long tradition of kinship studies in anthropology, and I tangled with long-standing kinship terminology I had inherited from my field as I was writing my book." Linda noted that "I was handed a store of concepts in graduate school—some still inform my work. But, generations, the normative expectable life course, role theory, and theories of poverty and gender didn't offer enough plasticity or agency for me to situate what women and men were saying about family labor and what they were actually doing about it, and why."

Looking back on those early days, as we linger in our booth at Elmo's, we realize that we have been talking together about the work of kin for nearly thirty years now. The times have changed. As friends, scholars, and colleagues, we continue to revisit our data, and we consistently mull around in a sea of theories about poverty and family life. Kinscripts emerged from these early musings, but our cycle of discovery and rediscovery around the labor of kin was never quite satisfied by this initial product. As times changed, and as we eventually made forays into the politics of science and public policy, which we will address shortly, we have slowly been moving our storyline on the work of kin from a focus on girls and women to the necessary spotlight on boys and men.

Adolescent Boys and Slow Ethnography

As we consider the question of why it has taken us so long to produce detailed narratives about the lives of males using the lens of kinscripts, we assert that *we have never excluded them in our ethnographies or our written work*. Their stories, however, have been sprinkled throughout much of what we write and talk about rather than positioned center stage. During our breakfasts at Elmo's, we debate with ourselves and with each other about why this is so, particularly because males have been part and parcel of our ethnographies from the start. One hypothesis that we entertain frequently is that the creation of ethnographies of adolescent males and the labor of kin is very slow-going. We know from our fieldwork experiences that women studying adolescent males require excessive amounts of time and physical and emotional labor to carefully identify gendered behaviors and their meanings in context (Burton, Garrett-Peters, and Eaton 2009). It also necessitates traversing expansive temporal and physical spaces and having some theoretical mastery of adolescent development to disentangle the paradoxical demands that impoverished families (and mothers, in particular) often place on their adolescent male children (Burton 2007; Stack 2001). We both understood these issues from our initial ethnographic work when we, as young mothers and budding scholars (albeit at different points in historical time), sought to participate in the lives of and build relationships with adolescent boys inside families.

Not surprisingly, in the course of our engagements with adolescent boys and their families, we became inevitably enmeshed in social relationships with them by virtue of participating in their everyday lives (Asher and Fine 1991). To develop these relationships, we quickly understood that we had to "be there" and "linger" in our research sites over extended periods of time. Being there allowed us to see behaviors other researchers who were short-timers in the field may not have normally seen, such as the nuanced and sometime covert rules and courses of action in families' daily routines. We exerted tremendous effort in identifying and trying to understand the rules and routes of families' everyday lives and how families present themselves to others in the situations they encounter (Goffman 1959). This was not an easy task by any means. Nonetheless, being in the field over long periods through different seasons and at different times of the day and night (see Burton 1991) allowed us to observe how adolescent boys learned about and assumed family caregiving roles that were in stark contrast to what others believed about them after observing only the boys' public personas.

As we have noted, the lives of many teen boys in poor families have been part of our ethnographic purview in all our studies (see for example Burton 1990, 1997, 2007; Burton, Garrett-Peters, and Eaton 2009; and Stack 1974, 1996, 2001). When we met these young men, they were often characterized as problems at school by their teachers and principals. But, when we stayed with them long enough, we found that the very same boy the principal labeled as no good was in charge of a toddler in the family every day after school, or worked two jobs to help his mother pay the light bill and rent.

Linda's (Burton 1991) ethnographic work with adolescent males and their families in a midsized northeastern city provides a poignant example of the points we are attempting to make here. In the context of a local high school with a 25 percent graduation rate for African American teen males, Linda was introduced to James, an eighteen-year-old tenth grader who was labeled by school administrators as a "salty walking illiterate disaster." Linda came to know James over the course of several years, but not in the context of school. Rather, she interacted with him through a web of relationships that she built with his peers. Within several months, Linda learned that James was a "lite weight drug dealer" who sold "street pharmaceuticals" on a schedule that was not consistent with others who were also doing so. James sold drugs in three two-hour shifts: one in the morning, one in the afternoon, and one at night. After observing James's pattern, Linda queried him as to why he sold drugs in shifts. He told her that he would tell her when he was ready.

At the end of the first year, James invited Linda to his home to meet his family. When she arrived at James's home, she found him caring for his ailing grandmother, Ada, who was lying comfortably in a hospital-like room set up in the small apartment's dining area. Swaddled in a daisy-patterned comforter, Ada, dying of cancer, appeared to be all of seventy pounds. "I'm the only one who can take care of her," James said. "No one else needs to know about this. I figured that I could trust you and that maybe I could talk to you about this without you letting my homies know." Indeed, James carried the contradictions of his street persona and his gentle spirit of family caregiving on what an observant parent might see as "fragile man-child shoulders." Linda was able to gather these insights about James because she was there *over time* and *present* when he was ready to reveal the breadth of his life and family obligations, *on his own terms*.

Through our work, we have also come to know that there are circumstances that occur in single-mother households that demand considerable labor from adolescent sons. Robert Weiss (1979), a longtime mentor to both of us, has written eloquently about these issues in the lives of single divorced mothers and their children. The issue we have frequently observed in trying to identify our own "ethnographic truths" about these situations is that daughters are slightly more likely to receive "public credit" from their mothers for their kinwork while sons are frequently caught in variable webs of complex demands and mixed messages about their labor in ways that could lead a fast-paced ethnographer who does not linger in the field (e.g., spends merely one month there) to arrive at erroneous conclusions about these sons' contributions to their families. We have recognized the potential for such errors in our own fieldwork relative to what we know we would have missed if we had not lingered in the families in which adolescent boys had assumed the role of "the man of the house."

For example, Carol met Victor, a self-proclaimed man of the house, when he was working in a fast-food restaurant in Oakland (Stack 2001). This was not his first fast-food job, or even his very first job, as he had lied about his age and worked as a roofer when he was fifteen. That year he turned his earnings over to his mother and he beat up his stepfather, who had abused him and his mother for many years. "I guess he [the stepfather] thought I was never going to grow up," Victor said. Victor did grow up, and fast. He was, in his own words, "self-supporting" by the time he was fifteen.

Before long, Victor started dressing like a gangster and associating with gangsters. He found one job after another, and made good money. Victor gave his mother half of each paycheck, and he still had more money than he knew what to do with. By sixteen, between working and attending to his girlfriends and worrying about his little brothers, he had no time to go to school. Despite his mother's protests, Victor began to sleep in the daytime and run hard all night. He told his mother that he was "in charge of his own life." "I started working young," he wrote in his diary, and like a writer of a memoir, he added in bold letters that "a 15-year-old is very close to adulthood."

Later on in Carol's study, which followed her respondents over six years, Victor was working in a fast-food restaurant six hundred miles north of Los Angeles. When his mother decided to send his wayward thirteen-year-old brother, Santos, to live with him in Oakland, Victor confessed that he was excited. He wrote in his diary, "The main reason he is come to stay with me is because he is mess up by following my foot steps and joining a gang. . . . He is trying to be like me. I don't want him to do the same mistake and things I did." Victor repeatedly told Carol that he wanted his brother to "learn from my mistakes." Through her long engagement with Victor, Carol was able to document how an adolescent male who flirted with the life of a gangster also provided valuable kinwork to his family as he transitioned from boy to man.

Fifteen-year-old Antoine, one of Linda's adolescent male respondents, took on this role of man of the house at age thirteen when his mother, Sandra, started a job as a cafeteria worker in compliance with welfare-to-work regulations (see Burton 2007). Sandra's job required an hour-long commute by bus each way, long work hours, and very low pay. The considerable time Sandra spent being at and getting to and from work greatly decreased the amount of time she had to parent her eight sons (Antoine was the second oldest) and sustain relationships with a partner and her friends. As her partner and friend relationships dwindled, and her availability for parenting her sons all but disappeared, Antoine increasingly became her "spouse-apparent," serving as her confidante, consultant, and co-parent to his younger siblings. Antoine's fate as child-as-mate was sealed when his older brother, Dwayne, was arrested and jailed for attempting to contribute to the family economy by selling drugs.

Longitudinal observations of and interviews with Antoine and Sandra indicated that Antoine more than carried his weight as man of the house for several years, until at fifteen years of age he grew weary of his responsibilities. He had been responsible for getting his younger brothers and himself off to school every morning, and one day, according to him, "I just decided to stop." He and his brothers stayed home from school for almost two months before his mother was alerted to their truancy by school officials and was forced to quit her job and stay at home to ensure that her sons went to school every day. While Antoine's parenting responsibilities diminished somewhat because of the truancy incident and his mother's displeasure with his "failure as a co-parent," Sandra seemed to need him more than ever as an emotional confidante after she quit her job. She became increasingly depressed and anxious about the family's financial situation and struggled not to turn to drugs as an option to "settle her nerves."

Like Antoine and Victor, sixteen-year-old Alex served as the man of the house, providing solace and financial support to his mother and parenting for his fifteen-year-old sister and her one-year-old son. Alex's mother, however, was very ambivalent about his role and often sent him mixed messages about the importance of his contributions to the family (see Burton 2007). Whenever his mother started a relationship with a new boyfriend, she would "demote" Alex, requiring that he cease being her peer and "act like a child" in the presence of her boyfriend. On one occasion, his mother's boyfriend demanded that Alex take out the trash "like a good boy." Alex threw the trashcan at the boyfriend and demanded that the boyfriend leave *his* house "because he was the man of the house and helped his mother to pay the bills and raise his nephew." Alex's mother responded by telling him to go to his room. Instead, Alex left the house and moved in with a twenty-five-year-old woman down the street. He said, "Now, I am really the man of the house."

The point we are making here is that all these young men were engaged in extensive family labor that we, as ethnographers, would not have seen or been able to contextualize accurately if not for our long stay in the field and our attention to how adults in these boys' lives thought about their development and recruited them to or released them from family roles. In following James, Victor, Antoine, and Alex across various landscapes over time, we also became very aware of their public personas and how others perceived them in, for example, school settings. These young men were often labeled as "trouble." Working through the "trouble" label in our analysis is what led us to experience major disruptions in disseminating our narratives about them. Although the perspectives of social scientists and policy-makers about these teens and the work they do in families has shifted somewhat over time, during the earlier years of kinscripts some audiences found our insights on boys to be "too maternal," "potentially patronizing," and "likely exaggerated." Below, we discuss these points of view relative to the politics of science and how they shaped our kinscripts narrative on adolescent males.

The Politics of Science and Policy as Disruptions to Kinscripts

Indeed, in family after family, place after place, and study after study, we consistently observed adolescent boys engaging in the labor of kin. We lingered in the field and in families' and sons' lives long enough to witness the ungendered nature of their kinwork, to observe how expectations and practices around that labor were transmitted to boys sometimes as young as five years old, and to discover how boys' kinwork was often treated by institutional outsiders (e.g., school principals) as "fabrications" because males' laboring in poor families seemed counterintuitive to these boys' public personas. Most importantly, in our kinscripts journey, we experienced numerous disruptions in sharing these boys' narratives with scholarly and public policy communities. During the early and middle years of our work, the dominant discourse about poor men and boys, particularly those of color, never quite provided us with a comfortable academic entrée or a policy audience that would take this work seriously.

The dominant discourse across many years had cast urban poor minority boys and men into personas that made them irrelevant and almost invisible in families (Burton and Snyder 1998). They were regularly characterized in the scientific literature and in the media as human forms whose lives were pathological idioms tied to criminal justice systems, violence, unemployment, and a manifested disinterest in education and social mobility. As a consequence, our work on men and boys was often viewed as questionable and counterintuitive, or as anecdotal anomalies. It didn't help that we were women and mothers who prominently inserted ourselves in a discourse dominated by conservative male academics and policy-makers who saw no virtue in the family labor of men beyond that of family breadwinner.

Carol's engagement with disruptions in representing the labor of boys and men in families began in the 1970s when she and others, such as Joyce Ladner (1973), brought their ethnographic research on poor families to the academic and political debates surrounding the Moynihan thesis and the culture of poverty. Typically, these debates, which relied on relatively thin data, stigmatized poor men, mostly African Americans, as pathological deterrents to establishing "normative family forms" because of their histories of unemployment, family absence, and general malaise in caring for the children they produced. Alice O'Connor (2001, 269), in her now classic volume *Poverty Knowledge*, keenly described the disruptions Carol experienced in her attempts at integrating her research into the discourse of the time:

> [Unlike much of the existing research about men and poor families,] the pathology Stack and others emphasized lay not within the family [and men], but within racism and unemployment and a welfare system that made stable monogamous relationships between [men and women] difficult to sustain. Nor did "The Flats" [Carol's ethnographic research site] suffer from the absence of fathers—fathers were integrated within the kin networks, albeit *hidden from conventional research* when they

were not playing the "traditional" role of breadwinner or household head. By writing about gender relations from a female perspective, Stack complicated the [prevailing discourse] of wandering unemployed men and lone welfare-dependent women that had usually been told *by* and *about* men. . . . [Male scholars,] however, incorporated *none* of Stack's insights into the analysis of men in extended families.

Some of the initial dismissal of Carol's work went even further than O'Connor's account. Carol recalls, for example, that shortly after the publication of *All Our Kin*, she gave a talk on strategies for survival among low-income families residing in The Flats. A well-known economist in the audience banged his hand on the conference table after her talk, saying, "The trouble with ethnography is that it takes too long to find quick policy solutions, and I would add [that it is also] wrong-headed."

Nearly two decades later, Linda fared no better than Carol in using her longitudinal ethnographic research to put the labor of boys and men front and center in the discourse on poverty and families. By this time, the discourse had taken a slightly different slant, largely because of Wilson's (1987) *The Truly Disadvantaged*. The lens shifted dramatically toward neighborhood effects, violence, drugs, and gangs as producers of dysfunctional adolescent boys who were bound for lives in the criminal justice system. Ethnographies such as Sullivan's (1989) *Getting Paid: Youth Crime and Work in the Inner City*, Anderson's (1990) *Streetwise*, MacLeod's (1995) *Ain't No Making It*, Bourgois's (2003) *In Search of Respect: Selling Crack in El Barrio*, Venkatesh's (2008) *Gang Leader for a Day*, Bergmann's (2008) *Getting Ghost: Two Young Lives and the Struggle for the Soul of an American City*, and Harding's (2010) *Living the Drama: Community, Conflict, and Culture among Inner-City Boys* dominated the academic and public policy literature and airwaves. Linda vividly recalls the reaction of one senior White male academic when she presented her work on the labor of adolescent boys in families at a conference. He publicly scolded her:

> You have no idea what you are talking about. You are a Black woman studying Black boys in dangerous neighborhoods. There is no way you can gather the kind of data you present. What self-respecting man would tell you about changing diapers when he is a gangbanger? You need to stick with talking about women and that kinscripts stuff. That's something you probably know about. And, you only have subtle

intelligence so let the men handle the hard work. By the way, you will never get tenure if you start trying to convince people you know something about Black men. They will say you are biased and too emotionally invested to tell an accurate story.

Needless to say, Linda took this man aside and let him know that if he were ever going to garner an ounce of intelligent understanding about the lives of African American boys and men in families "in the 'hood," he should go into the field with her and see which one of them would come out unscathed and appropriately enlightened. She said: "Growing up in Compton, coupled with excellent graduate training, can provide one with fierce and accurate survival, observation, and analytic skills. Thus, as any good scientist should know, one should do his/her homework before making the clearly misinformed, ignorant, and disrespectful statements you made."

Unfortunately, this scholar's reactions to discussions of adolescent boys as kinworkers were fairly common among some public intellectuals during this time. It was more than difficult to engage these scholars and policy-makers in meaningful and contextually informed dialogues about young boys providing valuable family labor "in the 'hood." Such personas seemed inconceivable to many who could only conceptually and empirically configure these young men as readying themselves to become the next cohort to enter the criminal justice system.

The next phase of disruptions in Carol's and Linda's attempts to disseminate narratives about kinscripts and males appeared when scholars and policy-makers seriously turned their attention to the topic of fatherhood in the late 1990s. The major hiccup at that point, however, was that research on males' kinwork focused almost exclusively on how men participated financially, socially, and psychologically in families as *fathers* (see Booth and Crouter 1998). This narrow framing of men's family labor was encouraged by a national "call to arms" for research on responsible fathering and was reflected in (see Cabrera et al. 2000): (1) federal and private funding agencies redirecting their funding streams toward research on fathering (Federal Interagency Forum on Child and Family Statistics 1998); (2) rapid growth in the number of handbooks, anthologies, and special issues of scientific journals focused on fatherhood (Cabrera and Tamis-LeMonda 2002; Lamb 1987, 1997; Marsiglio 1995; Parke 1996); (3) the creation of several national research and information clearinghouses on fathering, such as the National Center on Men and Families at the University of Pennsylvania; (4) a notable rise in town hall meetings and activists' initiatives that championed responsible fatherhood, particularly among low-income men of color; and (5) the eventual launching of a specialty journal on the topic, aptly named *Fathering*.

Indeed, this flurry of attention and activities pushed scientific, political, and policy agendas on fatherhood forward at a rapid pace, but it did so almost to the exclusion of considering the other types of kinwork men and boys negotiated and performed in families (see, for example, Raley, Bianchi, and Wang 2012). We had observed in our ethnographic work that other forms of kinwork, such as providing care for younger siblings or ailing grandparents, were intricately connected to men's fathering roles. In fact, their kinwork as young boys and adolescents seemed to serve as "training grounds" for their future roles as biological and surrogate fathers. These data posed a dilemma for both of us. As we remained mindful of the focus of the times—which, by the way, also had a strong emphasis on "deadbeat dads"—it was not clear to us how we could present case studies of adolescent males' kinwork without once again engaging the politics of science that questioned whether poor adult men had the capacity to raise their children, especially if their sons were doing heavy lifting in their families that some deemed "a father's duty." We also knew from our work that the efforts of men were often minimized by women, who in much of the extant research were the primary informants about fathers' contributions to families, and who, in general, wanted much more from men than the U.S. economy and educational system could and would provide for them. So, again, we waited to launch our narratives on adolescent boys and kinscripts with these considerations in mind.

Fortunately, as the first two decades of the millennium have progressed, the field of study around kinscripts, poverty, and men and families is widening. The conservative, male-dominated points of view are at long last dissipating somewhat and new scholars are taking up the gauntlet of kinscripts and the labor of men in families. These scholars include, for example, Constance Dallas at the University of Illinois at Chicago (see Dallas and Kavanaugh 2010; Dallas et al., 2009; Dallas, Wilson, and Salgado 2000), and Kevin Roy at the University of Maryland, College Park (see Madhavan and Roy 2012; Marsiglio and Roy 2012; Roy 2004; Roy and Burton 2007; Roy, Messina, Smith, and Waters [forthcoming]; and Roy and Smith 2013). We are extending invitations to Constance and Kevin and others to join us for breakfast at Elmo's to discuss these issues. Perhaps the legacy of our work will indeed live on in the work of these trailblazers and others who find a theoretical home in the kinscripts perspective. We will continue to breakfast at Elmo's every Thursday and move forward in holding ourselves account-able for our work and in engaging with our younger colleagues who are clearly opening the door for us and others to proceed with this dialogue. It is such a good feeling when a plan comes together—even when it takes over thirty years. That's the magic of Elmo's!

Note

Writing and research for this chapter were supported by the National Science Foundation through grants SES-1061591 and SES-0703968.

References

Anderson, E. 1990. *Streetwise: Race, Class, and Change in an Urban Community.* Chicago: University of Chicago Press.

Asher, R. M., and G. A. Fine. 1991. "Fragile Ties: Shaping Research Relationships with Women Married to Alcoholics." In *Experiencing Field Work: Qualitative Research in the Social Sciences*, edited by W. Shaffir and R. Stebbins, 196–205. Newbury Park, CA: Sage.

Bergmann, L. 2008. *Getting Ghost: Two Young Lives and the Struggle for the Soul of an American City.* New York: New Press.

Booth, A., and A. C. Crouter, eds. 1998. *Men in Families: When Do They Get Involved? What Difference Does It Make?* Hillsdale, NJ: Erlbaum Associates.

Bourgois, P. 2003. *In Search of Respect: Selling Crack in El Barrio.* 2nd ed. New York: Cambridge University Press.

Burton, L. M. 1985. "Early and On-Time Grandmotherhood in Multigeneration Black Families." PhD diss., University of Southern California.

———. 1990. "Teenage Childbearing as an Alternative Life-course Strategy in Multigeneration Black Families." *Human Nature* 1 (2): 123–43.

———. 1991. "Caring for Children: Drug Shifts and Their Impact on Families." *American Enterprise* 2: 34–37.

———. 1997. "Ethnography and the Meaning of Adolescence in High-Risk Neighborhoods." *Ethos* 25 (2): 208–17.

———. 2007. "Childhood Adultification in Economically Disadvantaged Families: A Conceptual Model." *Family Relations* 56: 329–45.

Burton, L. M., R. Garrett-Peters, and S. C. Eaton. 2009. "More than Good Quotations: How Ethnography Informs Knowledge on Adolescent Development and Context." In *Handbook of Adolescent Psychology: Vol. 1*, 3rd ed., edited by R. M. Lerner and L. Steinberg, 55–92. Hoboken, NJ: Wiley.

Burton, L. M., and A. R. Snyder. 1998. "The Invisible Man Revisited: Comments on the Life Course, History, and Men's Roles in American Families." In *Men in Families*, edited by A. Booth and A. C. Crouter, 31–39. Hillsdale, NJ: Erlbaum Associates.

Cabrera, N. J., and C. S. Tamis-LeMonda, eds. 2002. *Handbook on Father Involvement: Multidisciplinary Perspectives.* Mahwah, NJ: Erlbaum Associates.

Cabrera, N. J., C. S. Tamis-LeMonda, R. H. Bradley, S. Hofferth, and M. E. Lamb. 2000. "Fatherhood in the Twenty-First Century." *Child Development* 71 (1): 127–36.

Dallas, C. M., and K. Kavanaugh. 2010. "Making Room for Daddy: Comparing Expectations of Unmarried, African American Adolescent Parents for Prenatal Father Involvement." In *What We Have Seen with Our Own Eyes: Social Work and Social Welfare Responses to African American Males*, edited by W. E. Johnson, 27–41. New York: Oxford University Press.

Dallas, C. M., K. Kavanaugh, B. Dancy, L. Cassata, and K. Norr. 2009. "Using Data from a Qualitative Study of Adolescent Fatherhood to Operationalize the Kinscripts Conceptual Framework." *Southern Online Journal of Nursing Research* 9 (1). snrs.org.

Dallas, C. M., T. Wilson, and V. Salgado. 2000. "Gender Differences in Teen Parents' Perceptions of Parental Responsibilities." *Public Health Nursing Journal* 17: 423–33. DOI: 10.1046/j.1525-1446.2000.00423.

Federal Interagency Forum on Child and Family Statistics. 1998. *Nurturing Fatherhood: Improving Data and Research on Male Fertility, Family Formation, and Fatherhood.* Washington, DC: Government Printing Office.

Goffman, E. 1959. *The Presentation of Self in Everyday Life.* New York: Doubleday.

Harding, D. J. 2010. *Living the Drama: Community, Conflict, and Culture among Inner-City Boys.* Chicago: University of Chicago Press.

Ladner, J. 1973. *Tomorrow's Tomorrow: The Black Woman.* Garden City, NY: Doubleday.

Lamb, M., ed. 1987. *The Father's Role: Applied Perspectives.* New York: Wiley.

———, ed. 1997. *The Role of the Father in Child Development.* 3rd ed. New York: Wiley.

MacLeod, J. 1995. *Ain't No Makin' It: Aspirations and Attainment in a Low-Income Neighborhood.* 2nd ed. Boulder, CO: Westview Press.

Madhavan, S., and K. Roy. 2012. "Securing Fatherhood through Kin Work: A Comparison of Black Low-Income Fathers and Families in South Africa and the U.S." *Journal of Family Issues* 33: 801–22.

Marsiglio, W., ed. 1995. *Fatherhood: Contemporary Theory, Research, and Social Policy.* Thousand Oaks, CA: Sage.

Marsiglio, W., and K. Roy. 2012. *Nurturing Dads: Social Initiatives for Contemporary Fatherhood.* ASA Rose Series. New York: Russell Sage Foundation.

Naples, N. 2003. *Feminism and Method: Ethnography, Discourse Analysis, and Activist Research*. New York: Routledge.

O'Connor, A. 2001. *Poverty Knowledge: Social Science, Social Policy, and the Poor in the Twentieth-Century U.S. History*. Princeton, NJ: Princeton University Press.

Parke, R. 1996. *Fatherhood*. Cambridge, MA: Harvard University Press.

Raley, S., S. M. Bianchi, and W. Wang. 2012. "When Do Fathers Care? Mothers' Economic Contribution and Fathers' Involvement in Child Care." *Journal of Sociology* 117 (5): 1422–59.

Roy, K. 2004. "Three-Block Fathers: Spatial Perceptions and Kin-Work in Low-Income Neighborhoods." *Social Problems* 51: 528–48.

Roy, K., and L. M. Burton. 2007. "Mothering through Recruitment: Kinscription of Non-Residential Fathers and Father Figures in Low-Income Families." *Family Relations* 56: 24–39.

Roy, K., L. Messina, L., J. Smith, and D. Waters. Forthcoming. "Growing Up as Man-of-the-House: Adultification and Transition to Adulthood for Young Men in Economically-Disadvantaged Households." *New Directions for Child and Adolescent Development*.

Roy, K., and J. Smith. 2013. "Nonresident Fathers and Intergenerational Parenting in Kin Networks." In *Handbook of Father Involvement: Multidisciplinary Perspectives*, 2nd ed., edited by N. Cabrera and C. Tamis-LeMonda, 320–38. New York: Routledge.

Stack, C. B. 1974. *All Our Kin: Strategies for Survival in a Black Community*. New York: Harper and Row.

———. 1996. *Call to Home: African Americans Reclaim the Rural South*. New York: Basic Books.

———. 2001. "Coming of Age in Oakland." In *The New Poverty Studies: The Ethnography of Power, Politics, and Impoverished People in the United States*, edited by J. Goode and J. Maskovsky, 23–42. New York: New York University Press.

Stack, C. B., and L. M. Burton. 1993. "Kinscripts." *Journal of Comparative Family Studies* 24: 157–70.

Sullivan, M. L. 1989. *Getting Paid: Youth Crime and Work in the Inner City*. Ithaca, NY: Cornell University Press.

Venkatesh, S. 2008. *Gang Leader for a Day*. New York: Penguin.

Weiss, R. S. 1979. "Growing Up a Little Faster: The Experience of Growing Up in a Single-Parent Household." *Journal of Social Issues* 35: 97–111.

Wilson, W. J. 1987. *The Truly Disadvantaged: The Inner City, the Underclass, and Public Policy*. Chicago: University of Chicago Press.

PART III

Reflections on Disruptions
Time and Craft

The essays in this last section cover a range of topics, centered on the theme of reflections and reexaminations. In some cases these reflections and reexaminations are occasioned by particular disruptive events experienced by an author: this is the case for Abel, Nelson, and Hertz. But in other cases, these reflections and reexaminations emerge as part of the process of writing an essay for this book: this is the case for Gerstel, DeVault, and Lareau.

Emily Abel, a historian, is less interested in the issue of "slowness" (she writes that what sociologists find slow, historians consider fast) than she is with how a disruption in her own life became the occasion for reconsidering, and rewriting. She notes that the experiences of her parents' illnesses and deaths and her own six months of grueling treatments for breast cancer were occasions for understanding the complexities of caregiving as both the provider and the recipient of care. But Abel goes beyond that observation to explain how her "brief foray into the world of religion" led to a transformation of her understanding of the role of religion in the lives of caregivers in the nineteenth century while her experiences with social support helped her understand how social networks could be of great significance to those caregivers, enabling them to make better sense of suffering.

Margaret Nelson's chapter is a reflection on method—a reflection occasioned not by a personal event (or privately experienced disruption), but rather by the serendipitous reinterviewing of a woman after an interval of fifteen years. Nelson focuses on differences in the accounts this woman gave during the two interviews—differences she attributes to attempts to conceal unpleasant issues. But even as Nelson acknowledges these differences, and acknowledges as well errors in her own research techniques, she emerges with a renewed confidence in hearing and understanding the stories she is told.

Rosanna Hertz describes both a life and a scholarly interpretation disrupted by the arrival on her doorstep (complete with backpack, duffel, and plans to stay for a year) of the son of one of her closest informants from the kibbutz in Israel she had studied over twenty years before. Whereas Nelson takes a disruption as the opportunity to reflect on issues of methodology, Hertz uses *her* disruption to reflect on the relationships entered into during the process of fieldwork; this process of reflection leads to a reengagement with her key research findings. More explicitly than others with long-term involvements with informants, Hertz (like Hansen) asks what scholars owe the people they study. She also, reflexively, turns back to herself and her knowledge as she asks what we learn about "ourselves when we look through their eyes" and what we "learn about our culture refracted through their experience."

In the title of her chapter, "Rethinking Families: A Slow Journey," **Naomi Gerstel** not only harkens back to the very first chapter (Black), but she also raises the issue of changing understandings that was at the heart of so many of the essays in the previous section. As Gerstel looks back over her own research trajectory (like Hunter) she notices both continuities and shifts in the analytic frameworks on which she can draw and the research strategies available to her. She also considers an issue raised by others that is central to this section as she muses about how her own life trajectory caused disruptions in, and led to a different understanding of, the research she was conducting. Finally, Gerstel writes about collaboration as a process through which scholars can learn from others and have company on a "slow journey," an issue of central importance in the essay by Burton and Stack.

Words are central to our craft as social scientists. Each of the three sections of **Marjorie DeVault**'s essay deals with the issue of words as they reflect on an aspect of her lifelong love of language. Like Gerstel, DeVault reflects on a career rather than a single piece of scholarship. In the first section, DeVault discusses the complex decisions she made about words as she wrote her book and titled it *Feeding the Family*. A second section is oriented more toward issues of methodology as she writes about her fascination with conversation analysis and the lessons she carries with her as she seeks to make sense of interviews collected in a range of projects. The last section focuses even more closely on issues of understanding as DeVault describes working with people who are culturally Deaf as they interact with health-care providers. Her own account of being misunderstood when she reported on this research in Taiwan offers one of those rich ironies that are the hidden treasures of the collection.

Annette Lareau's account of the issues that emerged as she wrote *Unequal Childhoods* also reiterates themes addressed in many other essays. She acknowledges the complexities of the relationships involved in long-term ethnography as well as relationships with others involved in the research process, including but not limited to her research assistants. She describes the disruptions of "real life" as she cares for a friend who is ill and experiences the demands (and gifts) of a new partner and the children he brings into their marriage. She evokes the difficulties of finding one's way through data, even for a seasoned researcher writing her second book. Finally, she notes the speedup in the academy that makes it ever more difficult to engage in "high-quality" scholarship, an issue that brings us back to our Introduction. We have now come full circle.

11

History on a Slow Track

Emily K. Abel

What is slow to a sociologist is fast to a historian. Like qualitative sociologists, historians weave together in-depth analyses of material from disparate sources to compose a coherent narrative. Historical research also takes a long time. Especially before thousands of documents became available on the Internet, most of us traveled to distant archives and worked in them for weeks, months, and occasionally years. I thus assumed that my book *Hearts of Wisdom: A History of American Women Caring for Kin, 1850–1940* might well consume a decade. The topic was vast, compelling me not only to trace changes across ninety years but also to discuss women in diverse social positions, with very different relationships to the care recipients. Although caregiving today is concentrated on the elderly population, nineteenth- and early-twentieth-century women cared for people of all ages. I needed to examine large numbers of reports of charity workers, public health nurses, and government officials; the personal diaries and letters of a broad array of women; and slave narratives.

What I could not anticipate was that a set of personal experiences also would lengthen the process. Shortly after I began the project, my mother was diagnosed with lymphoma and turned to her five children for emotional, practical, and occasional nursing assistance during the five months she battled the disease. Her death left me and my siblings responsible for my father, who had suffered from a series of disabling strokes for over a decade. He experienced a number of major medical crises until his death six years later. Because I lived in California and my parents in New York, their care frequently involved cross-country trips. In addition, a year after my mother died, I was diagnosed with breast cancer and lost another six months to its grueling treatment. But if those events interrupted my project, they also enriched it. In the introduction to the book, I wrote that as both a provider and a receiver of care, I had seen firsthand how caregiving can reignite family conflicts, impose financial stress, and encroach on both work and leisure. But I also had gained a deeper appreciation of caregiving as a profound human experience.

Looking back, I realize that other aspects of my experience affected my project more profoundly. The first was a brief foray into the world of religion. When cancer struck, I had just finished writing a chapter about nineteenth-century women's care. It would have been impossible to miss the spiritual component of caregiving during that period, especially when sickness led to death. As Drew Gilpin Faust (2008) eloquently has explained, the nineteenth-century ideal of the "Good Death" can be traced to fourteenth-century Catholic manuals. In 1651, the Anglican bishop Jeremy Taylor published his enormously influential book *The Rule and Exercise of Holy Dying*, which both drew on and revised those texts for a Protestant audience. By the early nineteenth century, Taylor's notion of the Good Death had spread widely through American society, reaching people of various social and religious backgrounds. The basic elements were consciousness and lucidity, resignation to God's will, and fortitude in the face of physical pain and emotional suffering. Caregivers thus had to ensure that dying people were adequately penitent, "sensible" of their sins, and prepared to face death with equanimity. The role of caregivers was especially critical at the moment of death, when they were expected to discern the state of the soul and the prospect of everlasting life.

Family and friends occasionally detected signs of eternal damnation. Mary Ann Owen Sims, an Arkansas woman, could "never forget" the terror she experienced at the "death seane" of her uncle in 1843. "For he was a wicked man and oh the agonies of a lost soul usher[e]d in to the presence of its Maker was truly heart rend[e]ring even to my youthful minde" (1976, 150). Fortunately, such incidents were relatively rare. Although Mary Ann Sims's husband endured "sevier" suffering, his behavior conformed to the cultural code. He exhibited "Christian fortidude and resignation knowing that he who governed the universe had done all things well," and "not a murmer escaped his lips" (176). Sarah Connell Ayer's journal entry for July 10, 1827 read: "Mrs. Carpenter died. We have reason to hope that she has exchang'd this world for a better. She suffered much pain during the last two, or three weeks of her life, but appear'd calm and resign'd to the will of her Saviour, and gave cheering evidence of her preparation to meet death" (1910, 274). Mary E. Sears described her sister's death this way:

> Eliza was unconscious to apperance much of the time, but always recognized the voice of her *dear James* [her husband], and to his questions to her readiness to go home to Jesus, she would reply in monosyllables, of ready "happy, yes, yes, happy" was Jesus calling for her? "yes, calling, calling," when a heavenly smile would light her countenance: ah! What a sweet consolation to the stricken friends to hear from her own lips the words, "ready, willing"! . . . About *four o clock* P. M. she seemed to arouse somewhat. And calling for each of us by name bade us *farewell* and *kissed* us then was soon lost. . . . God had indeed called her; and in mercy had granted her consciousness enough to recognize us for the last time on earth; for this we will praise Him, for twas indeed a consolation to hear her once more call our names so sweetly and smile so gently "don't weep for me don't weep." (1970, 228)

But if I could not avoid knowing intellectually that religion had a major place in nineteenth-century caregiving experiences, I could not understand it experientially. Thus, I tended to agree with historians who argued that accounts of peaceful deaths bore little relation to reality. Lawrence Stone (1978), for example, asks rhetorically, "How many were so physically ravaged by pain and by disease that they were either beyond caring or a foul-smelling embarrassment to the onlookers?" Although the linguistic turn in scholarship might have encouraged me to try to understand the cultural values that shaped contemporary accounts rather than to discern the truth about how people actually experienced death and dying, I assumed most descriptions of death had little meaning.

I also misinterpreted the spiritual work in which nineteenth-century caregivers engaged after death occurred. A vast "consolation" literature arose in the nineteenth century. Many authors were ministers, but others were women who wrote primarily for other women and typically focused on the death of children. Both groups urged the bereaved to accept the death as the will of God and express gratitude that the patient was now free of suffering. In addition, survivors were told to find comfort in knowing that they could look forward to ultimate reunions in heaven.[1]

In private letters and journals, many survivors couched their chronicles of family deaths in conventional religious rhetoric. "God has again called my only son," wrote Mary Adams to her mother in April 1863, "and now our little Frankie sings with his angel brother the new song of redemption." After recounting the events that occurred during the terrible days preceding his death, she described the final evening. Mary "took him on a pillow on my lap and held him till he breathed his last mortal breath. . . . In all his life he never went to sleep easier or waked up happier. I was so glad the Savior so gently took him." She urged, "Do not grieve for me, Mother. I am quite well." Reading that letter, I assumed that the language was simply formulaic. Only the wail at the end sounded genuine: "Oh, how can I live without him?"[2]

After many months of illness, I no longer dismissed all spiritual expressions as inauthentic. Having grown up in a Reform Jewish household in the 1950s, I had not immediately assumed that religion might have something to offer when I received a cancer diagnosis. My own experience seemed to support the theory of the secularization of society, which argues that confidence in scientific theory gradually eclipses faith in religious authority. I was quite confident that neither of my parents had even remotely considered consulting a rabbi as the end approached. Judaism, after all, was what my father had most wanted to flee when he left his immigrant parents' home to seek higher education. The headache that descended whenever he could not avoid a family bar mitzvah was our only indication that Judaism still had some hold over him. Although my parents enrolled me in a Reform Jewish Sunday school, they also encouraged me not to take it too seriously—and, indeed, it offered little of real substance or meaning. The few relatives who still kept kosher seemed like throwbacks to an earlier, unenlightened era. Now that a life-threatening illness had greatly intensified my sense of vulnerability, it seemed especially imperative to place my faith in the certainty of science and endow my physician with almost miraculous powers.

But immersion in sickness also compelled me to confront a new set of issues. I had always assumed that a job at a major research university meant that no significant intellectual current could pass by me by. Suddenly I could not think of any way contemporary academic theory could help. While scientific medicine tried to fix my body, perhaps religion would enable me to participate in different conversations and thus make some sense of my terrifying experience.

What I then undertook was far too tentative and disorganized to deserve the name "spiritual quest." I read the books a friend who was a Unitarian minister recommended, participated in meetings of a group of women from diverse faiths seeking to integrate feminism and religious doctrine, attended a few evening classes conducted by a somewhat offbeat rabbi, and even flirted (for a day or two) with the idea of joining a congregation. Two close friends and I then organized a Torah study group and held occasional Shabbat dinners together.

Although all those activities gradually dwindled away, I gained some understanding of what religion could offer people confronting serious illness and death, either as patients or as family members. When I returned to my manuscript after my cancer treatment ended, I ripped up what I had written about the nineteenth century and began again. I now saw that many women understood their care experiences within the framework of religion, even as they struggled against it. To be sure, many bereaved relatives often acknowledged that intense grief retarded efforts to fulfill pious expectations. Fannie Tenney described her response to her husband's death this way: "I could not look away from earth to heaven as I want to. It all seemed so terrible to me. I do say 'God's will be done.' But I cannot look up as I want to" (quoted in Hampsten 1982, 141). And in a few instances, religion deepened rather than attenuated despair. Some bereaved parents berated themselves for having become too attached to their children. Others feared that the intensity of grief revealed the insufficiency of faith. "This shadow of death should not rest upon our spirits if we *truly believed*," Mary Wilder Foote confided to her sister. "The bursting life around me should remind me of immortality instead of calling up sorrowing thoughts of the precious bud." (Foote and Foote 1918, 95).

Nevertheless, women also testified to the support religious teachings provided. Although Fannie Tenney failed to "look up" as much as she wished, she emphasized that "there is no other for me to go to but to God. If I did not know that there is help in him I should despair" (quoted in Hampsten 1982, 141). After blaming herself for having loved her daughter "too well," a Georgia woman continued, "The thought of being reunited with our darling is indeed a blessed, comforting one it weakens the pang of present separation" (Lines 1982, 207). As novelist Catharine M. Sedgwick wrote to a sister whose oldest son had died, "The Holy Spirit is your comforter, and let us acknowledge the ineffable consolation with which he has softened your calamity" (1871, 110). If religion could not entirely stifle unbearable emotions, it could "weaken" or "soften" them, thus enabling the bereaved to gain at least a modicum of critical distance.[3]

Participation in a support group gave me a window on a different feature of nineteenth-century caregiving. The very idea of joining such a group initially had been anathema. If the other members were close to death, they would be intimations of my own mortality. And some undoubtedly would have the wrong politics or lack the extensive education I considered prerequisite to the acquisition of wisdom. But when a rabbi said that he considered sharing one's life with others to be a spiritual act, I thought I could try at least one meeting. And then, on that first night, I found myself saying that my new awareness of life's contingency had made me hesitate to return to a long project; perhaps I should just write a series of articles. The next speaker was a woodworker who said he understood; he had been able to undertake only small projects since his diagnosis. Others then described the ways a heightened sense of uncertainty had transformed their lives. Suddenly, I realized, these are my people.

I previously had written about nineteenth-century obligations of neighborliness primarily as burdens. Because mutual aid was often a requirement of participating in social life as well as a form of insurance, sickness among members of a broad community pulled women away from their homes, often for extended periods. Housework accumulated and children were left alone. Caregiving also reopened wounds. Women who had endured intense physical pain during childbirth had to tend other women laboring in agony. During epidemics, mothers nursed neighbors' children through the same illnesses that had struck their own offspring.

My support group experience suggested that if caring for a large social network forced women to reexperience losses, it also helped them make sense of suffering. The widely distributed consolation literature encouraged women to transcend suffering by reaching out to others. According to the biographer Joan D. Hedrick (1994), Harriet Beecher Stowe offers one example. When her fifteen-month-old son Charley died of cholera in 1849, Stowe turned for support to her friend Mrs. Allen, who had sustained a similar loss. After giving birth to another baby, she asked, "How is it with you in your heart of hearts when you think of the past—I often wonder how your feelings correspond with mine" (199). Three years after suffering a second crushing blow—the drowning death of another son—Stowe sent a letter to a friend who had just lost a daughter. "Ah Susie," she wrote, "I who have walked in this dark valley for now three years, what can I say to you who are entering it? . . . I know all the strange ways in which this anguish will reveal itself—the prick, the thrust, the stab, the wearing pain, the poison that is mingled with ever bright remembrance of the past—I have felt them all—and all I can say is that, though 'faint,' I am 'pursuing,' although the crown of thorns secretly pressed to one's heart never ceases to pain" (278–82). Hedrick notes that Stowe's novels depicted "an informal 'priesthood' of women who have suffered" (316). Once again I had to revise a large section of my work.

Barbara Ehrenreich (2002), one of the most trenchant critics of today's relentlessly upbeat breast cancer culture, reminds us that the costs inflicted by the disease far outweigh whatever benefits it confers. In her view, the possibility of personal transformation has been greatly exaggerated. But if breast cancer does not lead automatically to spiritual renewal and new forms of human connectedness, it can enhance our understanding of the experiences of the many groups in the past who lived in extremely close proximity to serious illness and death. For that, a historian must be grateful.

Notes

1. See Douglas (1977) 1988; Halttunen 1982; Landerman 1996, 60–61; and Simonds and Rothman 1992.
2. Mary Ann Weber to her mother, June 11, 1871, Parker Family Letters, in the possession of Marianne Parker Brown, Santa Monica, California.
3. I also discuss these issues in my book *The Inevitable Hour: A History of Caring for Dying Patients* (Baltimore: Johns Hopkins University Press, 2013).

References

Abel, E. K. 2000. *Hearts of Wisdom: American Women Caring for Kin, 1850–1940.* Cambridge, MA: Harvard University Press.

Ayer, S. C. 1910. *Diary of Sarah Connell Ayer.* Portland, ME: Legavor-Tower.

Douglas, A. (1977) 1988. *The Feminization of American Culture.* New York: Anchor Press/Doubleday.

Ehrenreich, B. 2002. "Welcome to Cancerland." In *The Best American Essays, 2002,* edited by S. J. Gould, 66–87. Boston: Houghton Mifflin.

Faust, D. G. 2008. *This Republic of Suffering: Death and the American Civil War.* New York: Knopf.

Foote, C., and M. W. Foote. 1918. *Caleb and Mary Wilder Foote: Reminiscences and Letters,* edited by M. W. Tileston. Boston: Houghton Mifflin.

Halttunen, K. 1982. *Confidence Men and Painted Women: A Study of Middle-Class Culture in America, 1830–1870.* New Haven, CT: Yale University Press.

Hampsten, E., ed. 1982. *Read This Only to Yourself: The Private Writings of Midwestern Women, 1880–1910.* Bloomington: Indiana University Press.

Hedrick, J. D. 1994. *Harriet Beecher Stowe: A Life.* New York: Oxford University Press, 1994.

Landerman, G. 1996. *The Sacred Remains: American Attitudes toward Death, 1799–1883.* New Haven, CT: Yale University Press, 1996.

Lines, A. A. 1982. *To Raise Myself a Little: The Diaries and Letters of Jennie, a Georgia Teacher, 1851–1886,* edited by T. Dyer. Athens: University of Georgia Press, 1982.

Sears, M. E. 1970. "A Young Woman in the Midwest: The Journal of Mary Sears, 1859–1860." *Ohio History* 82 (3–4): 215–34.

Sedgwick, C. M. 1871. *Life and Letters of Catharine M. Sedgwick,* edited by M. E. Dewey. New York: Harper and Brothers.

Simonds, W., and B. K. Rothman. 1992. *Centuries of Solace: Expressions of Maternal Grief in Popular Literature.* Philadelphia: Temple University Press.

Sims, M. A. O. 1976. "Private Journal of Mary Ann Owen Sims," part 1, edited by C. D. Whitman. *Arkansas Historical Quarterly* 35 (4): 142–87.

Stone, L. 1978. "Death in New England." *New York Review of Books* 25 (16). *www.nybooks.com.*

12

A Serendipitous Lesson

Or, How What We Do Shapes What We Know

Margaret K. Nelson

I have always been an "in and out" qualitative sociologist, by which I mean I go "into" the "field," conduct my interviews, and then come "out" and analyze the material I've gathered. Rarely do I go back and interview someone more than once, and if I do, it is not because I am trying to overcome the hesitancy of a participant to reveal herself in a single interview (Seidman 1991), but because we didn't quite cover all the questions the first time around. In any case, because there is often a long gap between collecting data and transcribing, and an even longer gap between transcribing and analysis, by the time I have questions about just what the material means, it would be problematic to go back.[1]

And so I make do. I strive for the best interview possible with each respondent and I strive for a sufficient number of respondents to allow for analysis of themes across the range of relevant variables involved in the project. Cross-checking (or validation, if you will) derives from the number of individuals in a particular position who make particular claims, rather than from the assumption that any individual's words can serve as an accurate representation of the issue under investigation. So, for example, when most of the middle-class respondents respond differently from the working-class respondents about an issue such as the domestic division of labor, I assume that I have captured, if not a class difference in what people actually believe, feel, or do when the door closes behind me, a class difference in attitudes about what they want me to believe about them when that door closes. And if, on occasion as I write up my findings, I slip from arguing the latter (that I have found class differences in what people want me to believe about them) to the former (that I have found class differences in what people actually feel, believe, and do), I'm probably not alone in that.

I also, quite happily, have relied on research assistants to conduct interviews for me as researchers sometimes do to get around differences between myself and my respondents in race/ethnicity (Lee 2002) and social class. Equally often, I have relied on assistants simply to cover a broader geographical area (Nelson 2010) or, even more simply, to get the work done more quickly. And although research assistants have sometimes ignored my concerns, I have also found that their concerns, which may be quite different from my own, lead them to follow pathways I might not have pursued. To take just one example, many years ago when I was collecting oral histories from women who had taught in one-room schoolhouses, I hired research assistants who were themselves teachers. They were interested in finding out about how the women had handled discipline, a topic that I thought would be of no interest to me. As I listened to their interviews and read their transcripts, however, I realized that fear and isolation lay at the heart of an experience I was approaching from an entirely different set of concepts, and I made these new ideas the centerpiece of an analysis (Nelson 1988).

Of course, I've read the many critiques of interviewing as a method, as well as of my particular approach to this practice. In fact, because I am in a joint sociology/anthropology department, I hear such comments almost daily from the anthropologists who go "into the field" and stay there over an extended period of time and, in the case of several of my colleagues, return again and again to fine-tune their understanding. Indeed, for decades now, the methods of social science have been subject to critiques from a broad range of commentators who argue that these methods are contaminated at every stage, from the formulation of a research project, through the collection of what passes for data, to analysis, interpretation, and even publication.[2]

With reference to data collection, scholars have been especially concerned with the power differentials of interviewing and the relevance of the identity and position of the researcher (Oakley 1981; Smith 1987; Mishler 1986). Some of the more recent scholarship on data collection methodology continues these discussions of what happens in the interview itself. For example, Ezzy (2010, 164) focuses on being attentive to the relationship that emerges in the interview: "It is the emotional structure of the relationship, as much as a well thought out cognitively articulated approach to questions, that underlines good interviewing practice." Tanggaard (2007, 172) goes perhaps one step further when she notes that "interviewing is not a mere technique of data collection but a methodology involving some analysis in the very process of collecting the material" (see also Parker 2005).

Even more relevant to the issues I will discuss below are debates about what we can infer about what has happened from the information we obtain in an interview. Polkinghorne (2007, 479), citing Spence (1982), suggests that we never get at "historical" truth and that the best we can hope for (and what we might, in fact, seek) is a kind of "narrative" truth: "Storied texts serve as evidence for personal meaning, not for the actual occurrence of the events reported in the stories." But what does that mean in terms of our use of those stories? Can we embrace them fully? Or, conversely, do we have to discount them wholesale? Lieblich, Tuval-Mashiach, and Zilber (1998, 8) suggest a kind of middle-ground approach to making sense of texts garnered from interviews: "We do not advocate total relativism that treats all narratives as texts of fiction. On the other hand, we do not take narratives at face value, as complete and accurate representations of reality. We believe that stories are usually constructed around a core of facts or life events, yet allow a wide periphery for freedom of individuality and creativity in selection, addition to, emphasis on, and interpretation of these 'remembered' facts."

A recent, serendipitous series of events offered me the opportunity to evaluate the nature of the data I obtained by comparing interviews conducted at two points in time. Unlike the example of Josselson (2009), who had purposely asked a single woman to tell her story at repeated intervals over thirty-five years, or Black (this volume) and Romero (this volume), who followed the same respondents for many years, I happened on two interviews conducted with a single woman, asked to tell her story two times to two different interviewers with a fifteen-year hiatus between those two events. Even though these two interviews, taken together, offer evidence of concealment, revision, and outright contradictions, what I learned from this example is that changes in the storyline emerged because each representation could only reflect who that woman understood herself to be and how she chose to portray herself in relation to a specific interviewer asking a specific set of questions at a specific moment in time. Curiously, perhaps, as I consider these findings, I walk away with more rather than less confidence in the viability of the data I obtain from the practices in which I normally engage.

The Role of Serendipity

In 2011, Karen V. Hansen asked if I would help organize a session having to do with "slow sociology" for an upcoming conference. I said yes, and for some reason—probably pure chutzpah—I said I would also like to present a paper at the session. As the conference approached, I found myself tossing and turning in bed one night, full of anxiety about what in the world I was going to do. Sometime close to morning I woke up from a delightful dream: in it, I had previously written a paper that would fit this session to a "T," and since it had been presented only once at a very informal student conference, I could in all fairness to the discipline present it again. I jumped out of bed with enormous relief and enthusiasm, ready to locate the paper (whose name had curiously escaped me) among the many files on my computer, only to realize (to my great chagrin, and amusement, too) that, of course, there was no such paper—that it was all just a dream.

But here's the lucky part. The paper in the dream was about having interviewed someone more than once and about what multiple interviews could tell us about interviewing and about the validity of the responses our respondents give at any moment in time. And it turns out that there is one such person in my (very real) files, the result of my having remained in the same place for over thirty-five years and having mined that place for interview subjects on a range of different issues. A woman I will call "Joanna Darling" was captured in my research net three times.[3] I interviewed Joanna in her role as an unlicensed family day care provider in the mid-1980s (Nelson 1990); my research assistant had interviewed her again in 1996 for my research on single motherhood (Nelson 2005); and I had interviewed her once more in October 2011 for my current project on "making kin." Unfortunately, I have no records from my first interview and therefore won't be able to discuss that one; I draw only on the next two.

If there has been some bad luck along the way (in my losing utterly the transcripts from the mid-1980s), there has also been some good luck (or another piece of serendipity, if you will). A few days before my dream (and the occasion that in all likelihood gave rise to the dream itself), I had been cleaning the locked storage in my office and I had (at long last) done what should have been done years before and destroyed the dusty tape recordings from the 1990s. As I held in my hand a recording from a woman whom I had referred to in my writing as "Joanna Darling," I realized that she was in fact the very same woman I had interviewed just a few months before. I had not remembered during the 2011 interview that she had been interviewed in 1996. Had I done so and read the 1996 transcript *before* the 2011 interview, this chapter would be entirely different.

Joanna Darling and Me

Because it might help make sense of the methodological (and substantive) lessons learned from comparing the two interviews, I want to say a brief bit about Joanna Darling herself and a bit about my relationship with her.[4] Joanna is a White woman, born sometime in the mid-1940s, who has lived most of her adult life in Vermont. For approximately thirty-five years (from about her twenties through a substantial part of her fifties), she was a family day care provider; most recently she has been running a program that serves women who have recently been released from incarceration.

Joanna has been married twice and has five biological children. One child was born into the first marriage; no children were born into the second marriage, which was brief and occurred when her youngest child was about six. Each of the five children has a different father—although, as will be discussed further below, at least one of these fathers has taken a great interest in, and provided parental care for, some of the children who are not his own. Table 1 provides information about the ages and living situations of Joanna's children in 1996 (at the time of the first interview I discuss below) and (where known) fifteen years later (at the time of the most recent interview). Joanna now also counts as one of her children Verawati, an Indonesian girl by birth, who came to her through a program that everyone I have interviewed calls "Indo-Kids." No longer in existence, in the 1990s Indo-Kids provided the opportunity for Indonesian children whose parents worked for a mining company to come to the United States and learn English while attending a private high school in Vermont.[5] In 1996, Verawati and her brother Irwan were living in a home with about eight other children from the program; apparently, both children were quite unhappy there.

TABLE 1: Joanna Darling's Household at Two Points in Time

	1996		2011	
	Age	**Living arrangement**	**Age**	**Living arrangement**
Noah	20+	Not living in Joanna's home	35+	Living somewhere in Vermont
Ben	19	Hadn't quite left Joanna's home but not there much	34	Living in Coolidge County, Vermont
Natasha	17	Before summer: lived with Keith (Celeste's father) During summer: lived in Joanna's home After summer: moved to her own father's home, near Rochester	32	Living in Coolidge County, Vermont
Celeste	13	Living in Joanna's home	28	Living in Coolidge County, Vermont
Clarissa	4	Living in Joanna's home	19	Away at college
Verawati	14	Living in Joanna's home	29	Living in Dubai

In that same year, my research assistant independently, through her own networks, identified Joanna as a single woman who was appropriate for the research I was conducting at that time on how single mothers accumulated the necessary resources for daily living. During that interview, the research assistant followed my interview guide, which asked about engagement in the formal and informal economy, reliance on state programs, household composition, and internal family dynamics.

Fifteen years later (in 2011), I interview Joanna for a study on how families "make kin" out of people to whom they are not related by blood, marriage, or adoption. One might say I am interested in "fictive kin" (Stack 1974) or "families we choose" (Weston 1991) or what has most recently been called "voluntary kin" (Braithwaite et al. 2010). Of all the research projects I have conducted, this has been the one in which I most rely on a storytelling and least on a structured or even semi-structured list of questions: I have started each interview by asking my respondents to "tell me the story" of their relationship with a particular individual. In the summer of 2011, as part of this new project, I had interviewed a woman who had had an Indonesian girl living with her through the Indo-Kids program. That woman gave me Joanna's contact information. Thinking back to the time I had known her in the 1980s (and *not* to the 1996 interview, which I associated with the pseudonym and not her real name), I sent an e-mail to Joanna: "It's been a long time since we've met, but my research interests seem to circle back to you periodically and it will be a pleasure to meet up again." She responded quickly: "Cycles are pretty prevalent in living, aren't they? Next week is very full. How about Monday, the 3rd around 4 or 5? Is that doable for you?" Monday the 3rd was indeed doable for me, and so we met again on a raw October afternoon in a café midway between our two homes.

Telling Stories

A close comparison of two interviews with the same individual, conducted by two different people for two very different reasons, leads to some very interesting lessons about the process through which we gather material for what we call qualitative sociology and the kind of "truth" we obtain from that material. The central lesson is the most obvious: that method and substance intertwine in curious ways, and ultimately it is in the ways that we practice our craft that we learn what we need to know. But there were other, more specific, lessons too—about concealment, revising history, and the validity of details.

Modest Concealment

The first of these more specific lessons is that you only get told the pieces of the story the interviewee wants to tell and not those pieces the interviewee wants to conceal (unless you ask specifically, which you cannot do if you don't know that concealment is an issue). While many have noted the power of the interviewer, we should also consider the ways in which the respondent holds power in her hands as well. Indeed, it would be a mistake to view the respondent as passive; it would also be a mistake to view the respondent as hesitating out of shyness or discomfort rather than from her own concerns about what she does—and does not—want to reveal about herself.

As I mentioned, when my research assistant interviewed Joanna in 1996, she did so because I was interested in Joanna's experiences as a single mother trying to make ends meet. At that time, Joanna was still raising several of her five children, and Verawati had been living with her for almost a year. When asked by my research assistant to list the members of her household, Joanna did so easily: "My three daughters [Natasha, Celeste, and Clarissa], and I have another daughter [Verawati], who is Indonesian." The interview protocol then asked her to describe each of the members of her household, and more specifically to say something about the relationships between each of her children and their (biological) fathers. Her response to this question as it concerned Natasha (her third child) seemed quite open:

> Natasha, my oldest [daughter], has had a very difficult relationship with her father. Mostly because he has been very negligent. . . . And she's struggled very hard to get into his life but he just has not been responsible or there for her. [Celeste is my fourth child and her father] Keith, however, has always fathered Natasha. . . . [Natasha is] actually going to go and live with her [own] father [near Rochester] for her senior year because she figures it's her last chance of creating a relationship with him. . . . Natasha lived with [Keith last year] and she was very difficult for a while. . . . We often got together as a unit [Keith, his wife, and me] to talk about what was going [on]. . . . It was really [*pause*] a hard year.

As this narrative makes clear, because she had lived with the father of her younger sister, Celeste, Natasha had not been in the household during the previous school year when Verawati first came to live with Joanna. Moreover, Natasha would not be living in the household the following school year either, because she was going to be trying to work things out with her own father. Indeed, although she was living at home during the summer, she was a "temporary" resident in the household, which had been reconfigured (to include Verawati) in her absence. All of this moving around was probably emotionally difficult for Joanna: it seems likely that Joanna and Natasha had been at loggerheads; Joanna had to resolve complex issues about Natasha with Keith and his current wife; and Joanna had to help Natasha negotiate a relationship with her biological father (and deal with him herself over the arrangements for Natasha to move there for her last year of high school). And these difficulties are acknowledged by Joanna ("It was really [*pause*] a hard year"). These difficulties are also part of the story Joanna tells because the interview is *focused* on and *asks specifically about* how she manages her relationships with her children, how the children relate to their fathers, and how the different people who have contributed to the household (as fathers, as friends) get along.

Fifteen years later, in 2011, when my interest is quite different, so is the story. Now I want to know how many children were living in the household when Verawati first came to stay (during the school year of 1995–1996, which was right before the 1996 interview). When asked how many of her biological children she had in her home that year, Joanna answers: "Four, four, wait a minute, no I think I had three at the time, I have an older son [Ben, and] I'm trying to remember if he was actually living there. I think he was at that age where he hadn't quite left, if he was there he wasn't there much of the time. So there were three." By "three," she means Clarissa, Celeste, and Natasha. Noah, the oldest, is long gone and doesn't enter her counting. Ben is the fourth ("four, wait a minute") but he was there so rarely that perhaps, she suggests, he doesn't count ("no I think I had three"). In fact, as will become clearer below, it is probably *Natasha* and not Ben who was not there and who doesn't count, although Joanna conceals that fact. But because we haven't discussed Natasha in *this* interview (and I hadn't yet reread the 1996 interview), I take this enumeration at face value.

Later in the same (2011) interview, I ask Joanna about how her older children responded to Verawati. Joanna again ignores Noah entirely but now she (re)introduces Natasha as she says this about her (Natasha's) attitudes: "Natasha was the next daughter and she, um, was busy with her life, she didn't focus a lot on Verawati, she liked her but she didn't focus on her." She then rushes on and describes the attitudes of Ben (her second child): "And Ben was, I think Ben was living at home, I think he was in and out a lot, so he would tease her, he treated her like he treated his other sisters." Curiously, then, Ben—even though he doesn't really count—is described more fully than Natasha, who Joanna suggested had been living at home. Joanna is not being deceptive. She's not telling the full story either (as the "um" indicates): "she, um, was busy with her life." But then, dunce that I am, I was not *asking* for the full story and I do not ask her the obvious question: Why was Natasha too busy with her own life to interact with a scared fourteen-year-old? Nor do I wonder why Joanna is telling me more about Ben (who is on his way out) than Natasha (who is younger and still, theoretically, at home).

And I don't know enough in 2011 (because Joanna has concealed the fact that Natasha was not there when Verawati first came to live in her home) to ask whether Natasha's absence was the reason why Joanna had room in her home—and in her heart—to take on another "daughter." However, I do ask

Joanna the related question of whether she had wanted an additional child to take in at that time, and she punts: "I wasn't particularly looking for a child. . . . Truthfully, I'm not sure why Maddie [who had an Indo-Kid living with her] called me." Had I read the earlier interview *before* this second one, I might have pushed here a bit more to uncover the ways in which Natasha's defection had relevance for Joanna's willingness to make room for another child; without that information, in 2011, I get an incomplete story.

In fact, in 2011 Joanna clearly does not want to raise the issue of how difficult Natasha had been as an adolescent. And because I don't ask, she does not have to raise it, even though Natasha's distance from her mother and sisters might have been relevant to what was happening on a daily basis when Verawati first came to live with Joanna. In fact, the household re-formed itself around the two remaining daughters and Verawati and thus, in a way, rejected Natasha: "[Verawati] just fit in and she loved us back with all of her heart, and she was—it ended up that my next daughter grew up, so in the end it was Verawati, Celeste, and Clarissa who was a baby, and the three of them were like, it was just a really wonderful household, and Verawati was like this golden nugget in the midst of it, this heart, this heart person." So I learned about the new household, but I had missed the opportunity to find out how the absence of Natasha was viewed by her sisters and her mother: Were they lonely? Feeling abandoned? Anxious to have someone fill the space Natasha used to occupy? I had also missed the opportunity to find out how Natasha felt about this newcomer who had "replaced" her while she lived in the household with Keith and his wife. None of the relevant questions were asked—or answered.

Rewriting History

If the first point is relatively straightforward—that our respondents will conceal uncomfortable truths—the second point is slightly more complex, with two related components. First, the interviews I collected from Joanna are sharp evidence that our respondents are no different from anyone else insofar as they will rewrite their own histories to tell the story that is most consistent with the person they want to present themselves as being at a given time. Second, the interviews are equally sharp evidence that who anyone wants to be (or wants to appear to be) will change over time. Joanna's interviews give two such examples of an altered story to support an altered self-conception.

The first example of revision has to do with names. When Joanna was initially interviewed in 1996, she referred to her Indonesian daughter as "Vera," which was what most people called the girl. It was, "Well, people help me get clothes together for Vera, my Indonesian girl." When I interviewed her fifteen years later in 2011, she was very explicit about calling the child (now a woman) she had come to consider her daughter by her full name as a practice of *both* the past and of the present: "Most people call her Vera but *I* called her Verawati because I felt she had to have culturally as much of a name as she possibly could, and I felt that was really important and I started to understand what happened to her culture, which is very typical like what happened to the American Indians." In 2011, she believes that she rescued Verawati, and she tells me that as part of that rescue she helped Verawati retain (and recover) her own past. Indeed, Joanna goes on at length about this issue not only in the quote above, but at several points during the interview.

The second example is even more telling. In the 1996 interview, when asked how Verawati has come to live with her, Joanna suggests that Verawati had simply been placed in Joanna's home because Joanna had expressed some interest in the Indo-Kids program and one of the children needed a home:

> And actually Maddie is the one who got me connected into it. And they, a year ago the woman who did the program asked—I belong to a group that [works with the homeless] . . . and we were having a [meeting] at Maddie's house, and this woman was there and she asked if anybody was interested [in Indo-Kids]. And I said, you know, "I'm interested." And then a year later Maddie calls up and says, this girl needs a place to live right now. [I say,] "Okay!" And within a few days she was in my house.

The next time she tells the story, in 2011, it is quite different in some, but not all, of the details. Maddie is still involved, but what is needed is a home for a boy, not a girl, and there are some intermediate steps that the first telling left out (including the fact that Irwan had substituted his sister for himself as the child in greatest need):

> Maddie called me one day, and told me that there was [an] older boy who needed a home . . . and, I, um, I said I would be happy to meet with [the boy whose name was Irwan] and he was like . . . sixteen or

seventeen at the time, I can't remember. A few days went by and she called me back and said Irwan said that he wants you to take his little sister, he's more worried about her, so I said, [that would be] okay. You know, I hadn't been attached to either one because I hadn't met them yet, and so I said I'll meet with her, and she happened to be going to the same school that my daughter was . . . and I went—

Unfortunately, I interrupt her here to ask a question (about how old the sister was) and she answers that Verawati was fourteen, about to turn fifteen. And then she continues describing that first meeting with Verawati. But this time—in 2011—the story is not just about a girl placed in Joanna's house ("Okay!"). Rather, in this story the girl clearly makes her own decision to be with Joanna. It is not just random chance that brings them together, but Verawati's having chosen Joanna after Joanna carefully explained what she had to offer:

> So I sit with Verawati outside on the hillside and she's this chubby little girl with Coke-bottle-glass glasses, and she cut her own hair, and she's a funny looking girl—she's absolutely gorgeous now—and I knew that she had a really hard time understanding English so I had some plus on my side because I could at least know that, and I sat with her and spoke as simply and as clearly as I could, and I kept checking with her, and I said to her right out, "I know you don't understand English, I'll explain anything I'll say to you," but it was as simple as I could, so I told her about my home, the children . . . I described to her that whole situation and we spoke for half an hour and I knew that she wasn't understanding a lot so first of all, she had my youngest, [the] four-year-old to interact with, that was helpful, she really liked little kids and that was obvious. So I just tried to give her as much reassurance as I could like just how I was. So I asked her, "Do you want to come live with me? Do you want me to come get you tomorrow?" She didn't blink an eye and she said, "Yes." There was no hesitation whatsoever.

Joanna wants, now, to see herself as having been selected for "how I was" and not as having been the casual recipient of a child in need.

In both of these stories—about what she called Verawati and about her first contact with Verawati—Joanna differs from one interview to the next. In 1996, she is casual about what she calls this child she has not yet claimed as her own; in 2011, she has fully embraced her, renamed her, and helped her reclaim her Indonesian identity. In 1996, a child was placed with her because she had a general concern about the children in the Indo-Kids program; in 2011, Verawati distinctly chose to live in her family. Each new presentation of self differs slightly from the one before. But each presentation is true to the present moment.

The Devil Is in the Details

A third lesson about the narrative truth of interviews is that details matter, but they may not always be precise, or matter in the way they seem to at a superficial level. In 1996, my research assistant (given the topic of how single mothers got by) quite appropriately asked Joanna how she acquired clothing for this new addition to her family. Joanna answered, "Well, people donate, help donate. A friend of mine . . . who is a chiropractor donated money to help me get some clothes together. People just gave me things. I asked around, 'You got a pair of winter boots?'"

One would think that these winter boots were simply Joanna's way of being precise—of focusing on the concrete material needs Verawati presented when she came to live with her and was about to face her first cold Vermont winter, and of showing that she could call on her community to help her out if needed. In the second interview, in 2011, I am again interested—albeit for a very different reason—in how Joanna got together the necessities of daily living for Verawati. And here as well, Joanna's response is equally precise; it is also quite different. She says, "If I wanted to give her clothes that was okay, *anything that she had in my home, I gave to her*, it was either what I had already, or—*I remember giving her my boots*—or my friends helped" (emphasis added). As was the case during the first interview, there is a specificity, and in fact this second time she interrupts herself to get to that specificity. But the content of that specificity changes from the first time to the next.

Perhaps the difference between the two narratives can be simply accounted for by faulty memory; perhaps Joanna no longer can remember a time when she didn't share her household possessions with the girl she had long since come to consider her own. But I think there is something more at stake. Consider that the first time Joanna was interviewed, when Verawati had been with her for less than a year, Joanna wasn't sure that she *alone* could (or would) be able to give Verawati the wherewithal to take sturdy footsteps out into the world—and she hoped others would help ("I asked around, 'You got a pair of winter boots?'"). However, fifteen years later, Joanna firmly believes she made a difference and in retrospect she insists that she alone had been fully capable of providing what Verawati needed to make her way in the world ("anything that she had in my home, I gave to her. . . . I remember giving her my boots"); at most, Joanna admitted, she needed but a little help from her friends to launch Verawati.[6]

As an alternative reading (one that is less psychological), we might think of how Joanna in 1996 was being asked about how she survives as a single mother. She was about forty-five and deeply embedded in a community that supported her in material and nonmaterial ways. And she was proud of the fact that this community was there to support her as she helped a child in need ("people donate, help donate"). In 2011, Joanna is at a very different place in her life, assessing her accomplishments as an individual and finding that while she has relied on others, she has relied just as much on herself. Not surprisingly, she now emphasizes this self-reliance ("I remember giving her *my* boots") while embedded in, but not entirely dependent on, a generous community.

Either way we want to interpret these details, it is clear that Joanna has changed over time. And it is not surprising that her story has changed too.

Discussion

I have outlined the three lessons about the narrative truth of interviews I learned through comparing two independent interviews with the same person. As noted, this situation is different from what Josselson (2009), Romero (this volume) and Black (this volume) describe because they are fully aware each time they interview one of their respondents of the earlier occasions of interaction. In my case, in 2011, I am an essentially naive interviewer (aside from the fact that I had some information about Joanna dating from the mid-1980s).

At one level, the lessons are not all that surprising: taken together, we learn that people conceal information they don't want to provide, that people rewrite history in order to present themselves in a way that fits a current self-image, and that people provide details that might be misleading (even if they accurately represent a deeper truth or truths). Of course, taken as a whole, these lessons cast doubt on any remaining notion any of us might hold about the objective notion of the "truth" interviews reveal.

They remind us that we should always be careful to "qualify" our conclusions because they stem from information that we know to be partial at best.

But do they mean that we have to take a fuzzy middle ground between relativism and accuracy? I think not. In fact, on reconsideration of what the two interviews with Joanna suggested, I might lean further toward "face value" in spite of the concealment, rewriting, and contradictory details. At the very least, I think that the lessons do *not* need to be taken so seriously as to undermine the more basic project (of gathering stories to be used as "data") in which we are engaged. Let's think, for a moment, about the issue of the boots—the one place where there is seemingly the most overt contradiction. Each time Joanna talked about the boots, some of what she said was the same. If the emphasis shifts from one moment to another, we can still rely on Joanna to tell us that that she draws on her social resources to manage her daily life and the challenge that life presents ("a friend of mine . . . donated money"; "friends helped"). But more importantly, each version is, in a sense, *profoundly true to the topic under consideration.* When I want to know (in 1996) whether Joanna has occasion to create a "social economy," she tells the research assistant that yes, she does. When I want to know whether (in 2011) she believes she has made a difference in Verawati's life and feels a sense of responsibility, she tells me again that yes, she does. Or, take the issue of names. It is interesting that Joanna changed the story over time, and that change helps me understand that something happened over the course of her relationship to Verawati to make her want to view herself as the person who helped Verawati make sense of her cultural past. But it is not more important for me to identify the precise moment that she began that process any more than it is necessary for me to identify the source of the winter boots. In short, while I suggest that we be attentive to the limitations of our data as objective accounts of whole truths, I also suggest that partiality and subjectivity do not necessarily undermine our research interests.

The lessons to be gathered from a comparison of the two interviews also serve as a sharp reminder that the person conducting the interview is part of the process: the presentation of self is directed, at least in part, to a specific interviewer probing about a specific issue at a specific time. But once again we should not assume from that understanding that the respondent is powerless or passive. In fact, I would suggest that the interviews suggest something quite different. In 1996, my research assistant was a good twenty years younger, and a great deal less experienced in life, than Joanna; much of the power on that occasion clearly lay with the respondent in that interview.

Joanna tells enough to indicate that she and her daughter are having difficulties but she is unwilling to reveal anything that she cannot package in a fashion that is acceptable to her. Fifteen years later, Joanna and I are more evenly matched in age and experience but that does not make me all that powerful. Joanna knows from many years of conducting interviews herself that we are creating knowledge together and she is both willing to allow me to ask questions and equally willing to push back (and punt). Both her concealment and her revisions of the historical record are evidence of this.

And even as we recognize the concealment and revisions, we need also to remain attentive to our usual practices of care in conducting interviews. And I mean "care" in two senses. First, and most obviously, we need to take care to ask the questions that will get us the information we want to know; if we are good at our craft, we will carefully follow up on discrepancies, hesitancies, and lacunae within the interview, as I should have done in 2011 with respect to the issue of Natasha's attitude toward Verawati.

Second, and even more important, I would suggest that we also need to exercise care in the asking so that we honor both the fragility and the strength of the respondent and so that we do not probe too deeply into areas best left to psychology. To illustrate this point, I want to go back to the incomplete story of Joanna and Natasha and why it is of substantive importance to me as a sociologist who wants to exercise caution in interviewing and who believes that we can get the information we need without probing too deeply into someone's psyche.[7] After all, my real interest is *not* in why Joanna *as a particular and unique individual* needs to keep a full house but rather in the range of motivations people have for "taking on" people who are not their own kin (and clearly needing to fill absences is one of those motivations). For that interest, it is sufficient to learn that Joanna pulls in someone else each time someone leaves—recently, as Clarissa went off to college (just before the 2011 interview), Joanna made room for one of Celeste's friends who was in need of a safe haven. I learned this in part *because* I had access to two separate interviews. But even without the first interview, I could or *should* have learned this if I had listened carefully enough in the second interview where she said, "It ended up that my daughter grew up."

Colleagues who read earlier drafts of this chapter wondered whether there isn't a contradiction between this point and my close interpretation of the issue of the boots. I think not. I believe there is a difference between a nuanced, careful reading of the texts we create with our respondents, and asking those respondents to provide us with their interpretations for what they do and say. And I believe, though I acknowledge that this is a fine line, there *is* a difference between even asking someone to explain what I will call the "intermediate why" of what they do and asking them to delve into their subconscious. In Joanna's case—the one now on the table—that difference could well be between asking *whether* she wants to replace children when they leave and asking *why* she needs, constantly, to make these replacements. As a sociologist, I feel comfortable working with (and gaining access to) "replacement" as a motivation; I am distinctly uncomfortable with whatever probing might lead to answering the deeper reason for that motivation (e.g., not feeling loved or mothered or something like that).

In short, what I am arguing, then, is that my serendipitous lessons have not thrown into question my usual practices or indicated that I should always reinterview my subjects (at fifteen-year intervals). Rather the lessons have taught me that what I normally do—what I referred to as "in and out"—is sufficient, but that I have to be conscious (reflexive, if you will) about what I am doing. And this means being exquisitely careful in conducting interviews (asking and listening both) and in analyzing the data I've got. Indeed, when you get right down to it, more of the problems with "validity" stemmed from my end than from that of what Joanna Darling herself had to say.

Notes

1. By "problematic," I mean many things: respondents might be hard to locate; they may live too far away to easily reinterview; and a second interview after a long period of time would be an entirely different event that might not even be of use in clarifying what was said some time before.
2. Some relatively early, general discussions of these issues were raised in the debates surrounding the publication of Jaber F. Gubrium and James A. Holstein's *The New Language of Qualitative Method* (1997). Pieces by Denzin (1998), Dingwall (1998), and Oakley (1998) open a range of issues for consideration, as does Gubrium and Holstein's response (1998).
3. All names are pseudonyms; the names for the Indonesian youth are chosen from a website that lists Indonesian names (*www.csupomona.edu/~pronunciation/ indonesian.html*).
4. I am changing many of the details here to protect Joanna Darling's anonymity.
5. Theoretically, the children were supposed to return to Indonesia and work for the mining company. Verawati did not; neither did the "daughter" of another woman I interviewed. I don't know what happened to most of the children, or

even how many came to the United States through the program. Nor do I know whether the program operated in any area other than Coolidge County.

6. I am grateful to my sister, Elizabeth Hersh, a psychiatrist, for her help with this interpretation. I return below to the issue of psychological interpretation.

7. One of my interviewees called me on this, saying that she had her own "shrink" and didn't need me going into private territory. I am grateful to her for having done so.

References

Braithwaite, D. O., B. W. Bach, L. A. Baxter, R. DeVerniero, J. R. Hammonds, A. M. Hosek, E. K. Willer, and B. M. Wolf. 2010. "Constructing Family: A Typology of Voluntary Kin." *Journal of Social and Personal Relationships* 27 (3): 388–407.

Denzin, N. K. 1998. Review of Gubrium and Holstein 1997. *Journal of Contemporary Ethnography* 27 (3): 405–15.

Dingwall, R. 1998. Review of Gubrium and Holstein 1997. *Journal of Contemporary Ethnography* 27 (3): 399–404.

Ezzy, D. 2010. "Qualitative Interviewing as an Embodied Emotional Performance." *Qualitative Inquiry* 16: 163–70.

Gubrium, J F., and J. A. Holstein. 1997. *The New Language of Qualitative Method.* New York: Oxford University Press.

———. 1998. "Standing Our Middle Ground." *Journal of Contemporary Ethnography* 27 (3): 416–21.

Josselson, R. 2009. "The Present of the Past: Dialogues with Memory over Time." *Journal of Personality* 77 (3558): 647–68.

Lee, J. 2002. "From Civil Relations to Racial Conflict: Merchant-Customer Interactions in Urban America." *American Sociological Review* 67 (February): 77–98.

Lieblich, A., R. Tuval-Mashiach, and T. Zilber. 1998. *Narrative Research: Readings, Analysis, and Interpretation.* Thousand Oaks, CA: Sage.

Mishler, E. G. 1986. *Research Interviewing: Context and Narrative.* Cambridge, MA: Harvard University Press.

Nelson, M. K. 1988. "Sexual Harassment and Schoolteachers in the Early Twentieth Century." *Educational Foundations* 2 (2): 61–79.

———. 1990. *Negotiated Care: The Experiences of Family Day Care Providers.* Philadelphia: Temple University Press.

———. 2005. *The Social Economy of Single Mothers: Raising Children in Rural America.* New York: Routledge.

———. 2010. *Parenting Out of Control: Anxious Parents in Unsettled Times.* New York: New York University Press.

Oakley, A. 1981. "Interviewing Women: A Contradiction in Terms." In *Doing Feminist Research*, edited by H. Roberts, 30–62. London: Routledge and Kegan Paul.

———. 1998. "Gender, Methodology and People's Ways of Knowing: Some Problems with Feminism and the Paradigm Debate in Social Science." *Sociology: The Journal of the British Sociological Association* 32 (4): 707–31.

Parker, I. 2005. *Qualitative Psychology—Introducing Radical Research*. Buckingham, UK: Open University Press.

Polkinghorne, D. E. 2007. "Validity Issues in Narrative Research." *Qualitative Inquiry* 13: 471–86.

Seidman, I. E. 1991. *Interviewing as Qualitative Research*. New York: Teachers College Press.

Smith, D. E. 1987. "Women's Perspective as a Radical Critique of Sociology." In *Feminism and Methodology*, edited by S. Harding, 84–96. Bloomington: Indiana University Press.

Spence, D. P. 1982. *Narrative Truth and Historical Truth*. New York: Norton.

Stack, C. B. 1974. *All Our Kin: Strategies for Survival in a Black Community*. New York: Harper and Row.

Tanggaard, L. 2007. "The Research Interview as Discourses Crossing Swords: The Researcher and Apprentice on Crossing Roads." *Qualitative Inquiry* 13: 160–76.

Weston, K. 1991. *Families We Choose: Lesbians, Gays, Kinship*. Between Men—Between Women. New York: Columbia University Press.

13

Paying Forward and Paying Back

Rosanna Hertz

Most of us think a *lot* about the people we study. After all, our careers are built on what we know and write about them. But what do our respondents think about what we write? What if they showed up in our classrooms or at our front doors looking for an accounting? In a tongue-in-cheek essay entitled "The Last Seminar," Stanley Cohen (1979) imagined just such an improbable (and potentially nightmarish) scenario. Former subjects visit him and other faculty in their classrooms. Peasants, factory workers, gang members, and the like invade the researchers' turf, demanding the return of their native identities and challenging the theories the authorities have advanced about them.[1]

I have never shared Cohen's hallucinations, but about a decade ago the son of one of my closest informants showed up on my front door with a backpack, a duffel bag, and plans to stay for a year. His arrival occasioned a host of questions for me, particularly about what can happen when the "field" comes to you. In this article, I examine three questions about the relationships we enter into when doing fieldwork. First, what, if anything, do we owe the people we study? Second, what do we learn about ourselves when we look through their eyes? Third, what do we learn about our culture refracted through their experience?

In January 1999, I received an e-mail from Ari, the eldest son of an Israeli couple whose kibbutz I had studied over twenty years earlier.[2] His note read, "I am finishing the military in a few months. I would like to know if it is possible to come and live with you and work in the U.S. I want to make money so I can travel." The past flashed before me. I recalled my job as a child care worker on the kibbutz and how each day I bent down to double-knot the shoelaces of one particular toddler. I remembered his big gap-toothed smile and his warm hugs. Soon, if my husband and I consented, he would show up at our front door.

Different Interpretations of the Reality That Was

Ari's request prompted the first of several episodes in which I revisited understandings I had negotiated while in the field. None of these episodes of self-reflection led me to dramatically revise, or even reject, conclusions I had reached at the time of the original research. However, each in its own way underscored just how tricky perception is and how deeply rooted assumptions and ideological preferences can challenge even the most ardent efforts at openness.

Friend or Family?

I became a volunteer in 1977–1978 to gain insight into gender relations in an Israeli kibbutz. The role of volunteer is a popular one for participant observers since it is socially sanctioned and appreciated. Participating in the kibbutz's host family program, which assigned me to a family, would enhance my study of the community. My kibbutz host family was very appealing from that perspective: both the father and the mother had been born on the kibbutz; they were a settled married couple with two children; and although they were only a few years older than me, they were not my peers (e.g., I was single and a student). By coincidence, I wound up working at the children's house in which this couple's son lived.[3]

From the outset, I viewed my relationship with my host family as a transaction bound by the length of my stay on the kibbutz. They gave me data and connections; I provided them with the opportunity to speak English and to learn more about the world beyond the gates of their fairly insular community. As one kibbutz member put it, volunteers like me kept gossip from becoming stale. It seemed to me like a "workable identity" (Maines, Shaffir, and Turowetz 1980, 278), a role definition that made sense to me and to the people with whom I would routinely interact. Moreover, I felt like I had struck a bargain that would leave me largely unencumbered when it came time to leave (cf. Maines, Shaffir, and Turowetz 1980).

I did not anticipate that my host family would come to see me as a family member or that, some twenty years later, their son would make a request that presumed deeper, familial ties (or obligations). I had kept in touch with Ari's parents over the intervening years through birthday cards and letters and occasional brief visits. Still, I did not think of them as family. Family is a permanent set of mutual obligations with love as a binding tie. I was one of a series of volunteers whom they "adopted" for a short time. I thought of myself as interchangeable with the other foreigners: I filled a slot in their family, but I always wondered what place, if any, I had in their hearts. They used to tease me, saying, "You'll leave and we will never see you again." The defiant part of myself wanted to prove them wrong, but I *also* felt vaguely like a foster child whose attachments were supposed to be severed when she moved on. Ironically, I was an adult cast as a child in the host family program. When another kibbutz member had a complaint about me or just wanted more information, they would ask my kibbutz parents. They spoke for me and my actions reflected on them. I was very conscious of this; yet I presumed they acted out of duty, not love.

Although Ari had always been a warm and loving child, it had been two decades since I had spent time with him. My husband and I agreed to host Ari in a spare room in our home, but we were surprised that immediately on arrival, he behaved toward me not as a guest but more like I was his older sister or a favored aunt. Our offer of a place to stay did not shape his assumptions, we came to learn, but his parents' view had: I was not a friend, I was family. This might seem like a contradiction, but I think it took Ari's stay with us to cement our mutual obligations and responsibilities to one another as family members, including his parents and siblings. Since I was no longer in the role of field-worker and had decided that I would not write about the kibbutz again (or so I thought), I could allow myself the necessary emotional space to discover a more authentic view of this particular family. I emphasize "particular" because I thought the research project was frozen in time, even though my thoughts about it were not and even as my correspondence with this family continued. Skeptical readers will argue that I still needed to prove to this family that I differed from all the other volunteers who passed through their house.

Research, then, is not static, but a process of ever-changing bargains between one's own needs and those we study. Certainly Ari's stay demonstrated familial reciprocity. I now realize that agreeing to have Ari live with us proved that I shared feelings of family obligations. I had mistaken my role of field-worker for that of a detached participant, although I now know this is a fieldwork myth (see Kleinman and Copp 1993).

As I looked back on my days in the kibbutz, however, I realized that I had been drawn deeply into the rhythm of this family's life—enough to qualify in their eyes as a family member. By sharing their rituals, maintaining the family pace, and synchronizing my routines with theirs, I tried to earn a place in their family. For example, before Shabbat dinner in the communal dining room, I would join the rest of the family to visit grandparents, who served us small cakes or other specially prepared foods and coffee. These ritual family gatherings always included uncles, aunts, and their children. During the week, I visited the family when I had time. If I did not see them a few days, my kibbutz father would show up at my place of work and tell me the children missed me. Without saying it directly, he was telling me that I was being lax about my priorities and that I needed to make time to visit.

Twenty years later, I recognized that even as I attempted to maintain a level of detachment, I slipped into family-like behaviors. For example, after only a few weeks with my adoptive family, I stopped writing fieldnotes about them. Being with them became a haven from the fieldwork. Shabbat gatherings not only provided opportunities to question more kibbutz members about gender and work, they also served as a way to give and receive laughter and caring. I did not go "native"—a perennial source of concern to fieldworkers and those who supervise them—because I continued to write fieldnotes about everything else and to doggedly pursue insights related to my theoretical interests.

My definition of our relationship as one of friendship rather than family helped me to manage the duality of my roles in the community—participant *and* observer, insider *and* outsider—and also to fulfill my own needs for affiliation. At the time, I understood the obligation of a social scientist (at least in my fieldwork training in the 1970s) to be fairly modest and restricted. I imagined that most field-workers developed relationships that resembled the ones I had (e.g., William Foote Whyte and Doc maintained contact). Even as my relationship to this family changed from formality to friendship (one that I hoped to maintain when I left the community), I clung to the idea that this was still a transaction—a quid pro quo.[4]

Agreeing to host Ari in our home initially did not feel like a "family thing" to do (even though we had not hosted long-term guests before), but Ari interpreted it as such. He referred to us as his "American family" when explaining our relationship to other Israelis he met in the United States. He sought our advice on personal and deeply felt matters, such as how to cope with homesickness, how to respond to his parents' desire for more letters and phone calls, and how to ask an American woman for a date. Ari admitted that he was not a particularly open or revealing person, yet he felt he could share his worries and questions with us because we were family.

The Meaning of Motherhood

From the outset of my research, I was interested in how the social and economic organization of the kibbutz, especially the system of communal child care, influenced gender roles and power. I hypothesized that the children's houses gave women freedom to achieve gender equality. Free and continuously available child care meant that women could participate fully in the kibbutz. Because they did not have to care for children in the evening, women could attend the community meetings in which kibbutz policies were set. Moreover, with child care obligations detached from motherhood, men and women could take on much more equal roles in childrearing.

Since my attention was focused on gender relations in an egalitarian community, I underplayed the meaning of motherhood in the kibbutz. However, I had had a child of my own since leaving the field, and Ari's presence in our home caused my memories to surface and to make connections that had eluded me twenty years earlier. For example, I recalled that when I visited my kibbutz sponsor's home, Yael (Ari's mother) often asked me how her son's afternoon had been. She told me that she could tell when I had been the child care worker on the last shift because I was the only one who made double-knots in her child's shoelaces to keep him from tripping. Moreover, she could tell from Ari's mood and behavior who had worked the afternoon shift on a given day. As a mother, she had limited control over her children's caregivers. The kibbutz ideology of socialization gave child care providers quite a lot of power in those days.

Not until Ari took up residence in my home and I compared his child care experiences with those of my daughter did I fully comprehend how closely my adopted kibbutz mother looked for clues about who had cared for her child each day. I remembered that communal child care was such a source of tension for my kibbutz parents that they had considered leaving the kibbutz. I had not learned about this until several months into being adopted into their family, after I had learned enough Hebrew and had earned Yael's trust. She told me that she hated relinquishing her children to the care of others so much that she would sit outside the children's houses where they slept to make sure they did not cry out in need of her comfort. Her anxieties about parent-child separation were not uncommon and caused some families to leave the kibbutz. The nightly separation stoked in Yael a deep yearning to watch over her children as they slept. I did not understand that her pain resulted from her inability to embrace this core ideological component of kibbutz life. She hungered for her children because she never had enough time with them. Yael's desire to nurture conflicted with the organization of communal life, despite her own experience as a kibbutz daughter who had been born and socialized into this system. She wanted more control over her children's lives than was allowed by the communal system, wherein committees made all the decisions about childrearing, including how to address talent, personality, and intelligence.

In short, our shifting personal experiences enable a similar shifting of our fieldwork analyses. The conclusions we draw, I learned, are at best partial and situated in historical moments that reflect our own life circumstances as much as those of the people we study.

Independence and Dependence

When I was a field-worker in the late 1970s, I observed that household work in the kibbutz—work that women in the United States did in the privacy of their homes—was accomplished in a communal fashion, and no one received pay for their labor. In this socialist community, a woman's economic well-being was not dependent on her spouse's ability to earn a living, although at the time I conducted my fieldwork, jobs were divided along gender lines. It was only after Ari arrived in our home that I began to recognize I had overlooked other kinds of trade-offs—of dependence and independence—that men and women make in a socialist community.

Despite three years of military service, Ari depended on us to help him negotiate the world of transactions most of us take for granted in a capitalist society. Whereas our eleven-year-old daughter had learned from an early age that virtually everything gets valued in one currency or another (e.g., time or money), Ari thought in terms of one big exchange: work for life. In the kibbutz and in the military, he had little experience with money and felt no need to calculate the equivalence of exchanges. Quite simply, his clothes got washed and his food got cooked and served because he belonged to the community. While living in our home, he behaved as if Coca-Cola, his favorite drink, just appeared by itself in the refrigerator. He knew that someone had to go to the grocery store, pay for it, and stock the shelves. However, in the kibbutz, someone else had done it; it was their job. Likewise, I had to show Ari how to work our washing machine and dryer. He grasped the process easily enough, but then he asked me, "How do I get my jeans ironed?" His question startled me at first, and then I told him, "I have an ironing board and an iron. You can use it to iron your jeans, but to be honest, few people I know iron blue jeans." He acknowledged my point but replied that the kibbutz needed to create work for people, especially old people, and ironing allowed them to continue to feel productive. What I had seen twenty years earlier as a breakthrough for women may have had less to do with an ideology of gender equality than with the need to employ older members.

Governance in kibbutz community and economy looked different when I viewed it through the lens of Ari's experience. Kibbutz members, I recalled, did not enjoy a full range of choices when it came to consumption and material objects. I concluded that members traded individual choice for collective well-being. Ari was accustomed to having a committee make most consumer decisions. Certainly, he had likes and dislikes, but he had learned to live within the parameters set by committees. Individuals like Ari who ventured "outside" the community remained less able to choose on their own. Bedeviled and sometimes embarrassed by his discomfort with making choices from a restaurant menu, Ari would ask us to choose for him.

These three instances of insight that occurred when the "field returned" both heartened and chastened me. I was heartened to discover that I could "revisit" the data—my memories as well as my fieldnotes—and recognize my omissions. I was chastened to see again how complex my obligations actually were and how incomplete my observations had been.[5]

Different Interpretations of Current Reality

When the field returns, it can bring a feeling of disorientation—akin to the feeling you get when you see yourself in a television monitor but do not know the location of the camera capturing your image. In this case, Ari was the observational instrument observing me, my family, and our society. The disorientation came from recognizing the images he described but not always recognizing myself (or ourselves) in the description.[6]

A Planned Life

As Ari became a member of our family, he began to reveal more to us about ourselves. For example, he grew more openly critical of our lives: "You work too much" and "You have to make a plan to see anyone" were common complaints wrapped in the language of observation. At first, his comments jolted me. But then I realized his astuteness. These two observations characterized our daily life as part of the dual-career lifestyle that ruled us. Time was scarce and friends were scheduled, as was everything else. Academic work is endless, and I had allowed it to overtake my life. During the months Ari lived with us, my husband, Bob, worked in India as a consultant a great deal. Ari viewed us as slaves to our jobs. While he criticized "lazy" people who took advantage of the community by working only when they felt like it, we represented the other extreme: people who are starved for leisure and thus a full life.

Ari was also right about our friendships. We make a plan. We leave little to spontaneity. I know what I am doing six months in advance. No one just stops in without phoning first, not even neighbors. Our daughter played in an after-school program where she selected from activities that adults supervised, and on weekends she, too, scheduled playdates. In the kibbutz, people just stop by all the time. They do not have appointment books that control their lives. Children play unsupervised, though all the community members watch out for them.

The Underground Economy

Not unlike the writings of Alexis de Tocqueville and Wu Tingfang, Ari's observations revealed facets of American culture that were only dimly visible to me or that had become so much a part of my world that they had disappeared from view and from *memory*.[7] The most profound revelations were triggered by Ari's adventures in the underground economy.

Ari's tourist visa made it difficult for him to find work, as it prohibited employment. I figured that among my friends with small businesses, someone would hire Ari and pay him under the table. Had his sister been the child living with us, she could have found work as a nanny, but for a man it was different. Though Help Wanted signs were everywhere in 1999, cash work was hard to find. I placed an ad in my daughter's school newspaper and a call on the college's e-mail bulletin, saying that a young man living in our home was available for any kind of work from weeding to child care. Ari found a few weeks of gardening work, but gardening was not a lucrative occupation. Also, Ari did not like working by himself because he was used to working on teams; it made him even lonelier.

Ari found a local Israeli café where he felt comfortable. Similar to other ethnic groups in the United States, Israelis rely on each other to learn the local culture and to find employment, especially when the work is illegal. At the café, Ari met an Israeli who worked for a local moving company owned by an Israeli (who was married to an American). The man offered Ari a job, and Ari thought it would pay good money (in cash). His boss knew illegally employed Israelis had no recourse, so he exploited his employees. He paid eight dollars an hour for backbreaking work moving furniture. Ari thought he would get rich quick. However, he was paid per job and often had to sit around most of the day doing nothing but waiting. His boss did not guarantee him a set wage per day or week, and his boss knew he would need additional employees in a month's time when leases turned over. The hours he did work caused back pain; fellow employees said that his body would eventually get used to the heavy lifting.

Ari made more in tips than in hourly wages. After a month, he became fed up with the limited hours and thought about finding another job. When the boss heard rumors that Ari might go to work for a rival Israeli moving company, he offered him a promotion. Moving season would soon begin, and Ari was a good worker. Now that Ari spoke fairly decent English, he became a foreman. This meant that he would be in charge of the crew (which always consisted of at least one other man). As it turned out, the boss hired undocumented Mexicans who did not speak English to do the heavy work of moving furniture. Ari told us the Mexicans never moved up because the Israeli boss did not trust them in the same way that he trusted someone from his own country.

To continue to drive the moving truck, Ari needed to get a U.S. license. His international driver's license was about to expire. To complicate matters, Massachusetts requires proof of U.S. citizenship or long-term status (i.e., a green card) to apply for a license. Ari's boss knew how to get his illegal employees licenses and permits in Florida but did not want to pay the full airfare (or expenses) for Ari to get a U.S. driver's license; Ari had to work to pay for half of the trip's costs.

After three months of driving, a brush with the law convinced Ari he needed to obtain a U.S. license or risk being deported. The police stopped him because of a broken headlight and fined him for not having a valid driver's license. Ari's boss had coached him to tell the police that he was doing his "uncle" a favor. Ari was not taken to the police station for working illegally.

Ari flew to Florida to take the test. He listed the hotel he stayed in as his residence on the application form. Once a person has a U.S. driver's license in one state, he can obtain a driver's license in Massachusetts (without a green card or citizenship). Ari told us that the system works like this: after a few weeks had passed, he would report his license as lost and tell the Massachusetts authorities that he had just moved to Boston; he would then use our address as his new home. The computer system would allow the authorities in Massachusetts to confirm that he has a valid driver's license from another state; they would then issue him a new license from the state of Massachusetts. His lack of U.S. citizenship and his entry into the United States on a tourist visa would get lost in the transfer process. Ari could not believe that the United States has no uniform requirements for a license. Neither could we.

Ari stayed with the moving company even though his boss continued to exploit him because of his illegal status. Ironically, although the boss trusted Ari more than the Mexican illegals, he did not think twice about taking advantage of Ari. Often it took the form of threats: if Ari wanted a day off, the boss would threaten to fire him. Therefore, Ari once worked ten hours or more every day for three weeks during a heavy moving period. Despite his working conditions, Ari applied to extend his tourist visa because he was earning money more quickly in the United States than he would have been able to do in his country.

Late one night, he came home from work and said, "I have a favor to ask. I want to extend my stay in the U.S. and I would like you to sign this paper and write that I am an employee in your home." I surprised myself by how easily the "No" came out. I was not willing to lie about the place of his employment to a U.S. government agency. I recommended that he ask his boss for such a letter. He said his boss would not do it; he applied, instead, to extend his tourist visa. However, while his request was pending, pressure from his parents to return home, coupled with the cold weather in New England, changed his decision to remain in the United States.

Why was I suddenly not willing to continue to help with his illegal work? Ari's request made it clear to me that I could not cross this particular legal boundary to help him further, because this would escalate my involvement by including a government agency.[8] My family has agreed to make an inside-outside distinction about hiring practices; that is, we do not hire undocumented people in our house, but we ignore what goes on outside of our house. Zoë Baird withdrew her nomination as attorney general under President Clinton when it surfaced that she had undeclared, not fully documented live-in help for her child. There were laws, and then there were *laws*. Just about everyone—until Zoë Baird—ignored declaring domestic help and paying taxes and benefits for such help. We drew the line at nannies and placed our daughter in a day care center. Not only had I written about the politics of career women hiring poorer, often undocumented women to care for their children (Hertz 1986), but I also felt I should align my scholarship and childrearing practices. Despite the greater financial cost of the day care center, we decided to go this route, which made me feel more politically correct than my academic friends who had live-in nannies during the day but expected them to become invisible or "disappear" during the evening (Macdonald 1998). Equally important, my child care work in the kibbutz had taught me how important collective practices of childrearing are for children to create a deep web of social ties and community obligations.

Until Ari lived with us, I had never given much thought to the legal status of the people who worked in and around our house. My husband had worked in the fields of California and written a book about undocumented agricultural workers (Thomas 1985), so we knew about underground economies. However, we were not paying much attention to the underground economy by the time Ari arrived on our doorstep, because when I hired businesses or contractors, they hired other people to do the actual work. My main concern was that the work got done, and the person or business I hired was responsible for seeing to it. My attitude was probably not all that unusual, but Ari's work experience forced me to dig beneath the surface of contracts and civility and to wonder about the labor practices of those businesses. Ari simultaneously found employment and exploitation by a member of his own ethnic group who had also once lived at the margins. His boss had had to figure out the system from the margins and how to manipulate it himself. It is not new news that undocumented workers have no recourse—as Ari's experience confirmed—but we did not realize how widely dispersed the underground economy is. It is not confined to certain categories of workers (e.g., nannies, migrant farmworkers, drug dealers). Further, tourist visas make it relatively easy to find such work through a shared ethnic group and to skirt around various regulations barring those holding tourist visas from U.S. employment. We were not hiring Ari ourselves, so we did not think of ourselves as housing an illegal worker in the United States. After September 11, 2001, ignoring illegal workers is no longer an option.

Conclusion

In *Dancing at Armageddon*, Mitchell (2002, 208–9) asks two questions that bear directly on the central issue of this article, the return of the field: "Do we visit the field one last time to acquire final facts? Or is it to liberate ourselves from unquiet memories?" Before Ari visited, I never thought I would write about him or his family again (Baker and Hertz 1981; Hertz 1982; Hertz and Baker 1983). Since his visit, however, I have given a great deal of thought to what I learned from him—what I learned when I realized that the field never leaves. I conclude with three implications.

First, we cannot lose sight of the personal obligations that bind us to our subjects. These may appear small, temporary, and tactical at the moment they are negotiated, but they and their consequences can affect many generations across many years. I deliberately included "paying" twice in the title of this article to signify that I felt haunted by an obligation until Ari's e-mail arrived. U.S. relationships are built on credit and debt as the basis of interaction. People do not base intimate relationships in the kibbutz on a similar set of exchanges; instead, a collective consciousness emerges as an obligation (Baker and Hertz 1981). U.S. hospitality translated into time and money and coaching in practical matters. My hospitality to this young man discharged a debt that I could not ignore simply because my fieldwork had ended. I could only pay back the knowledge I had received with hospitality. Ari's involvement with our family, on my turf, forced me to juxtapose the hypercommodified life I led against the one I had studied and tried to forget as impossible in the United States. "Paying forward" has a double meaning: I may be tipping the economic scales again to aid my daughter in a cross-cultural experience. I would prefer to believe that our two families established emotional and intimate ties as I experienced the transformation of possible selves.

Second, we never truly bring closure to the field, and that is good. We never truly liberate ourselves from those we study. They transform us as much as we might transform our understanding of them over time. They are not simply the studied but an intrinsic part of ourselves. The return of the field may cause surprise (and even consternation), but it should sharpen a researcher's observational and analytic skills in much the same way that aging and environmental changes can make it necessary to adjust an eyeglass prescription. The field-worker, then, needs to reconcile divergent interpretations of the past and present realities that can come about only through a deliberate (albeit occasionally uncomfortable) process of self-reflection. In a sense, when the field returns it does us the service of illustrating just how selectively we perceive the world around us even when, as qualitative researchers, we try to be open and observant.

And third, with both communication and transportation technologies making the world a smaller place, and with the spread of democratic principles and market transactions increasing the permeability of national boundaries, we all have increased opportunities to become observers. Likewise, the opportunities for us to be observed increase. In the best of all possible worlds this might lead to greater mutual understanding and respect for differences. However, interaction does not always lead to understanding and respect. To the extent that nations, populations, and classes find their identity and advantages challenged or threatened by interaction, the distinctions between legal and illegal and friendly and unfriendly will become more important. Opportunities for foreigners to visit and study indigenous cultures of all sorts may become severely limited when it is not easy to distinguish between friend and foe. In Ari's case, particularly post-September 11, it is hard to imagine his being able to manipulate the immigration bureaucracy to extend his stay beyond the limits of a tourist visa. Imagine how much more difficult it would be for an Afghani student to attempt what Ari accomplished. So, despite what the technologies and markets encourage, we may be becoming far more bunkered and selective in our interactions and therefore less knowledgeable about the world and about ourselves as a result.

Epilogue

On July 17, 2002, we received an e-mail from Ari, who was trekking around parts of Asia with his younger brother. I had written him a week earlier and told him that I was finishing up summer school and had a few weeks off before the fall semester began. He teasingly wrote back, "p.s. Rosanna: What are you gonna do with some spare time on your hands?? Maybe fly with Bob to a short visit in Thailand?" I responded that perhaps we could make a plan to meet in Asia in three years' time.

He knows the contours of my life well. We never did connect in Thailand, but we see him every few years in either Israel or the United States—reunions that are always planned. His sister and another brother have visited us a few times, and we have traveled to Italy to meet his sister's new baby, the first grandchild in the family.

Meanwhile, he and my daughter began to correspond shortly after his stay with us. He wrote, "Now we can gossip about your parents!" While I had thought when Ari left us that at some point in high school or college our daughter would go to Israel for an extended stay with his family, this did not happen. However, they continue to exchange e-mails and write on each other's Facebook walls, and when serious events happen in the United States or in Israel (or where he presently lives), we all quickly contact one another. When the Boston Marathon bombing happened in 2013, Ari immediately wrote our daughter at college. He also checked on my husband and me since he knew we often cheer on the runners close to the finish line. He now lives in Australia with his wife, who is completing a PhD, and we use social technology to talk frequently. We most certainly are family.

Notes

An earlier version of this article appeared in *Symbolic Interaction* 26 (3): 473–86, in 2003. I thank four anonymous reviewers for their critiques. I also thank Kathy Charmaz, Robert J. Thomas, Norman K. Denzin, and Richard G. Mitchell for their sharp insights. I take responsibility for telling this story: it is mine.

1. In an e-mail to me, Stanley Cohen wrote that, according to the editor who accepted his paper for publication, it "was the first time that the journal had *knowingly* published a work of fiction." Cohen's account questions the authority of the researcher as the godlike interpreter and theorist while challenging older ideas about objectivity in social research. Such stories told are now no longer dubbed fictional accounts (or published under pen names for fear of professional reprisal; see, for example, Laura Bohannon's novel [Bowen 1954]); they are part of a broader shift in ethnography and participant observation that transforms social science knowledge (see Atkinson and Hammersley 1994). Two decades later, a significant literature has emerged that attempts to connect the self with their storied lives. For instance, Richardson (1997) illustrates the connection between her emotional life and her autobiography and intellectual life; Romero and Stewart's (1999) collection gives voice to those who have been silenced by "master narratives." In this article, I further reveal how we confront ourselves through our respondents' cultural vision (see also Glassner and Hertz 2003).

2. I have changed the names of my kibbutz family members.

3. Kibbutzim have undergone numerous changes since I conducted the original fieldwork; however, this kibbutz maintained the founding ideology for years beyond other kibbutzim. For instance, this kibbutz was one of the last to agree to children sleeping in their parents' homes. The children's houses have since

been modified ideologically. In short, they are day care centers and no longer the primary source of socialization for children.

4. Feminists writing about methodology have argued that researchers need to give back "some thing" to the people we study (see DeVault 1996 for a review that includes new ways feminist scholars are approaching ethical and moral questions of what we owe). In short, while scholars may say they owe and have lifelong obligations to their respondents, I do not know of any who have written about hosting individuals from their former field studies. Usually, the giving back in a research project has a social action or policy component (see, for example, Reinharz 1992 for a feminist perspective; see Whyte 1991 for a social action call to social scientists). Wayne Baker and I gave the kibbutz a report, which included recommendations for various practical changes. It did not fulfill the feminist obligations or the social action call that followed decades after this study. In the late 1970s, I thought this was what I owed.

5. A contemporary tension in ethnographic research is epistemological: can we develop a science out of social life? Knowledge itself has come to center stage as social scientists attempt to more fully represent social reality. Reflexivity, one such attempt, implies a shift in our understanding of data and its collection; it is to constantly and intensively scrutinize "what I know" and "how I know it." To be reflexive means to engage in ongoing conversation about experience while simultaneously living in the moment. By extension, the reflexive ethnographer does not simply report "facts" or "truths" but actively constructs interpretations of his or her experiences in the field and then questions how those interpretations came about (see especially Rabinow 1986). The outcome of reflexive social science is reflexive knowledge-statements that provide insight into the workings of the social world and insight into how the knowledge came into existence (Myerhoff and Ruby 1982). The best definition I have found of reflexivity is Helen Callaway's (1992, 33): "Often condemned as apolitical, reflexivity, on the contrary, can be seen as opening the way to a more radical consciousness of self in facing the political dimensions of fieldwork and constructing knowledge. Other factors intersecting with gender—such as nationality, race, ethnicity, class and age—also affect the anthropologist's field interactions and textual strategies. Reflexivity becomes a continuing mode of self-analysis and political awareness." By bringing subject and object back into the same space, authors give their audiences the opportunity to evaluate them as "situated actors" (i.e., active participants in the process of meaning creation).

6. Horace Miner's classic essay, "Body Ritual among the Nacirema" (1956), is unmatched in his dissection of American bodily rituals. I am reminded of it as I write this article. Ari focused in on a self I prefer not to see. Asked for advice on how to get through daily life, I recently told a friend with young children she

should think of it as putting her foot down on the gas pedal: fast forward your life by speeding it up.

7. I am indebted to Richard Mitchell for guiding me to Wu Tingfang's remarkable book, *America through the Spectacles of an Oriental Diplomat* (1914), on his travels to America. It includes Wu's commentaries on the enormous but often only dimly visible differences in culture, tastes, and social mores—differences that stood out to him because he was Chinese.

8. See Tamar El-Or (1992), who argues that intimate and reciprocal field relationships end when the informant feels that she has become the object of someone else's interest. In an interesting twist, I could no longer be Ari's informant, and I felt this request invaded the intimacy we had developed.

References

Atkinson, P., and M. Hammersley. 1994. "Ethnography and Participant Observation." In *Handbook of Qualitative Research*, edited by N. K. Denzin and Y. S. Lincoln, 248–61. Thousand Oaks, CA: Sage.

Baker, W., and R. Hertz. 1981. "Communal Diffusion of Friendship: The Structure of Intimate Relations in an Israeli Kibbutz." In *Research in the Interweave of Social Roles*, vol. 2, edited by H. Z. Lopata and D. Maines, 259–83. Greenwich, CT: JAI Press.

Bowen, E. S. [pseud. L. Bohannon]. 1954. *Return to Laughter: An Anthropological Novel*. New York: Harper.

Callaway, H. 1992. "Ethnography and Experience: Gender Implications in Fieldwork and Texts." In *Anthropology and Autobiography*, edited by J. Okely and H. Callaway, 29–49. New York: Routledge, Chapman and Hall.

Cohen, S. 1979. "The Last Seminar." *Sociological Review* 27 (February): 5–20.

DeVault, M. L. 1996. "Talking Back to Sociology: Distinctive Contributions of Feminist Methodology." *Annual Review of Sociology* 22: 29–50.

El-Or, T. 1992. "Do You Really Know How They Make Love? The Limits on Intimacy with Ethnographic Informants." *Qualitative Sociology* 15 (1): 53–72.

Glassner, B., and R. Hertz. 2003. *Our Studies, Ourselves*. New York: Oxford University Press.

Hertz, R. 1982. "Family in the Kibbutz: A Review of Authority Relations and Women's Status." *Marriage and Family Review* 5 (2): 29–50.

———. 1986. *More Equal than Others: Women and Men in Dual-Career Couples*. Berkeley: University of California Press.

———. 1997. *Reflexivity and Voice*. Thousand Oaks, CA: Sage.

Hertz, R., and W. Baker. 1983. "Women's and Men's Work in an Israeli Kibbutz: Gender and the Allocation of Labor." In *Sexual Equality: The Israeli Kibbutz*

Tests the Theories, edited by M. Palgi, J. R. Blasi, M. Rosner, and M. Safir, 154–73. Darby, PA: Norwood Editions.

Kleinman, S., and M. A. Copp. 1993. *Emotions and Fieldwork*. Newbury Park, CA: Sage.

Macdonald, C. 1998. "Manufacturing Motherhood: The Shadow Work of Nannies and Au Pairs." *Qualitative Sociology* 21 (1): 25–53.

Maines, D., W. Shaffir, and A. Turowetz. 1980. "Leaving the Field in Ethnographic Research: Reflections on the Entrance-Exit Hypothesis." In *Fieldwork Experience: Qualitative Approaches to Social Research*, edited by W. B. Shaffir, R. A. Stebbins, and A. Turowetz, 253–81. New York: St. Martin's Press.

Miner, H. 1956. "Body Ritual among the Nacirema." *American Anthropologist* 58 (3): 503–7.

Mitchell, R. G. 2002. *Dancing at Armageddon: Survival and Chaos in Modern Times*. Chicago: University of Chicago Press.

Myerhoff, B., and J. Ruby. 1982. "Introduction." In *A Crack in the Mirror: Reflexive Perspectives in Anthropology*, edited by J. Ruby, 1–35. Philadelphia: University of Pennsylvania Press.

Rabinow, P. 1986. "Representations Are Social Facts: Modernity and Post-Modernity in Ethnography." In *Writing Culture: The Poetics and Politics of Ethnography*, edited by J. Clifford and G. E. Marcus, 234–61. Berkeley: University of California Press.

Reinharz, S. 1992. *Feminist Methods in Social Research*. With L. Davidman. New York: Oxford University Press.

Richardson, L. 1997. *Fields of Play: Constructing an Academic Life*. New Brunswick, NJ: Rutgers University Press.

Romero, M., and A. J. Stewart, eds. 1999. *Women's Untold Stories: Breaking Silence, Talking Back and Voicing Complexity*. New York: Routledge.

Thomas, R. 1985. *Citizenship, Gender and Work*. Berkeley: University of California Press.

Whyte, W. F. 1991. *Social Theory, Social Action: How Individuals and Organizations Learn to Change*. Newbury Park, CA: Sage.

Wu T. 1914. *America through the Spectacles of an Oriental Diplomat*. Reissued by IndyPublish.com, 2001. 1914 version available at *members.tripod.com/Ken_Davies/wutingfangcontents.html*.

14

Rethinking Families

A Slow Journey

Naomi Gerstel

I t is an honor for me to join with colleagues who are thinking about the value and facets of slow sociology. I agree that there is far too much pressure to push paper off one's desk—to write grants and to produce ever more publications rather than slowing down "to reap the creative fruits of intellectual crop rotation," as Judith Stacey (2007, 96) wrote in a book I coedited on public sociology. These pressures are mounting, as job markets constrict and universities become more dependent on external support (whether from federal institutes, private foundations, or wealthy donors). Such pressures intensify as more women enter the profession and bring with them responsibilities to the partners, children, relatives, and friends who so often can "disrupt" what Arlie Hochschild (1975) once called the clockwork of male careers. Because slowing down is becoming more difficult, it is all the more important to discuss it.

So many of the synonyms the thesaurus gives for "slow" indicate problems: "procrastinate," "mire," "retard," "bog down," "diminish," "handicap," and "loiter." I recently sat on a university committee refereeing tenure cases. To be sure, most of the committee members spoke of quality, but many of them also talked in terms of numbers, emphasizing how much those faculty seeking tenure and/or promotion had (or had not) published as a mark of success in their career. I sit in a department where the current advice to graduate students is: "Don't stay too long; just get something out." And like Judith Stacey, I often hear good graduate students say: "I want time to read, think, live and protest; I don't want [your] life of publish or perish" or just "I want to have a life; can I slow down and still become a sociology professor?"

Although I certainly have been guilty of trying to write fast, to move material out of my head or off my desk (including, ironically, for this book), I find it useful to reconsider this strategy. As I reviewed my own experience for this piece, I realized that I am already a practitioner of slow sociology in several different senses. First, I have been working to understand and analyze families since I first began my now long career. This long gestation period led me to rethink the varied meanings and practices of families and especially the inequalities within and across them. Second, some of the particular studies I have done, especially the most recent one, returned to some of the earlier issues that concerned me. The multimethod research that resulted has taken much longer than I anticipated. Third, I have a family. The members of that family—especially my partner, daughter, mother, brother, and close friends—sometimes slow me down.

In this piece, I reflect on these three meanings and pathways. Moreover, I stand back from my own life and argue that these meanings and pathways are likely unequally distributed. Some aspects of slowness remain gendered. Slowing down, while maintaining a place in the academy, also often seems a luxury of those who are already advantaged, especially those who enjoy the privileges associated with class and academic position. The right to do slow sociology, I will argue, is all too often tied to cumulative advantage.

The First Sense of Slow Sociology: Rethinking Families

Many years ago, I began my life as a sociologist by studying families and gender (what were then called "sex roles"). I began by doing research on professional women—young aspirant that I was—who lived apart from their husbands so they could both have jobs. I had learned and rejected the common view that the nuclear family "fit" with the demands of modern societies—a "fit" based on a wife who could and would just pick up and follow her husband's job anywhere it took the two of them. Coining the term "commuter marriage," I studied and wrote about professional couples who lived apart, arguing that they were rejecting neither marriage nor jobs but were refashioning both as a way to produce greater gender equality in their marriages. I enjoyed the first of many collaborations, coauthoring *Commuter*

Marriage (1984) with Harriet Gross; the book combined my research on dual-career professional couples with hers on couples in which one partner was a merchant marine.

Among the professionals, the families I studied each consisted primarily of husband and wife (they were like me: few had yet had children; few had much contact with relatives or friends). I chose this research site because I was interested in inequality within nuclear families, especially between husbands and wives, and I chose it because I had been shaped by the feminist movement and by Jessie Bernard's now classic book arguing that every marriage contains two marriages—"his and hers" (1972, 8). This led me to want to interview both the wife and husband in each commuter marriage: it was occasionally difficult to get both to agree and it was often time-consuming to travel to their separate homes (I sometimes commuted long distances, just as they did, to do the interviews—whether from California to New York or from Boston to Washington, DC). I discovered Bernard was right in several senses. Not only did the very act of commuting entail an attempt to equalize the response to both "her" and "his" careers, but commuter marriage also looked very different to the women and men married to each other. I would sometimes go away from an interview and wonder about even the details, asking myself if I had made a mistake. Was this woman really married to the man I spoke to last week?[1] This showed up in their broad assessments of commuter marriage. Most women disliked it less than most men (though very few really liked it). It was the men who lost more than the women, at least relative to the marriages that surrounded them. This was reminiscent of the old experiments of asking two children—one poor, one wealthy—to estimate the size of a coin. It seemed much bigger to the poor. Commuter marriage, in an analogous sense, seemed much worse to the men who compared themselves to other men. Clearly, interviewing both spouses slowed me down, but taking the time to interview both spouses rather than only one of them provided a much richer understanding of marriage.

The more I thought about family and gender—and the more I talked with Harriet Gross about the differences between the professionals and the merchant marines—the more I understood that focusing on a gender divide not only revealed but also concealed much, especially about differences among women and among men. Understanding inequality required movement from the study of inequality between spouses within families to inequality across different families. How did a comparison between working-class and professional women shape our understanding of family? Did class trump race, as some were arguing, or did middle-class Blacks and Whites practice family in different ways? Unpacking and reconnecting gender, class, and race is an arduous process. But these questions consumed me (and many others) for several decades.

I increasingly took a particular perspective, joining with a small number of others (e.g., Stack 1974; Hansen 2004) who were suggesting that too few of those who study work and family have looked beyond relations between spouse and partners or parents and children to examine kin connections. With a number of graduate student collaborators, I came to understand that this emphasis on marriage and the nuclear family—with its exclusion of the extended family—is narrow, even deleterious, and misses much of family life, especially outside the middle class. With a generous grant from the Rockefeller Foundation, we did interviews in Massachusetts that allowed us to examine the ways in which kin connections are not only gendered but tied to education, employment, marriage, and parenting—all of which, we argued, act as greedy institutions that interfere with broader kin connections (see, for example, Gallagher and Gerstel 1993; Gerstel and Gallagher 1995).

We were still focused primarily on gender and class, with little attention to race. Most of our respondents, all living in Massachusetts, were White. Earlier work (especially that of Carol Stack) led us to think that the focus on the nuclear family might be particularly likely to overlook the family experiences of women and men of color, and that an emphasis on the nuclear family promulgated a vision of family life that dismissed the social resources and community ties especially critical to the survival strategies of those in need.

To go further with the comparisons we wanted to make, we needed larger samples—those available in national data sets. I put together a work-shop with a number of graduate students interested in the topic to talk about the issues and data sets we would need. A key member of this group was Natalia Sarkisian, a graduate student who was already sophisticated in the use of quantitative methods. We decided to collaborate: she wrote a dissertation, and we jointly authored some articles. We located a national data set with some appropriate items (the National Survey of Households and Families) and used it to show that many Americans rely on extended family members for all kinds of support and help. But we also found—as we had hypothesized—that such reliance is not spread equitably across the population; instead, women, people of color, and those with fewer material resources are more likely to rely on and give to extended kin. (For summaries of work that came out of these analyses, see Sarkisian and Gerstel 2004; Gerstel and Sarkisian 2008; Gerstel 2011; Sarkisian and Gerstel 2012).[2]

We expected these differences, which were shaped by policy and politics; the myopic focus on the nuclear family was not a characteristic confined to academic research and media reports. Amy Armenia (another participant in the workshop), Kate McGonagle, and I again sought national data, this time to address policy that promotes particular kinds of families. A fortuitous invitation by the Congressional Commission on the Family and Medical Leave Act (FMLA) to examine employee use of the FMLA provided an entry point—a policy site, an audience, and some relevant data.[3]

As we told the commission, the FMLA allowed many people to take family leaves who would have been previously unable to do so. But we also had reason to remain skeptical about the actual reach of the FMLA, especially given our understanding that gender, class, and race jointly shape family patterns. We found that although gender neutrality in family leave taking was a primary goal of the FMLA, actual leave taking since the passage of the act has been far from gender neutral. We found that it is overwhelmingly women (especially those married) who say they need leaves, take leaves, and take longer leaves, especially for other people. These gender inequalities interact with race: it is White men who are particularly unlikely to take a family leave (Armenia and Gerstel 2006). Class position also affects the ability to take family leaves and the length of those leaves: while less affluent women are more likely to perceive a need for a family leave (Gerstel and McGonagle 1999), they take less time off than more affluent women. Worse, these data led us to expect that many organizations were not abiding by the act's mandate. But how to pursue this conjecture? Locating yet another data set (this time the National Study of Employers collected by the Work and Family Institute), that is precisely what we found. This data set did not provide direct data on actual noncompliance, but Amy Armenia and Coady Wing, my two younger colleagues, invented a way to use missing data to assess noncompliance. Our analyses showed that between 25 percent and 43 percent of corporations legally required to follow the FMLA *still* do not comply with it two decades after its passage (Armenia, Gerstel, and Wing Forthcoming). We came to argue that nonresponse with survey questions may represent a particular form of regulatory avoidance or defiance. I wondered if more direct data from observation at the workplace might be a way to explore these work-family issues in greater depth.

A Second Sense of Slow Sociology: Researching Jobs and Families

About seven years ago, Dan Clawson (a colleague with whom I had collaborated) and I were talking about our shared interests in inequality, work, and family. Along came a university offer for us both to take a semester off from teaching to write a grant proposal about families. We didn't object; we took the offer and eventually spent a year creating a long and consuming research agenda about the inequality of hours and schedules (another ironic twist). We probably would never have written a grant or done the resulting study if we had not been prodded by university largesse in the form of "seed" money. The money was part of the new institutional agenda being developed because of the growing pressure on the school to raise money and get support from somewhere outside the university.

We were turned down the first time we submitted our proposal to the National Science Foundation (NSF). The second time around, we got lucky; put another way, advantages were accumulating. Writing proposals is a time-consuming process that can be more "costly" than writing for publication. Although one can sometimes resubmit to the same funder, there is rarely a different place to resubmit the proposal when it is turned down, as most are. But in our case, the NSF was now calling for multimethod research. In other words, they were calling for slow sociology.

Following our joint interest and understanding of the underpinnings of inequality, we studied four occupations whose members vary by class and gender—physicians, registered nurses, emergency medical technicians (EMTs), and nursing assistants—all in health care, because that allowed us to look at the "webs of time" across occupations and organizations in a single system while ensuring variation in the families (the better to assess how they affect work hours and schedules). We collected five types of data: We mailed eight hundred surveys to those in each of the occupations and then observed at eight sites (including hospitals, nursing homes, doctors' offices, and EMT sites). We conducted over two hundred intensive face-to-face interviews, with respondents in the four occupations and with others who shape the hours and schedules of these occupations. Finally, we collected a variety of documents (including union contracts, official work schedules, and actual work schedules). Working on this multilevel, multimethod project, I learned still another meaning of "slow sociology," because our study of time took about a decade, absorbing the intense efforts of both of us (along with a number of graduate and undergraduate students who helped us out).

We designed the study around these four occupations because that allowed us to assess the ways in which the number and allocation of work hours and other scheduling decisions are the result of collective experiences and struggles, as well as products of relations between coworkers in the same occupation, among different occupations at a single workplace, among different workplaces, and among family members. The way to methodologically approach these issues, however, only gradually unfolded as we did the research. We initially thought (and proposed to the NSF) that we would do brief site visits at a couple of organizations. And that is what the NSF funded us for. As we did the interviews and conducted those abbreviated site visits, however, we realized that to understand both occupation and organization, we needed to do more (real) fieldwork. That way we could observe the same workers over a number of days. We could watch workers interact with other workers and with the managers who made decisions about their hours and schedules. And, we could see the differences and relationships among organizations (as they handed off patients and workers to one another). Consequently, what were initially conceived of as brief site visits grew into more extensive observations as we hung out in the organizations we studied.

As we came to the end of data collection, Dan and I were worried, feeling overwhelmed. We were swimming in data and asking, "Now what are we going to do with all of this?" It took many readings of transcripts and fieldnotes, along with analyses of the survey data, to make sense of what we had. We knew we needed time off and applied to the Russell Sage Foundation (RSF) for a year to get away from course and committee obligations so we could find time to draft the book, *Unequal Time*. Again, we got lucky—more "luck" for the already advantaged.

The RSF makes resources available only to a small number of scholars who then experience what Robert K. Merton long ago called "cumulative advantage." Updating the idea, DiPrete and Eirich argue that cumulative advantage produces an inequality among scholars that grows over time, for it is a "general mechanism for inequality across any temporal process (e.g., life course, family generations) in which a favorable relative position becomes a resource that produces further relative gains" (2005, 273). The other side of this: slowing down at an earlier stage may produce cumulative disadvantage; slowing down in the later stages (to collect richer data and analyze it) may depend on—as it produces—cumulative advantage.

Now, a little on the substance that came out of this long research process—a substance that is particularly appropriate for this anthology on disruption: As Dan and I culled the data, read and reread our transcripts and field observations, and cut and pasted from draft to draft, we came to see that a central theme was the pervasiveness of "normal unpredictability" and the inequality in strategies to deal with or control that unpredictability. We observed that all employers and employees, as well as their family members, deal with the pervasive unpredictability created by disruptions. All workers sometimes get sick; need time to care for a sick kid, mother, or friend; want a vacation or a mental health day; get stuck in a snowstorm; must stay an extra hour on the job because a day's work is unfinished or a coworker had to leave early; miss a ride; need to run unanticipated errands before businesses close; hit a traffic jam; wait on a delayed bus; or need to take a relative to a dental appointment. As one of our more articulate colleagues summarized it, "Shit happens."

Both class and gender shape how employees and their families can and do respond to these unpredictable events. We could, for example, observe what I had begun to tap in my earlier quantitative analysis of the FMLA: On the one hand, organizations often deny time off to low- wage women workers (who are often single mothers) and punish them for unpredictable events (a late bus, a sick child, or even a snowstorm). On the other hand, employers are much more likely to be lenient about such events when professional women encounter them (even though these women often also have more resources to cope with such disruptions). Professional women insist on and often get time off to take care of a sick child or are excused when a fire at home makes them late. Professional men use other strategies still: they turn to their others—like wives and nannies—to take care of what one called "life's little inconveniences." In short, we observed the ways gender and class interact when disruptions occur.

Understanding this unpredictability and the collective responses to it required a sociological vision that looks both vertically (say, looking at relations among employees) and horizontally (looking at hierarchies at the workplace and in families; examining linked organizations, linked occupations, coworkers, regular coworkers, and "irregular" workers).[4]

Understanding those networks required data that is multilevel (different occupations, different organizations) and multimethod (fieldwork, intensive interviews, a survey, and schedules). Dan and I came to believe that if we had studied only one occupational group (say, just doctors or just nursing assistants) or if we has studied only one organization (say, just a hospital), or if we had collected only one kind of data (say, just a survey or just face-to-face interviews), we would not have been able to understand the collective nature of time, the pervasiveness of normal unpredictability, or the inequality that sustains different degrees of control. However, both getting and analyzing all the data required sometimes had us feeling like we were moving at a snail's pace.

The Third Sense of Slow Sociology: Rethinking My Own Family

Much research shows that women are still responsible for more of the unpaid work of the home—whether it is housework, the care of children, or the care of extended kin. Women must juggle or "weave" (to use Anita Garey's [1999] evocative term) family and work. The "clockwork of male careers" still serves to deter and constrain women more than men. In this sense, doing slow sociology—because of family demands—is gendered.

I look at my vita. Pre-tenure, there is a speedup (as I commuted between a job and my partner). Post-tenure, there is a big gap. That gap occurred when we were raising my (adorable) daughter.[5] My daughter is out of college now, so she interrupts me less, but my mother stepped in to take her place. A few years ago, my now ninety-eight-year-old mother left her home in North Carolina to move to an assisted living residence near me in Massachusetts. She is no longer depressed, at least most of the time. We talk at least once a day and I visit her at least two or three times a week. But I never feel I do enough. While the pervasive norms about intensive mothering are oppressive, the absence of such norms for the care of elderly relatives is also oppressive. Both produce guilt, at least for women. From California, my brother calls about once a week and flies in three or four times every year. He spends much less time with our mother, and I doubt he feels guilty, at least most of the time. He reports that his friends are impressed by his commitment and willingness to come so often. My brother and I (with encouragement from our mother and friends) are doing gender in conventional ways.[6] When my mother first moved up to be near me, I said to my brother, "Oh well, I'll get less done; one less publication—so what?" He agreed. Sometimes, though, I not only feel guilty, I also get upset that I can't focus more on one piece or another.

I was surprised by the gaps in my vita, especially when my daughter was young, even though I had taught and written about the constraints that caregiving places on paid work lives. I was also surprised by how I felt about those demands. Much literature (including some of my own) on caring for children and elderly parents focuses on the burdens such work entails. And to be sure, caregiving is burdensome. But there are also great pleasures to be had from these intense relationships, including the sense of meaning and connection they provide, the sense of virtue that can come from being able to give care to the people you love, and the sense of fulfillment that can come from giving way to this part of gender norms after having resisted them for all these years.

To be sure, family slows you (and me) down; that is, it slows professionals down. Given my interest in inequality, I keep reminding myself that even this is unevenly distributed. Slowing down imposes relatively little penalty on professionals compared to low-wage workers. As Budig and Hodges (2010) show, earnings penalties for motherhood are significantly worse for women in low-wage jobs than for those in high-wage positions. The same is true for time and the control over it. That is, there is little penalty for doing slow sociology if one is an affluent professional, advanced in one's career, who has the luxury of responding to and controlling the normal unpredictability that intense family attachments routinely demand.

Conclusion

Let me confess: I am telling a linear story here. One study built on the previous one. One grant was made possible by an earlier one. One collaboration led to another. One advantage led to another. But that linearity is only a partial truth told in the interest of showing my pathways to slow sociology. There was far more happenstance—indeed, far more disruption—than this narrative would seem to imply. Moreover, thinking about slow sociology has alerted me not only to the connected pathways I have described here but also raised for me a number of additional questions I cannot answer. Let me conclude this piece with those questions.

First, what is the effect of technology? We hear arguments on both sides, and as far as I can tell, the data to answer this question are not very good. In my professional life, moving from one project to another, I have witnessed and used what seems like an avalanche of new technologies: I have shifted from cutting and pasting transcripts on the living-room floor to using NVivo to code, search, and organize data; from writing and revising on a typewriter to drafting and editing on a computer screen; from visits to the library to online searches; from tape recorder to digital recorder; from standing in long lines to enter piles of computer cards on a mainframe to running Stata software on my own computer. Astonishing. But it is not obvious how these technologies—some for quantitative analysis, some for qualitative research—affect the quantity and quality of writing and publication. Although typing up fieldnotes, transcribing, and coding may be faster with these technologies, collecting field observations remains just as slow. Although finding existing national data sets with relevant questions—typically available online—might be faster, combing through them and creating usable data remains slow. Although finding appropriate literature is surely faster, it is easy to get distracted by yet another find, and reading is just as slow. Of course, I experience the learning, using, updating, and fixing of this technology all too often as disruptions that slow me down. Overall, I suspect that none of these changes did much to speed up my thinking (and rethinking) and none erased the disruptions that interfere with the slow process of generating and assessing ideas.

Second, what kind of research is most slow sociology? I have heard arguments between those who do qualitative research and those who do quantitative work about which takes longer. Of course, almost everyone thinks that what they do is the more labor intensive and time-consuming. My experience doing both suggests it is a draw. Relying on national data saved us the time and money we would have had to spend on collecting our own data, but using these existing data sets meant we had to rethink how to empirically define family, class, and race, and to identify what items might help us tap, if only imperfectly, the issues we wanted to address. Relying on existing national data means having to rely on the conceptual choices that other researchers made about which items to include or exclude. With such massive amounts of data designed by someone else, it is easy to get distracted and go astray—to start "number crunching" ("I'll just run this and this and this . . ."). Doing both qualitative and quantitative analyses in a focused way demands constant revision and rethinking. This is, to be sure, a slow process—especially when the family one wants to study is not the family in vogue among the researchers who design and direct the collection of national data sets.

Third, what of collaborations? Noting my multiple collaborations, the editors of this book asked me if I could reflect on the ways in which collaborations might both speed up the process and slow it down. I collaborate because collaborators help me develop ideas. I collaborate because doing so allows me to use methods, especially the quantitative methods that Gallagher, Armenia, and Sarkisian know, that would otherwise be beyond my reach. I collaborate because I like the structure that collaboration provides. I collaborate because I like the company (most of the time). But does that speed me up or slow me down? I don't know. Another empirical question I can't answer.

Finally, when students say "I want to have a life; can I slow down and still become a sociology professor?" what do and should we say? A colleague of mine at an elite institution routinely gathers together her women students and tells them not to have kids until after tenure so they can work fast and furious before then. She is not alone. Narratives of success today still tend to emphasize the straight and narrow path—careers where there are speedups and little room for disruptions (harking back to Hochschild's clockwork of the male career).

This volume is important because it tells another story—one of the wisdom of allowing disruptions to do good research or disruptions to provide good care. Part of this message to slow down is gaining ground in the mainstream media. A recent *New York Times* article (Schwartz 2013), with the headline "Relax! You'll Be More Productive," pointed out that too many of us eat at our desks, leave work late, and work during vacations to maintain "a seemingly unsustainable pace." The article's punch line: those long, arduous hours not only make us sick but diminish the amount and quality of work we do. On reflection, I support that story. But as I have also tried to argue here, speedups are associated with gender and class, as is the right to slow down. It is often women, especially those who are advantaged, who are likely both to face the pressure and have the privilege to practice slow sociology, even if there remain some penalties they encounter when they do so. To return to where I began: as Judith Stacey reminded us, we must "revamp our institutional structures and the intellectual culture in our discipline and in the academy more broadly" (2007, 92). Advocating a slow sociology, then, requires revamping the institutional structures that we live and work in.

Notes

1. Such separation is still a dilemma that many professional couples today must face, although many universities and some corporations have become more sensitive to the plight of dual-career couples and are replacing outdated antinepotism rules with programs for partner hires.

2. This argument is based on a number of research projects, all collaborative, that I have developed with a number of graduate and undergraduate students, only some of whom I cite here (especially Amy Armenia, Shelley Erikson, Sally Gallagher, Mariana Gerena, Rachel Munoz, and Natalia Sarkisian).

3. Moving beyond prior legislation, which had allowed only maternity leave, the FMLA mandates job leaves for employees' own serious personal illnesses, including maternity "disability." It also guarantees twelve-week unpaid leaves to employees providing care for newborns or newly adopted children, as well as those caring for seriously ill dependent children, spouses, or parents. This act was an important step forward.

4. I want to thank Rosanna Hertz for this formulation of "vertical" and "horizontal."

5. I am not using the royal "we" here; my partner was and is an "equal sharer" in parenting, as Francine Deutsch (1999, 2007) refers to those relatively rare women and men who divide the labor of child care.

6. Some years ago, one of my older colleagues casually said to me, "Now that you have a kid, you will understand families." I thought he was being dismissive and sexist. And he might have been, given that he was invoking the old "insider" versus "outsider" debate that has now reappeared in both online and face-to-face sociological discussions of, for example, race (can White people write about Black history or Black culture?). Rarely, however, is it explicitly raised with regard to the study and talk of child or elder care issues. But now I think my colleague was in some sense correct (even if some of the best work on these issues comes from people without children). My caregiving responsibilities shape the way I think about and teach family. It also shapes how I think about slow sociology.

References

Armenia, A., and N. Gerstel. 2006. "Family Leaves, the FMLA and Gender Neutrality: The Intersection of Race and Gender." *Social Science Research* 35: 871–91.

Armenia, A., N. Gerstel, and C. Wing. Forthcoming. "Workplace Compliance with the Law: The Case of the Family and Medical Leave Act." *Work and Occupations* 41.

Bernard, J. 1972. *The Future of Marriage.* New Haven, CT: Yale University Press.

Budig, M. J., and M. J. Hodges. 2010. "Differences in Disadvantage: Variation in the Motherhood Penalty across White Women's Earning Distribution." *American Sociological Review* 75 (5): 705–28.

Deutsch, F. 1999. *Halving It All: How Equally Shared Parenting Works*. Cambridge, MA: Harvard University Press.

———. 2007. "Undoing Gender." *Gender & Society* 21 (1): 106–27.

DiPrete, T., and G. M. Eirich. 2006. "Cumulative Advantage as a Mechanism for Inequality: A Review of Theoretical and Empirical Developments." *Annual Review of Sociology* 32: 271–97.

Garey, A. I. 1999. *Weaving Work and Motherhood*. Philadelphia: Temple University Press.

Gallagher, S., and N. Gerstel. 1993. "Kinkeeping and Friend Keeping: The Effects of Marriage." *Gerontologist* 33 (5): 675–81.

Gerstel, N. 2011. "Rethinking Families and Community: The Color, Class, and Centrality of Extended Kin Ties." *Sociological Forum* 26 (1): 1–20.

Gerstel, N., and S. Gallagher. 1995. "Caring for Kith and Kin: Gender, Employment and the Privatization of Care." *Social Problems* 41 (4): 519–39.

Gerstel, N., and H. Gross. 1984. *Commuter Marriage*. New York: Guilford Press.

Gerstel, N., and K. McGonagle. 1999. "Job Leaves and the Limits of the Family and Medical Leave Act: The Effects of Gender, Race, and Family." *Work and Occupations* 26 (4): 510–34.

Gerstel, N., and N. Sarkisian. 2008. "The Color of Family Ties: Race, Class, Gender, and Extended Family Involvement." In *It's American Families: A Multicultural Reader*, edited by Stephanie Coontz, Maya Parson, and Gabrielle Rayley, 447–53. New York: Routledge.

Hansen, K. V. 2004. *Not-So-Nuclear Families: Class, Gender, and Networks of Care*. New Brunswick, NJ: Rutgers University Press.

Hochschild, A. 1975. "Inside the Clockwork of Male Careers." In *Women and the Power to Change*, edited by F. Howe, 47–80. New York: McGraw-Hill.

Sarkisian, N., and N. Gerstel. 2004. "Kin Support among Blacks and Whites: Race and Family Organization." *American Sociological Review* 69 (6): 812–37.

———. 2012. *Nuclear Family Values, Extended Family Lives: The Power of Race, Class, and Gender*. New York: Routledge.

Schwartz, T. 2013. "Relax! You'll Be More Productive." *New York Times*, February 9: Sunday Review, 6–7.

Stacey, J. 2007. "If I Were the Goddess of All Things Sociological." In *Public Sociology: Fifteen Eminent Sociologists Debate the Profession in the Twenty-First Century*, edited by D. Clawson, R. Zussman, J. Misra, N. Gerstel, R. Stokes, D. L. Anderton, and M. Burawoy, 91–100. Berkeley: University of California Press.

Stack, C. B. 1974. *All Our Kin: Strategies for Survival in a Black Community*. New York: Basic Books.

15

Time to Find Words

Marjorie L. DeVault

L anguage and language use have perhaps been less central to sociological investigation, which is more often undertaken "at home," than to anthropology, which has historically required immersion in "other" cultures, where language difference is both a barrier and also a route to understanding. Still, language has often been a resource for sociological analysis. I think of Chicago School (anthropologically inflected) fieldwork studies, in which researchers cataloged the argot of deviant groups (Shaw [1930] 1966) or occupational specialties (Cressey [1932] 2008), and of Howard Becker's famous account of "how [he] learned what a crock was" (1993). More recently, sociologists have joined scholars in communication studies, psychology, and education to develop approaches that make "talk" an artifact for study: conversation analysis (Goodwin 1981), discourse analysis (Fisher and Todd 1983), and narrative analysis (Riessman 2008). Symbolic interactionists understand language as the medium of meaning-making; institutional ethnographers examine language-in-use in order to map "conceptual practices of power" (Smith 1990). And a linguistic turn in the social sciences has generated lively and fruitful theoretical debates about the constructed, historically located character of "experience" (for a summary, see DeVault and Gross 2011).

Against this backdrop, I consider language use in research practice, focusing on the words chosen to label topics and analytic constructs, and the writing practices that communicate research results. I will embroider on the themes of craft and time in two ways: first, by discussing the time I've needed to find the words to convey my analyses as I intended, and then by considering how my interests and inclinations have shaped my scholarship over time.

(1)

I began my PhD in sociology without any background in the field; perhaps my lack of disciplinary knowledge at the time accounts, in part, for the time I spent "muddling about" to find a topic. But I did know feminism, and I knew that my topic might not yet have a name. I wanted to study—and bring into view—some of what women knew but didn't have words for. I wanted to challenge the connotations (of straightforward triviality) associated with a word like "housework," but I also wanted something more concrete than "caring" (which at the time carried connotations of emotionality, not work). Don't even ask about the title of my dissertation!—when I finished it, like many intelligent dissertators, I didn't fully understand what it was about (and didn't believe my teachers when they told me). But by the time I wrote the book (almost six years later), I had settled on the felicitous phrase "feeding the family." I held onto both "caring" and "work" as elements in the subtitle.

As I've noted in the book, I found a literary passage that helped me hold onto a sense of the topic before I found words for it. I don't recall why, at the time, I was reading Virginia Woolf's *To the Lighthouse*, but when I found the account of Mrs. Ramsay's dinner party, it spoke to me (see DeVault 1991, 6–10). From then on, I could say, "That's it," and remind myself of what I wanted to investigate, even if I didn't yet have the words for it. (Of course, this strategy isn't of much use at actual dinner parties, when people ask about one's dissertation topic—but that's a different problem.) Eventually, I came to refer to the kind of attentive emotional service Mrs. Ramsay provides at her party as "the work of sociability" ("sociability" was a word I'd picked up from my adviser, Arlene Kaplan Daniels, who used it in her writing on the instrumentally gala affairs thrown by high-level women volunteers in their civic fund-raising efforts [1987]). But part of the allure of the topic, for me, was my sense that "it" was there, pulsing with import, but also elusive, taking very different forms in different households and different moments, yet still in some sense an "it," recognizable by those who have learned to do the work.

As I talked with women, and a few men, about excruciatingly mundane details of household routines, it was comforting to have Mrs. Ramsay in my head, as an anchor and as reassurance that what I was studying was more significant than whether to buy Froot Loops or Cocoa Puffs. As I began to analyze these accounts, I applied labels. I didn't invent words, but I did try to use them creatively. I wrote about "monitoring" the stock of supplies in the kitchen, about "improvisation" at the supermarket, about "attending to preferences," and about "deferential service"—and I spent a good deal of time considering which words to use, and why. As I wrote, I discovered that I needed to explain not only what I meant, but why I'd chosen this word over that (often more common) one. I also discovered that explaining those decisions was always an opportunity to push the analysis a step or two forward.

I continue to have mixed feelings about some of these decisions. I'm delighted that the phrase "feeding the family," with its alliterative euphony, has had wide appeal. But I am also aware of its rosy, romanticized glow. Since writing the book, I've run across other *Feeding the Family*s, and they are either cookbooks or nineteenth-century domestic advice manuals; my own book is sometimes (mistakenly!) shelved in the culinary section. The phrase captures one part of my analysis (the part my grandmother liked the best), but not its sharper edge, my attention to inequity within the household. The word "provisioning" also gives me pause, with its military origin. I wanted a word that would do more than "shopping"—that would connect decisions in the supermarket with a broader strategy for what would happen later at home. I developed an analysis of shopping for groceries as work that linked a particular household with a wider market, and therefore as taken-for-granted work that is nonetheless essential to the operation of a market society, and capitalist food production in particular. Thinking about it now, I believe that analysis could be extended well beyond my initial arguments; I also see that the analogy of supplying an advancing army really isn't apt. Furthermore, although the phrase "feeding the family" has been taken up by other scholars, "provisioning" has not.[1] I can't help but think that the difference comes, at least in part, from the cultural resonances of "feeding the family"; the phrase suits a feminist analysis of invisible work, but it also works pretty well (to my chagrin) for a fundamentalist argument about women's place. Uncomfortable as it may be, I think scholars must acknowledge that the success and uptake of scholarly discoveries depend on the same kind of wordcraft that political operatives have come to deploy so skillfully, often shedding a lot more heat than light (on scholarly rhetoric in economics, see McCloskey 1990). I don't see how to avoid these dynamics, and that insight provides all the more reason to take the time to choose words with thoughtful care.

As I moved from dissertation to book, I developed an interest in copyediting. My line editor was excellent, and I appreciated and learned from the professional attention my manuscript received. But there were questions about consistency that caught my attention: on page _____, you discuss x; on page _____, you seem to refer to the same thing, but you call it y. My first impulse, as a young scholar, was to hear the comment as a straight-forward criticism, and make the correction. But at times that response didn't feel right, and I came to realize that I valued the nuances brought forward by multiple labels for activities. I don't remember exactly how I negotiated this issue with my copyeditor, but I know that the experience gave me a longstanding interest in copyediting as a routine practice of scholarship that deserves more attention. Writing about my analytic decisions, I argued that "strategic imprecision" could be useful: "If the language is 'man-made,' it is not likely to provide, ready-made, the words that feminist researchers need to tell what they learn from other women. Instead of imposing a choice among several labels, none of which are quite right . . . we should make our talk richer and more complex" (DeVault 1990, 111).

(2)

I discovered conversation analysis ("CA" to insiders) while working with the interviews I had conducted for my study of feeding the family, and I learned to think of "talk" as an artifact whose details could be explicated in order to illuminate the micropolitics of interaction.[2] Founded on the ethnometh-odological commitment to examine the "primordial" grounding and "every-day morality" of interaction (Garfinkel 1967), conversation analysis examines in microscopic detail how the many features of talk (not only its content, but its pace, inflections, overlaps, interruptions, and accompanying ges-tures, glances, etc.) are produced "artfully" in collaborative performance that "unfolds" moment by moment. Although I haven't taken up conversation analysis in my own work, I have taken advantage of opportunities to learn more about it, and I enjoy attending conference sessions where CA research is presented. Listening to researchers talk about the work makes it clear that the excruciatingly detailed transcripts in their articles—which outsiders like me struggle to interpret—are read by insiders only as markers for a conversa-tion that is kept alive through audio (and sometimes video) recordings. In a presentation, researchers and audiences hear the tape together and then con-sider the encounter. I learn a great deal from these sessions and I carry those lessons with me as I consider my own recordings and transcripts.

In working with my housework interviews (now see, there's an example—I've been sitting at the computer, struggling with what to call them! but sometimes one has to take the easy way out, and move on)—in working with my housework interviews, I became increasingly attentive to the details of talk. I began to read transcripts not only for content, but also for the way an account or story is put together. I came to see a speaker's "craft": there are language rules, but any speaker is also making in-the-moment choices about how to convey meaning, emotion, and significance to a particular audience. These insights grew in part from meditation on my data, and my studies of conversation and discourse analysis, but they were also fed by the burgeoning interdisciplinary field of narrative studies. It seemed, in the early 1990s, that stories were everywhere, and when I began a new series of interviews I asked explicitly for stories.

My studies of professional women—dietitians and nutrition educators—grew from my interest in household food work. But the topic is a very different one. "Feeding the family" is an activity that nearly everyone can talk about (and they want to—when I began to present my research, I was sometimes frustrated when audience members wanted to tell me about their grandmothers instead of discussing the analysis). By contrast, dietetics is a relatively small professional field whose practitioners bear the burden of stereotypes: the unattractive "cafeteria lady" or the forbidding disciplinarian who denies pleasure by enforcing the blandest of diets. Again, I can't say for sure why I was interested in this group; it's true that while I was contemplating a study of "food work," I had met some activist nutrition educators, but looking back I can't help but think that my cookbook-author grandmother and my home-ec-teacher aunt must also have had something to do with the direction of my research.

The field of dietetics and nutrition education was then—and remains—predominantly White, but I had learned by then that race matters everywhere, in different ways. I worked to recruit women of color as participants in my study and succeeded in interviewing several. Then I began to consider how we talked to each other, across racial and ethnic differences. I studied the transcripts, but here—as above—it is important to remember that the transcript stands in for our embodied encounter. I can't now remember where we met, but I recall vividly the feeling of one conversation, for me. I would characterize our talk as tentative, delicate, and hopeful—we were getting to know each other, and testing what could be asked and told. In the moment of the conversation, and even more as I studied the transcript, I was bringing to bear what I had learned over a lifetime of talking and listening, and over a shorter but substantial period of studying gender, race, and class inequalities and learning from work with students and colleagues of color (sometimes hard lessons, arising from my ignorance and blunders). In these analyses, too, I was interested in what the language at hand may not do easily, and how narrators use language strategically. For example, I considered the meaning of an African American nutritionist's comment that she wanted to work with "people like me," and suggested that she was using the phrase to reference "race" without using the word (DeVault 1995, 618). Perhaps—but readers point out that clients could be "like her" in various ways. Over the years, I've felt a bit less certain about my first interpretation. Thinking about it now, I recall other moments in that interview when this same participant speaks in this way—referring or pointing to understandings without labeling them explicitly. Would this expressive strategy be characteristic of talk across racial identities and the experiences associated with them? Or characteristic of a skilled public health worker, adept at navigating the subtleties of cross-cultural encounters? Of course, personality and interpersonal style and tone are also (always) at play . . . and I'm sure there is more to consider. Like other researchers who work with talk, I continue to find layers of meaning in the phrases that have captured my attention.

(3)

Over the last few years, I've been working collaboratively with two local colleagues (in law and health humanities) to investigate issues related to health care for people who are culturally Deaf—that is, people who use a signed language to communicate and understand the Deaf community as a linguistic-minority group.[3] My research partners bring distinctive disciplinary and personal resources to our collaboration: Michael Schwartz is a lawyer who directs Syracuse University's Disability Rights Clinic; he has years of experience litigating disability rights cases as well as a PhD in disability studies, and he is a Deaf person who is engagingly performative and charismatic. Rebecca Garden is trained in literature and disability studies and teaches at a medical university, where she deploys narrative to engage students with the ethical issues they will encounter as professionals; she is a superb networker and "bridge person," with a personal style that is both gentle and fierce. Most years, we have worked with law and social science graduate students on the team, and once with an undergraduate disability studies minor. Starting from Schwartz's research on Deaf people's accounts of their health-care experiences (Schwartz 2006, 2008), we have been interviewing local health-care professionals in order to explore their knowledge and understandings of Deaf culture and the strategies they deploy when they encounter Deaf patients, or in other encounters where communication access is at issue. Our project is built on the idea that litigation alone will not suffice, and we have organized or participated in a variety of educational outreach events for local health-care professionals, including a two-day symposium, panel discussions, ethical consults, guest appearances in classes, and independent study opportunities for medical and nursing students interested in Deaf culture and communication issues (DeVault, Schwartz, and Garden 2011).

Issues of language and expression are at the core of this project. At our team meetings, we rely on highly skilled sign-language interpreters; I have had to learn about and navigate some of the complexities of working with interpreters, which may not be evident to the casual observer. I have to remember that Michael listens by watching, so we need to arrange the room with sight lines in mind, to allow more time for multichannel communication (discussing a handout, for example), to distribute written material in advance, and to take more frequent breaks. Working together, and learning what works and what doesn't, is key to our analytic work: it helps me to understand what hearing professionals may not know about Deaf culture and communication, and what they might learn and do in order to work more effectively with Deaf patients. We also communicate frequently via e-mail, extending our face-to-face discussions. And since interpreters are also part of the health-care encounter we are studying, we sometimes ask them to "break frame" and participate in our discussions.

We are just beginning to analyze the narratives of health-care professionals we've interviewed. As we get started, I can see that language will continue to catch my attention. When Schwartz interviewed Deaf people about their health-care experiences, he found that they sometimes fought to receive interpreter services, struggling with doctors who weren't aware of their legal obligation to provide adequate communication access or who felt that providing interpretation was too expensive or simply unnecessary. In other situations, the same patients might make the judgment that for a small or routine matter, it wasn't worth the struggle and they would manage as best they could. Many of his interviewees expressed that experience with a distinctive sign, which Schwartz describes as follows (2006, 232): "arms raised, palms outward, arms going down, hands flicking downward—a universal gesture indicating the concept of letting go—'Live and let live.'" His

analysis makes clear that Deaf patients have different communication preferences and that they exercise agency in their interactions with health-care
professionals. But Schwartz points out that the strategy of letting go "carries
within it a kernel of anxiety. The Deaf patient wonders: 'Am I missing something that might come back to haunt me?' There is always a fear that the
information the patient is not obtaining by 'letting go' is exactly the information that is crucial to maintaining one's health" (2008, 967).

Interviewing health-care professionals, I've been struck by a phrase that
occurs frequently in their accounts of working across communication differences. They talk of "making do": finding ways to communicate in situations that are not ideal, such as in an emergency, before an interpreter
arrives; when the interpreter's skill may not match the patient's communication needs; or late at night, with no interpreter on duty. In these situations,
health-care workers may rely on visual assessment, rudimentary gestures,
writing notes, or pointing to visuals. I am often struck by the dedication of
nurses and physicians in these situations, their evident concern for patients,
and their artful improvisation. But these accounts certainly raise questions
about the situations in which "making do" is appropriate, and for how long.
More importantly, Michael, Rebecca, and I would like to juxtapose these
strategies in order to call attention to the significance of communication
access. If health-care providers are "making do," and a Deaf patient decides
to "let go," what kinds of critical information on both sides of the encounter
may fall by the wayside? And how might the resulting gaps in communication shape the course of a patient's diagnosis and treatment?

As in my previous work with interviews, I expect to spend a good deal
more time considering the meanings and uses of these two phrases. And as we
begin to share our findings with health-care professionals and educators, I'm
sure that we'll also need to consider the distinctive vocabularies and rhetoric of
medical culture. How will they hear and understand these phrases? I continue
to learn—and try to remember—that my words are heard differently by different audiences, in different contexts. Recently, I presented this small piece
of analysis, of making do and letting go, to an audience of Taiwanese faculty
and graduate students in a school of health policy. They listened attentively,
nodded, and applauded when I finished. Despite language differences (I spoke
in English), they clearly got it. But over the next few days, several approached
me individually to ask, "What does that mean, 'making do'?" I was abashed to
realize that I hadn't noticed or thought about how this idiomatic expression
would "play" half a world away from home, and that I had neglected to make

sure this audience understood one of my central ideas. But I am also thankful that at least some members of the audience had decided not to "let go," so that we were able to continue the conversation and I was able to learn a bit more about what I'm communicating, or not.

Conclusion

I am not trained as a linguist (unless we can count my undergraduate anthropology course in sociolinguistics), but I have been interested in language throughout my life. I think back to my sixth-grade teacher, who gave us the treat of a weekly creative writing session and encouraged me to think of myself as a writer. Or even further back, to my toddlerhood: When I was around five years old, my parents offered me up as a "guinea pig" for some university students who were learning to assess children's abilities—but they couldn't assess mine, because I refused to speak. After we got home, my mother asked gently, "Why didn't you answer? You know what a ball is, don't you? Why didn't you say?" "Well," I replied, sensibly, "I didn't know if they meant a round thing, or a fancy dance." While I've gained confidence with age, I've remained a relatively quiet and reserved person—more of a listener than a talker. I prefer writing, with its very different pace. I take pleasure in choosing words thoughtfully and deliberately, tasting and testing them as I write.

Of course, my account here—of a lifelong fascination with words—is a retrospective construction. Although I've been aware that I enjoy writing and find words and phrases interesting, I don't think I would have constructed this kind of "life story" without a nudge from Rosanna Hertz, who suggested this topic for my chapter. I've imposed continuity on a more contingent, accidental sequence of activities and encounters. That observation leads to another about research careers: I believe that most of us engage—choosing projects, pursuing lines of analysis, disseminating our work—in ways that are partly conscious and partly driven in less explicit ways, by our interests, our intuitions, and our capacity to notice this aspect of things more than that, along with accidents of history, and more. Those interests, intuitions, and capacities develop over time in the course of a career; they strengthen or wane in ways that one may not be able to control or even notice. As some strengthen over time, they deepen the craft knowledge that one brings to a project—the knowledge that is partly conscious and procedural but also intuitive, hands-on, and personal.

I learned from Howard Becker, one of my early teachers, to think of research as a craft, and my understanding of what that means has deepened over time in the course of reflecting on my own and others' practice. As I conclude this discussion, I think also of Susan Krieger's reflections in *Social Science and the Self* (1991). She was interested in how the self appears in social science, and she turned to the work of traditional Native American Pueblo pottery makers to consider how those craftswomen expressed individual visions within highly stylized community conventions for pot making. Each Pueblo community produces pottery with distinctive shapes and designs; outsiders may not be able to recognize the work of particular potters. But pottery makers themselves can easily identify the individual marks of their own creative work, and the distinctive designs of other craftspeople in their community. As one Laguna craftswoman explained, "So much of me goes into the pot."[4] Social science is a highly conventionalized practice; we are trained as researchers to follow the routine procedures that make our work recognizable, durable, and usable—like a good pot.

And still—whether I know it or not—so much of me goes into my writing.

Notes

1. One group of feminist scholars, however, does use the phrase "provisioning work" in a somewhat different way, to refer to all the paid and unpaid work through which women sustain families and communities (Neysmith et al. 2012).
2. For my discovery of conversation analysis, I owe thanks to sociologists at UCLA, where I gave an early talk on the research, and to Harvey Molotch, who included basic instruction on CA in a course on the sociology of the news, which he taught as a visiting professor at Northwestern University in 1981.
3. The convention in Deaf and disability studies is to use the uppercase "Deaf" to reference Deaf culture and the Deaf community as a linguistic minority, and to use the lowercase "deaf" for auditory impairment and people with hearing loss (such as later-life deafness) whose identity is not linked to a Deaf community.
4. Quoted in Stephen Trimble, "Talking with Clay," *New Mexico Magazine*, August 1986 (cited in Krieger 1991, 89).

References

Becker, H. S. 1993. "How I Learned What a Crock Was." *Journal of Contemporary Ethnography* 22: 28–35.

Cressey, P. G. (1932) 2008. *The Taxi-Dance Hall: A Sociological Study in Commercialized Recreation and City Life*. Chicago: University of Chicago Press.

Daniels, A. K. 1987. "Invisible Work." *Social Problems* 34: 403–15.

DeVault, M. L. 1990. "Talking and Listening from Women's Standpoint: Feminist Strategies for Interviewing and Analysis." *Social Problems* 37: 96–116.

———. 1991. *Feeding the Family: The Social Organization of Caring as Gendered Work*. Chicago: University of Chicago Press.

———. 1995. "Ethnicity and Expertise: Racial-Ethnic Knowledge in Sociological Research." *Gender & Society* 9: 612–31.

DeVault, M. L., and G. Gross. 2011. "Feminist Qualitative Interviewing: Experience, Talk, and Knowledge." In *Handbook of Feminist Research*, 2nd ed., edited by S. N. Hesse-Biber, 206–36. Thousand Oaks, CA: Sage.

DeVault, M. L., R. Garden, and M. A. Schwartz. 2011. "Mediated Communication in Context: Narrative Approaches to Understanding Encounters between Health Care Providers and Deaf People." *Disability Studies Quarterly* 31 (4). Online at *dsq-sds.org/article/view/1715*.

Fisher, S., and A. D. Todd. 1983. *The Social Organization of Doctor-Patient Communication*. Washington, DC: Center for Applied Linguistics.

Garfinkel, H. 1967. *Studies in Ethnomethodology*. Englewood Cliffs, NJ: Prentice Hall.

Goodwin, C. 1981. *Conversational Organization: Interaction between Speakers and Hearers*. New York: Academic Press.

Krieger, S. 1991. *Social Science and the Self: Personal Essays on an Art Form*. New Brunswick, NJ: Rutgers University Press.

McCloskey, D. N. 1990. *If You're So Smart: The Narrative of Economic Expertise*. Chicago: University of Chicago Press.

Neysmith, S., M. Reitsma-Street, S. B. Collins, and E. Porter. 2012. *Beyond Caring Labour to Provisioning Work*. Toronto: University of Toronto Press.

Riessman, C. K. 2008. *Narrative Methods for the Human Sciences*. Thousand Oaks, CA: Sage.

Schwartz, M. A. 2006. "Communication in the Doctor's Office: Deaf Patients Talk about Their Physicians." PhD diss., Syracuse University.

———. 2008. "Deaf Patients, Doctors, and the Law: Compelling a Conversation about Communication." *Florida State University Law Review* 35: 947–1002.

Shaw, C. R. (1930) 1966. *The Jack-Roller: A Delinquent Boy's Own Story*. Chicago: University of Chicago Press.

Smith, D. E. 1990. *Conceptual Practices of Power: A Feminist Sociology of Knowledge*. Boston: Northeastern University Press

16

The Days Are Long, but the Years Fly By

Reflections on the Challenges of Doing Qualitative Research

Annette Lareau

I n safe, comfortable spaces, such as in dark bars late at night, ethnographers and other qualitative sociologists often confide to each other about the remarkably *slow* pace of their work. Often talented researchers have been ashamed of being so slow. Yet, it is normal for a project to take years. I remember when I started the study that became *Unequal Childhoods*, other sociologists would ask me about it when we met at conferences; they expressed interest and enthusiasm about my planned book.[1] As the years ticked by, people looked more uncomfortable when they asked me about my book. (This was also probably because I looked embarrassed that my book was not done.) Then, a few years later, they stopped asking! I would meet people at a conference and they would ask about my teaching, my family, or the conference, but they wouldn't even mention the book. It was too embarrassing. There was a charming essay in the *New York Times* in 2004 about authors who take years to write a book. One author said, "Once the book is out you go from 'What a chump she can't finish that book' to 'Wow, what an incredible journey.'"[2]

Sometimes I think that sociologists interested in naturalistic studies of daily life have ceded too much ground to quantitative sociologists. This is not to say that quantitative sociologists aren't smart, interesting, and thoughtful. But the labor process is different. Although there are scholars who collect survey data, most quantitative scholars do not spend any time collecting data. Instead, the data set is given to them. In addition, the data set is established. There are a finite number of variables. The options are limited. Quantitative research also seems much more predictable than doing qualitative work. The pathways are established. This is not to say that quantitative scholars don't hit brick walls, have perplexing findings, or have findings that inexplicably vanish with the introduction of a new variable. It takes a long time for a researcher to get to know a complex data set. In addition, there is always the terror in number crunching that you might make a small error that would radically change the results. (It has happened.) But the key point is that the process of doing quantitative research is more predictable. It is also faster.

And qualitative work is chaotic as well as slow. Most of the time that I was working on *Unequal Childhoods*, I had no idea what I was doing. On paper it looked like I knew what I was doing. After all, I had written a grant proposal to the Spencer Foundation (which had graciously given me, as an advanced assistant professor, a major grant). I had read a fair number of books and articles on the relevant topics. I had completed an ethnographic study as my dissertation, published a heavily revised version of the thesis as a book, and even won an award for the book. Thus, you might think that I *should* have felt like I knew what I was doing. But I didn't.

Instead, I was stumbling along. Each situation was somewhat unpredictable. For example, each family that we observed had different ways of organizing their life; we needed to adjust to them. In addition, although I hoped to learn interesting things from the observations, I wasn't exactly sure about what I would learn. Even if you have a lot of years under your belt, the course of the research in each project is far from certain. This unpredictability makes the work exciting or terrifying depending on your perspective. Gaining access and maintaining access are huge hurdles; yet access is being constantly renegotiated. Multiple people need to be told about the study as you go along. And you need to build rapport with different people. As you get deeper into the study, you face new challenges. Sometimes people don't want you around. For example, one of the fathers in my study for *Unequal Childhoods*, Mr. Williams, was supremely unimpressed with the project when we visited his family regularly. As he told his wife somewhat angrily at one point, "It is your thing." Ms. Williams laughed merrily when he made this proclamation (as if he was being a recalcitrant child). His willingness to participate, despite his original reluctance, seemed to be part of a marital dynamic. Mr. Williams signed all of the consent forms, consented to be interviewed, and sometimes joked and laughed with field-workers, but other times (exhausted from a long day of work) he was grouchy. His grouchiness made me tense. I was afraid that one day he would come home, get mad at his wife, and end the study. (Fortunately, he didn't.)

And, of course, there is the emotional exhaustion. Quantitative researchers can work in their sweatpants, at home, late at night, while ethnographers have to travel to their sites, wiggle their way into complex social settings, help make others feel comfortable, and try to repair problems that pop up. This uncertainty—this pattern of taking three steps forward and two back—can make the progress seem slow as well as draining.

Some social scientists think that an entire ethnographic study can be done in two to three years: a bit of time to formulate the program, write the forms for permission to study human subjects (and submit them to the institutional review board, or IRB), gain access to the field, and collect data; one year to analyze the data, figure out the argument, and start writing; and one year to finish writing, go through the reviews, revise, and send a book (or, occasionally, a series of articles) to a publisher. Doctoral students want to do the entire process in two years. There have been people who have done that. But these people are rare. Doctoral students are generally faster than faculty because they have more time, sometimes they have more guidance, and they have urgency. I have seen doctoral students do a fine study in less than three years, particularly if during one of those years they don't have to work to earn money. For many faculty members or researchers who are juggling multiple demands in their lives, it takes several months to a year just to get the project going, and it takes another several months to a year to collect data for a qualitative project; sometimes it takes two or even more. It then takes months (not weeks) to figure out the argument, which is followed by writing the book, which often takes a year or more (if drafted at lightning speed) or two or three (at a more normal pace). The manuscript has to be reviewed, it has to be revised, it has to be reviewed again, and then it has to be finalized. There are many steps in the process. For most of us, it is slow.[3]

The hard reality is that ethnography is a greedy institution. With interviews, it is common for people to forget about the meeting. It can take many, many efforts to schedule one interview. Participant observation takes even more time. I usually budgeted two to three hours in the field and five hours for writing fieldnotes. When I paid graduate students to write field-notes, I encouraged them to write notes for five to twelve hours for each visit. This time doesn't count time I spend getting myself ready to go, figuring out what small gift to bring (i.e., a pie or tomatoes from the backyard), and traveling there and back. I also am constantly figuring out how to manage problems that surface in the field. For example, in elementary schools it is always a problem when a kid with whom you are trying to build rapport breaks a school rule by hitting another kid right in front of you. On the one hand, the adults expect you to enforce school rules; educators can withdraw permission for you to be there if they are sufficiently annoyed. On the other hand, you are usually trying to build a relationship with a kid; you don't want to damage that relationship. It is a balancing act. Usually unexpected dilemmas are routine during a study; each needs careful attention. Thinking about them is tiring.

Furthermore, I have never been one of those people who can get home, fix a cup of coffee, sit down, and start writing fieldnotes. Instead, I wander around the house, take a nap, work in the garden, or stall in other ways. My need to start to write fieldnotes looms large. I am anxious because the notes need to be written up that night and it takes hours to write the notes. Vivid, rich, and detailed fieldnotes are the life blood of an ethnographic study. But it is hard for me to force myself to get going. Finally, I settle down. I started following baseball while I was in the field in part so I would have something comfortable to talk about with my families; I now like to have a baseball game on the television or music playing while I write notes. (Television other than baseball, however, is too distracting for me.) As I begin, I have a habit of writing out (by hand) on a pad of paper the topics that I need to cover of what happened during the visit. Then, as I finish writing my field-notes on one topic, I decisively cross the topic off with a large X. It is satisfying. Topic by topic, I march along. In addition to the notes, I also write out the chronology of events, and I highlight the analytic themes raised by the visit. By the time I write an analytic memo (in which I try to link the themes in the notes to the broader general question of the study and the literature on the topic), I am exhausted. Each session of writing fieldnotes is slow. Still, it is deeply satisfying to print out each copy and pile them up, adding new visits to the pile. And, looking back, it seems as if the time in the field didn't last all that long of a period. The days are long, but the years fly by.

There are also difficult conflicts between work and family in doing ethnography. Your life (for better or worse) does not come to a screeching halt just because you have started a new study. But I would be lying if I didn't say that were times when I would wish that all of my life obligations would suddenly vanish so I could work 24/7 on my study. You have to create a balance. Sometimes it is tricky. I have a very good friend who, when I was in the middle of collecting data, got diagnosed with breast cancer. She had two children under the age of ten; it was a twelve-hour trip to travel to her home on the west coast. She went through chemotherapy and her prognosis was promising, but she was exhausted. Her husband needed to go on a long-scheduled work trip for two weeks. One summer evening I was talking with her by phone. She didn't sound good. I said, "I could come to visit." She said something like, "How about tomorrow?" My heart sank. We were in the middle of doing observations with an African American family below the poverty level. It was very hard to get permission to visit a family daily for three weeks, but it was crucial for the study. It was all going well, but it was intense. I was doing fieldwork too. But, abruptly leaving to go to see her just seemed to be the right thing to do. I left a few days later for a weeklong visit. I cooked, watched the kids, and hung out with my friend. While there, I also spent time on the phone each night with the research assistants. A crisis developed in the field. Money was stolen from the field-worker by the aunt of the kid. (The aunt was on dope). I personally would not have mentioned it to the mother, Ms. McAllister, but the field-worker (who as a graduate student was strapped for cash) did tell her. (I repaid the field-worker, of course, when I got home.) Ms. McAllister was humiliated and angry. It was a mess. And I wasn't there to pop by, bring some beer, and make jokes to help smooth it over. Instead, I coached the field-worker on the phone. It all worked out. But it was challenging. And throughout the project each day seemed long as I juggled not only the ethnographic visits and writing field-notes but the other considerable demands of my life. Having a large grant is a blessing, but it doesn't exactly solve this problem. I spoke on the phone to the field-workers after each visit from ten minutes to an hour. (I did this for many reasons: to learn what was going on, to guide the writing up of their fieldnotes, to help them feel emotionally supported, and to facilitate the data analysis and writing process.) Between writing fieldnotes, emotionally supporting the research assistants, managing the grant, teaching, doing committee work, and managing my personal life (when I was a single woman with elderly parents across the country), I had conflicting priorities. It always seemed like a lot to juggle on a good day, let alone a day when I was sick, my elderly mother wasn't doing well, or the car broke down.

And then, there is the pressure to publish. At many elite institutions, assistant professors are expected to publish two high-quality (well-placed) articles each year. Quantitative and qualitative scholars are expected, more or less, to have a similar profile. Book chapters do not count. A revised dissertation counts less than a new book (since doctoral students are considered to have had help in the project). Before tenure, people doing qualitative work are told that they need two books or one book, numerous articles, and a second project that is far along. It is crazy. Of course, one book that is high-quality (i.e., wins awards and is well reviewed) can offset a perceived lack in the number of publications. But it is a lot of pressure. The fact that qualitative scholars have spent months and years *collecting data* (while quantitative researchers were spared that time investment) is not, unfortunately, factored into the equations of evaluations. In some circumstances, having a slow research pace can be a career-ending matter.

There are really no easy answers to this "arms race" of publication, but being strategic can help. Everything that is on the CV when a young scholar accepts a job does not count toward tenure in the same way as new papers count toward tenure that are developed and published after a scholar begins a "tenure clock." Usually there is not enough time in the six years before tenure to collect a bunch of new data for a second project. Hence, my free advice is that young scholars should collect a lot more data than they need for their dissertation or first project. (Many anthropologists work with one data set for years.) Sometimes researchers have data on a related-but-distinct project that can be developed into a second set of articles or book. Often, young scholars can supplement the existing data set by adding a second site, doing a longitudinal follow-up, focusing on an analytic distinct topic, or doing interviews to flesh out a project. It is good to think about that ahead of time.

And, there is no such thing as a "quick" or "easy" publication. Everything is slow. Partly there are simply too much data. Each interview is around forty pages double-spaced in length. Fieldnotes can run twenty pages double-spaced per visit. There are documents too. Since a project can go in twenty different directions, it is hard to focus. And these computer software programs (e.g., ATLAS.ti) are essentially useless in my opinion when you have done all of the data collection. (They are excellent, however, if you have not done the data collection.) They do organize things, but they are sort of like a fancy file cabinet. They don't do the thinking for you. Most people I know don't find them very helpful. I do use them in some projects; other projects I don't. But the qualitative software packages certainly don't speed things up.

I find that even if I am diligently writing analytic memos as I am collecting data, there is still another very slow period as I am trying to figure out the argument. Sometimes a trial balloon gets shot down. For *Unequal Childhoods*, the most intensive period of data collection was 1993–1995 when we studied the twelve families; some interviews, including with African American middle-class families weren't finished until 1997. I remember that around 1997 I thought I had figured out the argument. I was invited to the University of California, San Diego, to give a talk. It was a friendly audience; most people in the room had liked my first book. They liked me. But I was hammered. They told me that I had a "culture of poverty" or "deficit" model where I made working-class kids look deficient compared to middle-class kids. Of course, I felt that it was not what I was saying. But that was what they *heard*. I was disheartened. I was also busy. During this time I was working at Temple University where the students were variable. Some were as strong as students anywhere in the country. Others, however, had never even heard of a "thesis." Teaching them how to write an essay was an uphill battle. Many, if not most, sociologists work in more challenging conditions. I was teaching four classes per year; many teach six or eight classes per year. Still, I had my classes, committee work, and other obligations. Finishing the book seemed daunting.

It wasn't until 1999 when I had a one-semester leave (funded by a presidential grant of the Alfred P. Sloan Foundation) that I began to gain ground. I was a visiting scholar at the Berkeley Center for Working Families (run by Arlie Hochschild and Barrie Thorne). In this vibrant intellectual climate, I began to settle on an argument that was received more positively. I spent a few months writing a paper (eventually published in *American Sociological Review*) that summarized the heart of the argument (Lareau 2002). I remember that in 1999 the group read a piece that eventually became a chapter on the Tallinger family. The responses were positive. I could tell that seminar participants really cared about the members of the Tallinger family. That was the first moment when I began to feel that this really might work.

Still, it is difficult to explain exactly how the core concepts of the book emerged. Mostly I read the fieldnotes over, over, and over again. I thought about the weaknesses in the literature. I thought about how I would answer the question "so what?" in the book. I was very impressed by the work of Melvin Kohn on class differences in child rearing values and the work of Basil Bernstein, Shirley Brice Heath, and Betty Hart and Todd Risley on class and language use. Yet, all of these studies seemed too narrow to me; they didn't seem to focus enough on the rhythm of daily life in families. (In other words, I had an emergent critique.) In our visits, the families seemed different to me in their approach to life; I gradually came to call this a different "logic of child rearing." I wrote a series of papers for conferences; I asked colleagues to read them. Many readers told me I was trying to do too much; they couldn't follow the argument. I kept "trying to keep my eye on the ball" in terms of the answer to this question, which I often asked myself: *what are you trying to explain?* Eventually I decided I was looking at variations in parents' organization of children's leisure time, parents' language use, and parents' intervention in education. (I would sometimes get confused about whether the children or the parents were the focal point. I was studying interaction, but eventually— in cases where there was a decision to be made—I decided to prioritize parents' actions.) Once I set my priorities in terms of the key research question, then some issues were simply less relevant.

I was in a writing group that was invaluable in giving me feedback. I would write drafts; they would "hold up a mirror" and tell me what they thought I was saying. Their feedback would help me get clearer about what I was trying to say and what I was not trying to say. I would revise to clarify the argument. I would then repeat the process. I do recall that I had trouble finding the right terms for what I eventually called "concerted cultivation" and "the accomplishment of natural growth." (It was a gardening analogy—I thought about the differences between wild flowers, including flowers that bloom on bridges and sidewalks, and flowers cultivated in greenhouses.) At one point I was using the term "hot house parenting," but the term seemed pejorative. I wanted terms that were neutral. I wanted to respect both approaches to child rearing. I also thought a lot about disconfirming evidence. Over and over again I would think to myself: "Imagine that you got it wrong. Maybe class doesn't matter. Maybe it is all about race." Then I would adopt that conceptual model that I was challenging and reread interviews to see if I could get the "disconfirming evidence conceptual model" to fit the data. I would look for any and all evidence that supported an opposing argument. This exercise had multiple goals. It helped reassure me that these data really did support the claims. It also highlighted moments where there was disconfirming evidence; reporting these pieces of data was crucial. These deviant examples showed more complexity in the data; they helped make the argument more nuanced. In addition, the examples helped the reader trust the argument (since it didn't make it seem as if I was "cooking" the data). But the manuscript also tried to show that these examples were unusual. In writing up the results, I had a rule of thumb where I would begin a new section with strong evidence showing three or four examples in support of a claim. I would then present one example of disconfirming evidence; in presenting the disconfirming evidence I would explain to the reader that this piece of evidence, while significant, should not distract the reader from the stronger evidence in support of the claim. I also tried to streamline the manuscript so it did not distract the reader with side issues. It was stressful to "let go" of other, related pieces of data since I was attached to them and since I wanted the story to be as complex as possible. But, as a reader, I strongly prefer to read a book that only has one main argument. I tried to write a book that I would want to read. I also tried hard to remember that an example could not speak for itself. A vivid, detailed, and rich example from fieldnotes was an example of something; it was illustrating an idea. I needed to state the idea before I introduced the example. There were countless quotes that could have been put in the manuscript. Given the effort that had gone into collecting them, it was hard to leave them out. But readers told me that the manuscript was repetitive. The quotes had to go.

I did not have a complete manuscript until 2001. It was reviewed. I revised it. I delivered the manuscript to the press in May 2002. I then had a "shoot-out" with the press over the length. (I had not read my contract.) The book would have been 420 pages. The editors at University of California Press (who were generally wonderful in promoting the book) wanted a book that was less than 350 pages because they felt it would impede the use of the book in the classroom, make the book more expensive, and so forth. In the end, I cut 75 pages (i.e., one chapter and eleven words per page) to bring the first edition of the book down to 340 pages. The final manuscript went to the press in September. I had a copy of the book in my hands in July; the official publication date was September 2003. It was out.

In *Unequal Childhoods*, I have a long acknowledgment on work-family relations. (The subtext of it is, "I know! I know! I know!" It has been almost ten years since data collection!) I worried incessantly that readers would ask themselves: "WHAT WAS SHE DOING?") The demands of my family life did impede the progress of my book, but my family members also brought me tremendous gifts. As I note in my acknowledgment to my husband (whom I had met at the end of 1994) and my two children by marriage: "In the clockwork of careers, wherein we are assessed for our productivity, families are not really counted as a legitimate force. But to be speedy is not everything, or even, when all is said and done, much at all. To have the gifts of companionship, nurturance, and good humor in daily life, however, is quite a lot. I appreciate having [my children, and my husband], in my life (2011, xiv)." I still think that being speedy is not really the point; I think that finishing a high-quality study that you care about it is the point. Family obligations often slow a project down, but family support is crucial to retaining one's sense of humor, recovering from a bad day on the project, and putting the enterprise in perspective. Also, except for a period when young scholars are under a tenure clock, speed rarely matters. When I was in graduate school I worried endlessly about my time to degree, but really it turned out that it didn't matter. And no one ever asked me, face-to-face, why it took me so long to finish my damn book. (They probably thought about it, however.) Over and over again, I run into people who, blushing, stammering, and looking down at the floor, say, "I am slow." Even senior scholars, for whom it shouldn't really matter, look distressed. I feel like saying: "Everyone who is doing a good study is slow. What matters is that there is great study."

To me, a great ethnographic study really helps us understand a social world. Although reasonable people disagree, I believe that outstanding ethnographic studies usually have two key features. First, excellent ethnographies are saturated with "thick description" where the ethnographers evoke the meaning and experience of research participants. The voices of research participants shine forth. Rather than presenting overly general descriptions of daily life, high-quality research is saturated with detail. To capture this level of detail, researchers usually need to do participant observation for a long time, but others have written fine books based on shorter periods of observation or based only on interviews.[4] Second, researchers make an effort to show the limitations of previous research. The unique contribution of the current work is clear. Put differently, there is an effort on the part of the researcher to answer the question, "So what?"

It is hard to write a good book. It requires a kind of "fire in the belly" to keep soldiering on—to keep going back, over and over again, to the pull of the field despite the chorus of people who want you to hurry, finish, and publish. And, it seems to me to be grossly unfair that as you are slogging away writing fieldnotes, none of the people—who surface years later—are around to tell you how much they like your book. Instead, you need to create your own cheering team in the form of a writing group, dissertation group, or cadre of friends to cheer you on and offer constructive, critical advice.

Ethnography can often be lonesome as well as chaotic, slow, and confusing. Usually you are alone in the field. It can be difficult to convey to your friends and family what it is like to be there in the field site; usually people in the field site have little understanding of your life when you are away from them. But ethnography can also be exciting and exhilarating. And usually there is a happy ending. Although building rapport is a slow process, ethnographers typically are able to build rapport. Although most ethnographers stumble along, interesting books and articles do often emerge from a study. Hence, although ethnographers often run a gauntlet of juggling multiple demands in the field, patching together a work-family balance during data collection and writing, not really knowing where the study is going most of the time, and struggling to finish a book, most do finish. Thus, I think that ethnographers should try to quell the self-criticism that can surface as projects take longer to complete than they had hoped. Ethnographers should not be perfectionists; after all, every study has flaws. But they should stay as long as they think they need to stay in the field in order to understand what they are trying to understand. They should also draw on the pieces in this book to educate others about the pace and nature of the work. Finally, they should try to remember that most scholars complete data collection on only one or two ethnographic projects in their entire *careers*. Being slow is routine. Good studies can and do emerge from the chaos. And most people don't carry out many ethnographies in their lives. The days are long, but the years fly by.

Notes

I am grateful to the Russell Sage Foundation as well as the Spencer Foundation for their support of my research. Tim Black, Maia Cucchiara, Kelley Fong, and Judith A. Levine provided helpful comments on an earlier version of this chapter. I also appreciate the suggestions of Rosanna Hertz and Peggy Nelson.

1. The book used ethnographic methods to examine differences in the day-to-day lives of African American and White families. Although the study included separate in-depth interviews with the mothers and fathers of eighty-eight children who were in third or fourth grade, the most unusual part of the book involved intensive case study observations with twelve families. Usually, a research assistant or I visited each family daily for three weeks. The families were paid for their participation. The study also included classroom observations in elementary schools, interviews with educators, and interviews with the twelve children (and their siblings) in the intensive study. *Unequal Childhoods* describes a cultural logic of child rearing where White and Black middle-class families engage in a pattern of "concerted cultivation," actively developing children's talents and skills. By contrast, the pattern for working-class and poor families—

"the accomplishment of natural growth"—sees parents caring for children but presuming they will spontaneously thrive. Since the middle-class strategy is more in sync with the standards of dominant institutions, middle-class children gain advantages even at the expense of the rituals of family life. Follow-up interviews with the young people at around age twenty suggest the continuing influence of social class and the growing power of race, especially for young Black men. An expanded edition of *Unequal Childhoods* was published in 2011 by University of California Press; it includes one hundred new pages describing the lives of the young adults. There is also an extensive methodological reflection on the (often angry) response of the families to their portrayals in the book. For more information, see Lareau 2011.

2. The quote is from Diane McWhorter, who spent nineteen years working on her book *Carry Me Home: Birmingham, Alabama; The Climactic Battle of the Civil Rights Revolution*, which was published by Simon and Schuster in 2001. The book won the Pulitzer Prize. McWhorter's comment appears in a thoughtful essay by Jonathan Mahler entitled "20 Years and 5 Editors Later . . . ," which appeared in the *New York Times* on September 26, 2004.

3. Getting permission from the institutional review board can be slow and daunting. For a discussion of how to manage this process, as well as for other concrete advice on doing ethnographic work, see Annette Lareau, "Doing Ethnographic Research: A Companion Guide" (unpublished book manuscript), Department of Sociology, University of Pennsylvania.

4. For an excellent, recent ethnographic study, see Black 2009. For a study that uses ethnographic methods to study families, see Cooper (forthcoming). For a classic book based only on interviews, see Rubin 1976.

References

Black, T. 2009. *When a Heart Turns Rock Solid: The Lives of Three Puerto Rican Brothers on and off the Streets*. New York: Vintage.

Cooper, M. Forthcoming. *Cut Adrift: Families in Insecure Times*. Berkeley: University of California Press.

Lareau, A. 2002. "Invisible Inequality: Social Class and Childrearing in White and Black Families." *American Sociological Review* 67 (5): 747–76.

———. 2011. *Unequal Childhoods: Class, Race, and Family Life*. 2nd ed. Berkeley: University of California Press.

Rubin, L. 1976. *Worlds of Pain: Life in the Working-Class Family*. New York: Basic Books.

Contributors

Emily K. Abel is Research Professor and Professor Emerita at the UCLA School of Public Health. Her most recent book is *The Inevitable Hour: A History of Caring for Dying Patients in America.*

Susan E. Bell is Professor of Sociology and A. Myrick Freeman Professor of Social Sciences at Bowdoin College. She is the author of *DES Daughters: Embodied Knowledge and the Transformation of Women's Health Politics.*

Timothy Black is Associate Professor of Sociology and a faculty affiliate of the Social Justice Institute at Case Western Reserve University. He is the author of *When a Heart Turns Rock Solid: The Lives of Three Puerto Rican Brothers on and off the Street*, which was named a best book of 2009 by the *Washington Post*, and won the 2011 Mirra Komarovsky Book Award given by the Eastern Sociological Society and the 2010 book award given by the Association for Humanist Sociology.

Linda M. Burton is the James B. Duke Professor of Sociology at Duke University. She recently served as coeditor of two volumes: *Communities, Neighborhoods, and Health: Expanding the Boundaries of Place* and *The Oxford Handbook of Poverty and Society.*

Marjorie L. DeVault is Professor of Sociology in the Maxwell School of Citizenship and Public Affairs at Syracuse University. She is the author of *Feeding the Family: The Social Organization of Caring as Gendered Work* and *Liberating Method: Feminism and Social Research.*

Joanna Dreby is Assistant Professor of Sociology at the University at Albany, SUNY. She is author of the award-winning book *Divided by Borders.*

Anita Ilta Garey is Associate Professor Emerita of Human Development and Family Studies and of Sociology at the University of Connecticut. Her book *Weaving Work and Motherhood* received the 2000 William J. Goode Book Award. She coedited *At the Heart of Work and Family: Engaging the Ideas of Arlie Hochschild* with Karen V. Hansen and *Who's Watching? Daily Practices of Surveillance among Contemporary Families* with Margaret K. Nelson.

Naomi Gerstel is Distinguished University Professor at the University of Massachusetts, Amherst. Her research, funded by NSF, Russell Sage, Sloan, and Rockefeller, examines time as a dimension of inequality, kinship, and work-family policies. A past chair of the American Sociological Association Family Section, she is a recipient of the Samuel F. Conti Fellowship and the Rosabeth Moss Kanter and Robin Williams Awards.

Karen V. Hansen is Professor of Sociology and Women's and Gender Studies at Brandeis University. Her most recent book, *Encounter on the Great Plains: Scandinavian Settlers and the Dispossession of Dakota Indians, 1890–1930*, was divinely disrupted by her collaboration with Anita Ilta Garey on *At the Heart of Work and Family: Engaging the Ideas of Arlie Hochschild.*

Rosanna Hertz is the Classes of 1919–1950 Reunion Professor of Sociology and Women's and Gender Studies at Wellesley College. Her latest book is *Single by Chance, Mothers by Choice: How Women Are Choosing Parenthood without Marriage and Creating the New American Family.* She is the coeditor (with Barry Glassner) of *Our Studies, Ourselves: Sociologists' Lives and Work.*

Albert Hunter is Professor of Sociology and Director of Urban Studies at Northwestern University. His books include *Symbolic Communities, The Rhetoric of Social Research, Multimethod Research,* and *Pragmatic Liberalism: Constructing a Civil Society.* He has served as an editor of *Urban Affairs Review,* chair of the Community Section of the American Sociological Association, and chair of the Plan Commission of the City of Evanston.

Annette Lareau is the Stanley I. Sheerr Term Professor in the Department of Sociology at the University of Pennsylvania. She is the author of *Unequal Childhoods: Class, Race, and Family Life.* A second edition of *Unequal Childhoods*, with a new, substantive follow-up of the children into adulthood, was published in 2011. She is also the coeditor (with Jeff Shultz) of *Journeys through Ethnography* and (with Kimberly Goyette) of *Choosing Homes, Choosing Schools.*

Margaret K. Nelson is the A. Barton Hepburn Professor in the Department of Sociology and Anthropology at Middlebury College. She is the author of several books, including *Parenting out of Control: Anxious Parents in Unsettled Times*, and the editor of collections such as *Who's Watching? Daily Practices of Surveillance among Contemporary Families*, which she coedited with Anita Ilta Garey.

E. Burke Rochford Jr. is Professor of Religion at Middlebury College in Vermont. He has researched the Hare Krishna movement since 1975 and published two books on the movement, *Hare Krishna in America* and *Hare Krishna Transformed.*

Mary Romero received the American Sociological Association Section on Race and Ethnic Minorities 2009 Founder's Award and the 2004 Society for the Study of Social Problems Lee Founders Award. She received the Américo Paredes Book Award for *The Maid's Daughter.* She is the author of *Maid in the USA* and coeditor of six other books. She is Professor of Justice and Social Inquiry at Arizona State University.

Carol B. Stack, author of *All Our Kin* and *Call to Home*, is Professor Emeritus of Social and Cultural Studies in Education at the University of California, Berkeley. She was chair of Women's Studies at UC Berkeley and assistant to the chancellor on the status of women. She is currently a research associate at the Social Science Research Institute of Duke University.

Pamela Stone is Professor of Sociology at Hunter College and the Graduate Center of the City University of New York. Her book *Opting Out? Why Women Really Quit Careers and Head Home* won the William J. Goode Award of the American Sociological Association and received considerable media attention, including stories on NBC's *Today Show* and the *CBS Evening News*.

Will C. van den Hoonaard, a sociologist, is Professor Emeritus at the University of New Brunswick and Research Associate at the Atlantic Centre for Qualitative Research and Analysis, St. Thomas University, Fredericton, Canada. He has authored or edited nine books, including *Essentials of Thinking Ethically in Qualitative Research* (with Deborah K. van den Hoonaard), *The Seduction of Ethics: Transforming the Social Sciences*, and *Working with Sensitizing Concepts*.